CW01662242

Bourdieu and Education

Specially selected by Diane Reay, this is a collection of innovative and thought-provoking recently published papers that 'use' Bourdieu to put theory into practice in order to understand and analyse educational problems. Bourdieu's work is renowned for its focus on inequalities and its centring of social justice.

The contributions utilise a wide range of diverse concepts in Bourdieu's theoretical 'tool-kit' and address educational inequalities across different aspects of the educational system – from higher education and parental choice of schooling, to teachers' professional development and the PE classroom. Illuminating key aspects of Bourdieu's scholarship, they reveal how good Bourdieu is 'for thinking with'; illustrate the merits of reflexivity, the move beyond binary ways of reading the social world; and demonstrate the significance of power in any analysis of education.

The chapters in this book were all originally published as articles in Taylor and Francis journals.

Diane Reay is Visiting Professor at the London School of Economics, UK and Emeritus Professor of Sociology of Education at the University of Cambridge, UK. Her main research interests are social justice issues in education, Pierre Bourdieu's social theory and cultural analyses of social class, race and gender. Her most recent book is *Miseducation: Inequality, Education and the Working Classes* (2017).

Education and Social Theory

Series Editor: Stephen J. Ball, Institute of Education, University College London, UK

Social theory can help us to make sense of many aspects of contemporary education by providing analytic concepts and insights. Social theories are tools of analysis and interpretation for educational researchers that enable us to make sense of the processes, effects and outcomes of educational experiences and institutions.

Drawing together selections from the best work previously published in Taylor and Francis journals to create powerful and effective collections, this series highlights and explores the social theories critical to educational writers, researchers and scholars. Each book focuses on a different key writer or field of theory, with the overarching aim of providing an overview of the social theories important to education research, but also of showing how these theories can be applied in a practical manner in the current education landscape.

Books in the Series:

Foucault and Education
Edited by Stephen J. Ball

Marxisms and Education
Edited by Noah De Lissovoy

Actor Network Theory and Education
Edited by Tara Fenwick and Richard Edwards

Feminist Posthumanisms, New Materialisms and Education
Edited by Jessica Ringrose, Katie Warfield and Shiva Zarabadi

Freud, Lacan, Zizek and Education
Exploring Unconscious Investments in Policy and Practice
Edited by Claudia Lapping

The Education Assemblage
Edited by Greg Thompson

Bourdieu and Education
Edited by Diane Reay

Bourdieu and Education

Edited by
Diane Reay

Routledge
Taylor & Francis Group
LONDON AND NEW YORK

First published 2019
by Routledge
2 Park Square, Milton Park, Abingdon, Oxon, OX14 4RN, UK

and by Routledge
52 Vanderbilt Avenue, New York, NY 10017

First issued in paperback 2020

Routledge is an imprint of the Taylor & Francis Group, an informa business

Introduction, Chapters 1, 4–12 © 2019 Taylor & Francis
Chapter 2 © 2015 David James. Originally published Open Access
Chapter 3 © 2007 Michalinos Zembylas

All rights reserved. With the exception of Chapters 2 and 3, no part of this book may be reprinted or reproduced or utilised in any form or by any electronic, mechanical, or other means, now known or hereafter invented, including photocopying and recording, or in any information storage or retrieval system, without permission in writing from the publishers. Copyright information for Chapters 2 and 3 can be found on the first page of the chapter.

Trademark notice: Product or corporate names may be trademarks or registered trademarks, and are used only for identification and explanation without intent to infringe.

British Library Cataloguing-in-Publication Data
A catalogue record for this book is available from the British Library

ISBN 13: 978-0-367-58598-3 (pbk)
ISBN 13: 978-1-138-33473-1 (hbk)

Typeset in Times New Roman
by codeMantra

Publisher's Note
The publisher accepts responsibility for any inconsistencies that may have arisen during the conversion of this book from journal articles to book chapters, namely the possible inclusion of journal terminology.

Disclaimer
Every effort has been made to contact copyright holders for their permission to reprint material in this book. The publishers would be grateful to hear from any copyright holder who is not here acknowledged and will undertake to rectify any errors or omissions in future editions of this book.

Contents

Citation Information

The chapters in this book were originally published in a variety of Taylor and Francis journals. When citing this material, please use the original page numbering for each article, as follows:

Chapter 1
The Practical Importance of Bourdieu's Analyses of Higher Education
Derek Robbins
Studies in Higher Education, volume 18, issue 2 (1993) pp. 151–163

Chapter 2
How Bourdieu bites back: recognising misrecognition in education and educational research
David James
Cambridge Journal of Education, volume 45, issue 1 (2015) pp. 97–112

Chapter 3
Emotional Capital and Education: Theoretical Insights from Bourdieu
Michalinos Zembylas
British Journal of Educational Studies, volume 55, issue 4 (December 2007) pp. 443–463

Chapter 4
The power of one? Conditions which challenge managerial professional development practices
Ian Hardy
Discourse: Studies in the Cultural Politics of Education, volume 35, issue 4 (2014) pp. 499–512

Chapter 5
Using Bourdieu in practice? Urban secondary teachers' and students' experiences of a Bourdieusian-inspired pedagogical approach
Louise Archer, Emily Dawson, Jennifer DeWitt, Spela Godec, Heather King, Ada Mau, Effrosyni Nomikou and Amy Seakins
British Journal of Sociology of Education, volume 39, issue 3 (2017) pp. 1–16

Chapter 6

Education and Cultural Capital: The Implications of Changing Trends in Education Policies
Diane Reay
Cultural Trends, volume 13, issue 50 (June 2004) pp. 73–86

Chapter 7

Fields and institutional strategy: Bourdieu on the relationship between higher education, inequality and society
Rajani Naidoo
British Journal of Sociology of Education, volume 25, issue 4 (September 2004) pp. 457–471

Chapter 8

Violent youth or violent schools? A critical incident analysis of symbolic violence
Kathryn Herr and Gary L. Anderson
International Journal of Leadership in Education, volume 6, issue 4 (October–December 2003) pp. 415–433

Chapter 9

Bourdieu and the Social Space of the PE Class: Reproduction of Doxa through Practice
lisahunter
Sport, Education and Society, volume 9, issue 2 (July 2004) pp. 175–192

Chapter 10

Mainland Chinese students at an elite Hong Kong university: habitus–field disjuncture in a transborder context
Cora Lingling Xu
British Journal of Sociology of Education, volume 38, issue 5 (2017) pp. 610–624

Chapter 11

Cultural capital as whiteness? Examining logics of ethno-racial representation and resistance
Derron Wallace
British Journal of Sociology of Education, volume 39, issue 4 (2017) pp. 1–17

Chapter 12

Student retention in higher education: the role of institutional habitus
Liz Thomas
Journal of Education Policy, volume 17, issue 4 (2002) pp. 423–442

For any permission-related enquiries please visit:
http://www.tandfonline.com/page/help/permissions

Notes on Contributors

Gary L. Anderson is Professor of Educational Leadership at New York University Steinhardt, USA. He is interested in doing research within the tensions between theory and practice in applied fields like education. He is the author of *Creating the New Democratic Professional: Beyond Corporate Management and Entrepreneurialism in Education* (2018, with M. Cohen) and *The Politics of Education Policy in a Era of Inequality: Possibilities for Democratic Schooling* (2018, with S. Horsford and J. Scott).

Louise Archer is Professor of Sociology of Education at King's College London, UK. Her work focuses on educational identities and inequalities, particularly in relation to gender, ethnicity and social class. She is the author of many books, including *Understanding Young People's Science Aspirations: How students form ideas about 'becoming a scientist'* (2016, with J. DeWitt).

Emily Dawson is Lecturer in Science Communication at University College London, UK. Her work focuses on how people engage with and learn about science, with an emphasis on equity and social justice. Her current research explores how to disrupt rather than reproduce social disadvantages in relation to science education, engagement and communication.

Jennifer DeWitt is Senior Research Associate in the Institute of Education at University College London, UK, where she is a member of the Centre for Sociology of Education and Equity. She is the author of *Understanding Young People's Science Aspirations: How students form ideas about 'becoming a scientist'* (2016, with L. Archer).

Spela Godec is Research Associate in Education, Practice and Society in the Institute of Education at University College London, UK. Her current research focuses on equitable practices in informal STEM learning settings, such as community centre, science centre, tech clubs and zoos. She holds a PhD from King's College London, UK.

Ian Hardy is an ARC Future Fellow in the School of Education at the University of Queensland, Brisbane, Australia. He researches and teaches in the areas of educational policy and politics, including teachers' learning. He is the author of *The politics of teacher professional development: Policy, research and practice* (2012).

Kathryn Herr is Professor of Educational Foundations at Montclair State University, USA. She is interested in qualitative and action research methods and recently completed a study of the first public middle school to move to single-sex academies/classes on a school-wide basis. Her research also covers youth violence and the fit/lack of fit between diverse youth and institutions of education.

lisahunter has researched, taught and published in areas of pedagogy, diversity, movement, health, gender and sexuality, teacher education, physical culture and sport and qualitative methodologies. Lisa's research, consultations and evaluations have contributed to a broad range of programs and organisations in education, health and sport and recreation. Lisa is the author of *Workplace learning in physical education* (2014, with T. Rossi, E. Christensen and D. Macdonald).

David James is Professor in the School of Social Sciences at Cardiff University, UK and Director of the ESRC Wales Doctoral Training Partnership. His research interests encompass governance, teaching, learning, assessment and learner identity across a range of educational settings, with a particular focus on the relationship between educational processes and social inequalities. His most recent edited book is *Masculinity and Education* (2014, with A.J. Coffey).

Heather King is Research Associate at King's College London, UK, where she is a member of the Enterprising Science team. Her research interests focus on the practice and professional development of science museum educators and the nature of museum pedagogy, and she is particularly interested in the nature of natural history teaching and learning.

Ada Mau is Research Associate at King's College London, UK, where she is a member of the Enterprising Science team. Her research focuses on issues and discourses of identities, 'race', gender, social class and social justice in education. She is also interested in heritage language learning, multilingualism, migration, social and cultural policy, informal learning and youth cultures.

Rajani Naidoo is Professor in Higher Education Management at the University of Bath, UK. Her research interests include public sector markets and new public management, transnational higher education and global governance, higher education and international development and the changing identity and nature of student participation in higher education. She is the editor of *The Sociology of Education: Reproduction, Transformation and Change in a Global Era* (2013, with M. David).

Effrosyni Nomikou is Research Associate in Education, Practice and Society in the Institute of Education at University College London, UK. Her work has appeared in journals including *Pedagogy, Culture and Society; British Journal of the Sociology of Education* and *Science Education.* Her research focuses on museums and visitor studies.

Diane Reay is Visiting Professor at the London School of Economics, UK and Emeritus Professor of Sociology of Education at the University of Cambridge, UK. Her main research interests are social justice issues in education, Pierre Bourdieu's social theory and cultural analyses of social class, race and gender. Her most recent book is *Miseducation: Inequality, Education and the Working Classes* (2017).

Derek Robbins is Emeritus Professor at the University of East London, UK. His research is centred on the work of Pierre Bourdieu and explores the relations between the philosophy of social science and empirical social scientific practice. His most recent book is *Cultural Relativism and International Politics* (2014).

Amy Seakins is Engagement Coordinator (Evaluation and Impact) at Imperial College London, UK. She supports staff and students in evaluating their public engagement activities and advises researchers on how they might achieve and evidence research impact through engaging wider audiences. She was previously a Research Associate at King's College London, focusing on science capital, science education and informal science learning.

Liz Thomas is Director and Chair of the Widening Participation Research Centre at Edge Hill University, Ormskirk, UK. She is committed to using research to improve policy and practice, and she is renowned internationally for her research on widening participation and student success. She is the author and editor of nine books on widening participation, including *Improving student retention in higher education: The role of teaching and learning* (2007).

Derron Wallace is Assistant Professor of Education and Sociology at Brandeis University, Waltham, USA. He is a sociologist of race, ethnicity and education and studies inequalities and identities in urban schools and neighbourhoods in global cities. His research examines the educational outcomes of working-class and middle-class Black immigrants in London and New York City. He is the editor of *Masculinity and Aspiration in the Era of Global Neoliberal Education* (2017, with G. Stahl and J. Nelson).

Cora Lingling Xu is Lecturer in Education at Keele University, UK. Her research interests revolve around mobilities of, in and through education. There are three major branches: inter-/intra-national student mobility, experiences of mobile early-career researchers of deprived backgrounds and transnational higher education programmes within and beyond China, underpinned by a strong agenda in achieving social justice through research and public engagement.

Michalinos Zembylas is Professor of Educational Theory and Curriculum Studies at the Open University of Cyprus, Latsia, Cyprus. He has written extensively on emotion and affect in relation to social justice pedagogies, intercultural and peace education, human rights education and citizenship education. His most recent book is *Peace education in a conflict-troubled society: an ethnographic journey* (2016, with C. Charalambous and P. Charalambous).

Introduction

Comprehension through Use: Working with Bourdieu in Educational Research

Diane Reay

Theory into Practice

One of the many attractions of working with Bourdieu, and perhaps the most appealing, is his insistence that his theoretical tools are not intended for theoretical commentary but should be put to use in empirical research. He has always contended that his research is characterised by reciprocal movement between theory and practice. As he asserts, his concepts are just as practical as they are theoretical (Bourdieu 1993). Over fifty years of committed empirical work he, in collaboration with his many colleagues, put together an impressive blueprint for empirical research. Over the duration of his academic career he was always immersed in empirical research projects and asserted that the theoretical tools that emerged out this work were meant not for theoretical explanation but rather to be put to work in new research.

In an interview with Beate Krais, Bourdieu suggested that the chief strength of concepts such as habitus lies in their empirical relevance:

> Ideas like those of habitus, practice, and so on, were intended, among other things, to point out that there is a practical knowledge that has its own logic, which cannot be reduced to that of theoretical knowledge; that in a sense, agents know the social world better than the theoreticians. (Bourdieu 1991: 252)

In emphasising empirical relevance, Bourdieu was also recognising the socio-historical and spatial contingency of concepts, including his own. While concepts such as habitus and field may work effectively to illuminate a particular historical juncture and a particular geographical region, that does not mean they will function similarly at a future moment in time or in a different space (Bourdieu 1985a). He argued that because his texts were the products of the application of method it was important to avoid the danger that they would be disseminated as if they were universally valid accounts of human reality. Rather, there was a degree of specificity about concepts such as habitus, field and capital that arose out of the particular conditions of the construction of the concepts.

Bourdieu argued in relation to his concepts:

> The main thing is that they are not to be conceptualised so much as ideas, on that level, but as a method. The core of my work lies in the method and a way of thinking. To be more precise, my method is a manner of asking questions rather than just ideas. This, I think is a critical point. (Bourdieu 1985b, quoted in Mahar 1990)

Bourdieu was using the term 'method' in a very elastic sense, but what he was stressing is that first and foremost his concepts are tools to be used in empirical research rather than theories to be debated in texts. They are lenses for understanding the world, incorporating aspects of both theory and method and, as such, have a degree of fluidity and openness. As Medvetz and Sallaz (2018: 12) point out, Bourdieu's concepts are founded on the logic of injunction, meaning they supply directives to carry out research in particular ways or provide protections against common errors and omissions'. Bourdieu invites researchers 'to decide deliberately and reflexively how to deploy his concepts' (Robbins 2006). This is in contrast to a spurious theoreticism where 'at conferences you can listen to these preconstructed concepts being exchanged, dressed up in theoretical tinsel, and having the air of scientific facts' (Bourdieu 1992: 42). Bourdieu himself saw his concepts as in a continual process of being reworked. Writing of his conceptual framework he commented:

> I blame most of my readers for having considered as theoretical treatises, meant solely to be read or commented upon, works that, like gymnastics handbooks, were intended for exercise, or even better, for putting into practice. One cannot grasp the most profound logic of the social world unless one becomes immersed in the specificity of an empirical reality. (Bourdieu 1993: 271)

Bourdieu rejected the view of his work as 'grand theory', arguing instead that it should be seen as 'a theory of action, or of practice' (Bourdieu 1990: 119). For Bourdieu all so-called objective knowledge can be seen to be constantly provisional, subject to testing and reformulation (Robbins 2006). As I have argued in earlier work (Reay 2004), paradoxically the conceptual looseness of Bourdieu's concepts also constitutes a potential strength. It makes possible adaptation rather than the more constricting straightforward adoption of the concepts within empirical work.

Although, sometimes, responses to Bourdieu's invitation to take his concepts and rework them have been viewed as excuses for artistic license (Atkinson 2011), conceptual moves beyond the limits of theoretical probity; they have also resulted in conceptual richness and creativity among an emerging group of new Bourdieusian scholars (Thatcher et al. 2015). While this edited collection comprises scholars with a long experience of working with Bourdieu, it also includes those who are just starting out on their academic careers.

Reflexivity and Socio-analysis

To take Bourdieu's work to the limits; to engage with his research affectively as well as intellectually is to recognise our own social and academic positioning in the same powerful way he recognised and worked with his own autobiography (Bourdieu 2004). This requires the deconstruction and reconstruction of his concepts in relation to our distinct experiences. The crucial aspect of reflexivity for Bourdieu lay in the recognition and articulation of the relationship between the researcher and the object of study, and the acknowledgement of the ways in which this relationship shaped all scientific endeavour. He was arguing for a rigorous epistemic, as opposed to a narcissistic, reflexivity.

Reflexivity for Bourdieu demanded socio-analysis. This entailed not only a socio-analysis of the research field but also a more demanding socio-analysis of the researcher, their positioning within the academic field as well as their relationship to the researched. Socio-analysis had a double dimension for Bourdieu. On the one hand it was a tool for social research, but on the other hand, it constituted a way of dealing with one's epistemological biases.

Turning the scientific gaze back upon researcher, according to Bourdieu, 'enables us to assume ourselves and even… to claim ourselves' (Bourdieu and Wacquant 1992: 199). Science was for Bourdieu an essentially practical enterprise. Instead of viewing science as a scholastic discipline enshrining academic principles he saw it as an ongoing practice of research and analysis. The concept of a neutral objective science is a fiction. As Craig Calhoun points out, for Bourdieu science is not simply the value-free expression of 'truth'; it is a project, but one organised, ideally, in a social field that rewards the production of verifiable and forever revisable truths—including new truths and new approaches to understanding—and not merely performance according to explicit rules and standards. (Calhoun 2002) A scientific gaze on the self offers the practitioners of socio-analysis 'the possibility of assuming their habitus without guilt or suffering' (Bourdieu and Wacquant, 1992: 199). Socio-analysis requires 'ripping the adherences and adhesions through which we usually belong to groups' and cannot be undertaken without unmasking 'the self-deception, the lie to ourselves collectively held and encouraged which, in every society, is at the basis of the most sacred values, and through it, of all social existence' (Bourdieu 2004: 93).

For Bourdieu, reflexivity is the principle that connects the epistemological security of the research project to the socio-analysis of the researcher as a cultural producer, and to the analyses of the conditions of possibility of education as a discipline. Socio-analysis, as the core of a reflexive social science, is the means by which the reflexive researcher can begin to make a break with common sense and the reigning doxa. Central to such a break is a rupture with the kind of 'scholastic bias', the objectifying and universalising perspective offered by a position within the academy (Bourdieu 2010: 180), which leads the social scientist to construct the social world as a set of theoretical conundrums to be interpreted and explained, rather than as real problems to be solved practically. To take Bourdieu's thinking seriously is to recognise we can never take any status quo for granted. Rather, even sociological explanation needs to be rigorously scrutinised. Consequently, working with Bourdieu is as much about raising questions about the way the world is as it is about seeking answers.

Moving Beyond Binaries

Paradoxically, for an academic who has repeatedly been accused of reifying binaries in his work, primarily those of agency and structure, objective and subjective, reproduction and resistance, science and affect (Jenkins 1982, 1992; King 2000), much of his scholarship has been an attempt to move beyond binaries, to reconcile problematic oppositions. A continuous theme in Bourdieu's scholarship is a preoccupation with the division between reproduction and transformation, reason and affect, science and feeling, and his efforts, particularly through the concept of habitus, to make sense of these dualities and begin to uncover connections and synergies as well as tensions. In contrast to the rigidity of binaries, an important part of the generativity of Bourdieu's concepts is their potential for highlighting unresolved conflicts and frictions in society rather than settled conditions or states of affairs (Medvetz and Sallaz 2018). For Bourdieu, choices between agency and structure, submission and resistance, are inevitably spurious. Rather, practices and situations are defined by their intrinsically double-skewed nature (Wacquant 1992).

When we analyse Bourdieu's scholarship it is struggle rather than reproduction that encapsulates its guiding tenet. His concept of field represents a social space characterised by competition and conflict. Social classes and other groups in society are constantly engaged in a struggle to realise their interests, to impose their view of the world as the dominant one over other social groups. Bourdieu's sociology is essentially relational rather than oppositional. At the core of Bourdieu's philosophy of knowledge is the belief that binaries represent outmoded perceptions of which sociology must rid itself. Rather, we need to understand the world in terms of relations rather than things, processes rather than states (Bourdieu 1990). But at the same time, it is important to recognise that interactions mask the structures that are realised in them (Bourdieu 1990: 126).

Power and Politics

A further key reason that Bourdieu's work has become so popular is its focus on inequalities and its centring of social justice. Of all the social theorists of the twentieth century Bourdieu had the most overt commitment to equality and social justice. He is perhaps the best known example of the academic as political activist, but even before he became well known for his activism, his work was viewed as a form of political as well as academic capital. In June 1968, students actually carried copies of his book, *The Inheritors*, onto the barricades. Fifty years on, at the beginning of the twenty-first century, at an historical juncture when dominant discourses of individualism, instrumentalism and hyper-competition proliferate, Bourdieu continues to provide us with a different way of looking and acting within the social world. So, for example, *The Weight of the World* (1999) written by Bourdieu and his colleagues was both exemplary ethnography and impassioned polemic. The publication of the book was a major social and political event in France, where it topped the best-seller list and triggered a wide-ranging public debate on inequality, politics and social solidarity. Bourdieu and his team of sociologists had spent three years researching the new emergent forms of social suffering that characterise contemporary societies. Declining housing estates; the school; families; the everyday world of social workers, teachers, policemen, factory workers and clerical assistants; and the universe of farmers, artisans and the unemployed were analysed as spaces where discriminations and recriminations, conflicts and contradictions, abound and accumulate, and where new forms of suffering are produced. *Acts of Resistance* (1998) took an even more politically committed stance. Sub-titled 'against the new myths of our time' the book is a series of essays that all in different ways stand up for the interests of the powerless and help to give a voice to those individuals and groups whose views are rarely heard in the dominant media. Employing an incisive, uncompromising rhetoric Bourdieu attacked neoliberalism and those who champion it from the International Monetary Fund to the President of the Bundesbank, from politicians to academic commentators.

But Bourdieu was much more than a passionate advocate of the left; he also produced an impressive body of sociological theory with an analysis of power and inequality at its heart. A Bourdieusian sociology of knowledge is a sociology of symbolic power. Whether Bourdieu was studying Algerian peasants, students, writers and artists, university professors or the socially excluded, a central unifying preoccupation emerges: the question of how stratified social systems of hierarchy and domination persist and reproduce intergenerationally without powerful resistance and without the conscious recognition of their members. For Bourdieu, power is not a separate domain of study but lies at the very core of all social life.

For Bourdieu 'what is problematic is the fact that the established order is not problematic' (1988: 56). He viewed research as not just about the production of knowledge but part of the struggle to generate social change through providing different ways of seeing the social world:

> scientific explanation should teach the researcher where his liberties are really situated and resolutely to refuse the infinitesmal acts of cowardice and laxness which leave

> the power of social necessity intact, to fight in himself and in others the opportunist indifference or conformist ennui which allows the social milieu to impose the slippery slope of resigned compliance and submissive complicity. (Bourdieu 1988: 4–5)

It is unsurprising then that Bourdieu's method emphasises the way in which 'the structure of social worlds is already predefined by broader racial, gender and class relations' (Bourdieu and Wacquant 1992: 144). As Derek Robbins points out, Bourdieu's world view turns Rousseau's contention on its head. 'It is not that we are born free but are everywhere in chains. On the contrary, we are born in chains and constantly strive to construct the functional fiction that we are free' (Robbins 2006: 347). As David James notes in his chapter in this book, Bourdieu's theory is largely a sociology of domination, grounded in a strong concept of power, and whilst there is plenty of scope for agency it centres the limits to agency. Individuals are constantly making and remaking the structures that limit their power and agency in everyday processes in which 'social structures and cognitive structures are recursively and structurally linked' (Bourdieu and Wacquant 1992: 14).

In 'For a scholarship with commitment' (Bourdieu 2010) Bourdieu rejects any opposition between scholarship and political commitment. Rather, he argues, remaining within the ivory tower and clinging to an 'axiological neutrality' constitutes 'a scientifically unimpeachable form of escapism' (page 180). Instead,

> The intellectual world must engage in a permanent critique of all the abuses of power or authority committed in the name of intellectual authority, or, if you prefer, in a relentless critique of the use of intellectual authority as a political weapon within the intellectual field. (Bourdieu 2010: 180)

As he cogently points out we academics must struggle against the typical academic propensity to confuse the things of logic with the logic of things; to mistake revolutions in words and texts for revolutions in the order of things.

> Nothing would make me more happy than to have succeeded in enablingsome of my readers, both men and women, to recognize their own experiences, difficulties, problems, sufferings, etc. in mine, and that they should derive from this realist identification, which is completely different from an exhalted imagination, the means to act and live a little bit better what they live and do. (2004: 142)

As Frangie (2009: 222) points out, Bourdieu's texts are not simply attempts at interpreting the world, but more importantly they are interventions aimed at changing it, challenges to the ways in which we perceive the social world and construct it.

The Collection

All the papers in this edited collection illuminate these key aspects of Bourdieu's scholarship. They are exemplars of putting theory into practice, illustrate the merits of reflexivity, the move beyond binary ways of reading the social world, and demonstrate the importance of power in any analysis of education. At the same time they are very diverse, covering topics as varied as higher education (HE), the science curriculum, the physical education (PE) classroom, whiteness and managerial practices. The Bourdieusian concepts they draw on are equally diverse, spanning habitus, field, capitals, doxa, illusio, misrecognition and symbolic violence.

In 'The Practical Importance of Bourdieu's Analysis of Higher Education' Derek Robbins argues that the strength of Bourdieu's analyses of educational practices lies in his refusal to remove them from their social contexts. Recognising the importance of Bourdieu's emphasis on specificity, Robbins' article relates Bourdieu's specific analysis of French HE to his own analysis of HE in the UK context, an exercise he claims is a project of applying Bourdieu's thinking pragmatically. In highlighting the contextual specificity of Bourdieu's theory, Robbins emphasises temporality as well as spatiality. Historical time and place both matter when we try and make sense of theory. The paper primarily works with the concept of field but like all good Bourdieusian analyses makes links to other concepts, in this case those of symbolic violence, habitus and capitals. It also underlines the transferability of Bourdieu's theory as long as analyses are contextually sensitive, making a sustained case that Bourdieu's analyses help us understand what is currently happening in UK HE. He argues for the importance of examining what is happening in HE in order to articulate the differences in cultural capital between staff and students. In particular, it is crucial to analyse how teaching and learning at the HE level modifies the habitus students have inherited. As Robbins concludes, 'Bourdieu's sociology undermines the notion of the anachronistic' (page 162).

That ability of Bourdieusian insights to reach beyond the anachronistic is evident in Derron Wallace's application of cultural capital as whiteness in his research on cultural capital among Black middle classes in the UK in the 2010s. His article highlights the enduring relationship between whiteness and cultural capital. His findings offer insights into the racialisation of cultural capital, challenging mainstream academic analyses that view cultural capital as exclusively a resource for Whites. Wallace reworks understandings of cultural capital to show how ethnicity and race are implicated in the formation and expression of cultural capital. Like many of the other papers included in the book, the paper extends the conceptual boundaries of cultural capital beyond Bourdieu's original conceptualisation. In a rigorous analysis that draws on Bourdieusian concepts of doxa and habitus as well as cultural capital, Wallace challenges what he calls 'the forced union between whiteness and cultural capital' (page 7), asserting that Bourdieu is a useful starting point for understanding how racism impedes the advancement of the Black and ethnic minority middle classes despite their cultural capital. Rather, as he concludes, race-conscious Bourdieusian perspectives are urgently needed to explore the complexities of Black and ethnic minority young people's class identities (page 14).

Liz Thomas' article on the role of institutional habitus in student retention in HE is a further example of the widespread conceptual development of Bourdieu's work. It attempts to provide a conceptual and empirical understanding of the ways in which the values and practices of an HE institution impact on student retention through the concept of institutional habitus. Power and the logic of practice are at the heart of a Bourdieusian analysis that concludes that relationships and positions are central to student success in HE. Thomas' research identifies internal structures of power and representation, including the spheres of governance, curricula and pedagogy as all contributing to processes of discrimination against non-traditional students. Like a number of the papers in this collection, it attempts to work with Bourdieusian concepts not only to examine practice but to detect ways in which practice can be improved.

Lisa Hunter's paper demonstrates the centrality of embodiment within Bourdieu's conceptual framework. The paper draws on Bourdieu's conceptual toolkit to develop a more dynamic understanding of teaching and learning as contextualised, contested and embodied, working generatively with concepts of field, habitus and capitals, but also Bourdieu's less well known concepts of doxa and illusio. The logic of practice is vividly brought to life in the PE classroom as the body operates 'below the level of consciousness ... it does not represent what it performs, it does not memorize the past, it enacts the past, bringing it back to life' (Bourdieu 1990b: 73). While some students in the PE classrooms Hunter researched are learning what they can do and who they are, many are learning what they can't do, who they are not or cannot be. Yet, again educational inequalities are foregrounded in the analysis. And, as with much educational research that works with Bourdieu, Hunter includes a powerful call to practitioners to challenge dominant discourses, arguing that in the PE field, and in schools and teacher education more generally, the excluding categories they maintain through the practices of PE are deeply damaging. Hunter argues that current configurations make impossible other ways of being and result in oppressing, marginalising or alienating young people from positive orientations to themselves and physical culture.

My own paper 'Education and Cultural Capital: The Implications of Changing Trends in Education Policies' uses cultural capital as a resource for gaining a deeper, richer insight into the way educational inequalities operate and are perpetuated. As with all the other capitals, Bourdieu's concern in relation to cultural capital was with its continual transmission and accumulation in ways that perpetuate social inequalities, and like many of the papers in this collection, Bourdieu's toolkit is deployed to map out inequalities within the field of education. The paper is also an attempt to elaborate, through the concept of cultural capital, affective aspects of inequality such as levels of confidence and entitlement. Cultural capital can be seen not just as a disposition to choose but also as the ability to get the choices one wants. The paper draws on a range of educational policies to show how they have prioritised micro-interactional processes that advantage middle-class cultural capital. All three case studies in the paper reveal a growing synergy between middle-class cultural capital and education policy in which the mobilisation of middle-class cultural capital both feeds into and has been fuelled by policy initiatives that prioritise the role of parents in the education of children.

Louise Archer and her colleagues' innovative paper also puts Bourdieu into practice but this time through a Bourdieusian-inspired pedagogical approach in the context of secondary science education. As Archer and her colleagues point out, working with Bourdieu is not an easy option. He doesn't make for good bullet points, but just as his concepts can shine a piercing light on educational inequalities they can also provide possibilities for praxis. They write that their motivation for employing Bourdieu's theory of practice was to investigate the potential for using Bourdieusian theory to inform the development of a teaching approach that uses an understanding of the reproduction of inequality in order to challenge the status quo. The resulting Bourdieusian-inspired pedagogical approach explored the emancipatory potential of such an approach, investigating how it affected student engagement, student 'voice' and student participation. There is a clear explanation of how Bourdieu's theory can be put into practice in which student engagement is seen to be produced as a form of practice that is generated at the interface of habitus, capital and field. In their own words, Archer et al. are using Bourdieu to 'speak truth to power and as a "critical partner", offering ideas for how things might be "done differently" in the ongoing struggle for a more socially just education system'. (page 283). As with much Bourdieusian-inspired educational research, they are seeking both to uncover educational inequalities but also to provide socially just alternatives.

In a stimulating paper, David James works with the little-used Bourdieusian concept of misrecognition to illuminate the misrecognition that lies at the heart of the relationship between educational inequalities and social class. But it also deploys the concept to examine a further level of misrecognition: the misrecognition of Bourdieu's theory by some educational researchers. In order to become critical social researchers, educationalists must subject themselves and their preconceptions to new forms of scrutiny that 'dislodge their thinking' (Stich 2012). There is no 'light touch' when it comes to applying Bourdieusian theory. James identifies four tensions between Bourdieusian-inspired research and some key characteristics of educational practice, policy and research. But, perhaps the most important tension he presents is the one between what he describes as the implicit pessimism of a Bourdieusian approach and the optimism of much contemporary educational research which continues to underline the importance of enthusiasm and other forms of positivity. As James points out, such enthusiasm and positivity can be seen to be a consequence of both an endemic reluctance to engage in problematising the ends of education and the tendency to prioritise technical over cultural aspects in collecting and using evidence of 'what works' (page 108). From a Bourdieusian perspective, in the absence of wider systemic changes, such optimism continually overestimates the capacity to act to bring about genuine change. But, as James wryly notes, until we have firmer grounds for optimism, a tendency to pessimism may be warranted. He concludes that putting Bourdieu to work in educational research is never the easy option as the findings generated through deploying his 'tool-kit' are often 'difficult to "hear", regardless of how ultimately practical or useful they might actually be'.

In 'Emotional Capital and Education: Theoretical Insights from Bourdieu' Michalinos Zembylas has two main objectives. First the paper outlines existing conceptualisations of emotional capital in educational research, and second, it undertakes a critical analysis of these conceptualisations, including a reflection on Zembylas' own explorations of teachers' and students' emotional practices. Bourdieu's later work often explored the psycho-social – the affinities of habitus and what Zembylas calls 'affective economies'. But it is the conceptualisation of emotions as resources through the notion of emotional capital that has been the most generative in thinking through the ways in which emotion practices are regulated within an educational context. As Zembylas points out, Bourdieusian understandings of emotional capital stand in sharp contrast to concepts such as emotional intelligence deployed in management and functionalist discourses as a set of resources stripped of social and political context. In order to understand and work with the concept of emotional capital, both its relational nature and context are key. And, as with all Bourdieu's concepts, the workings of power are central. Emotional capital illustrates the importance of emotions within habitus, but it also explains the significance of emotions and affects in the circulation of other forms of capital. The concept also reveals the part played by emotions in social and political practices, and the centrality of emotions in power relationships. As Zembylas concludes, 'using emotional capital as a conceptual tool ensures not only that emotions and the work of emotions are acknowledged in education, but also that the research focus becomes broader in terms of its socio-political implications' (page 459).

Cora Xu writes about a growing focus of research that uses Bourdieu's theory – the habitus-field disjuncture – but deepens her analysis by examining how it is exacerbated by the hysteresis effect. Her research looks at two dissonant fields, those of Hong Kong and Mainland China HE, and identifies two levels of habitus-field disjuncture experienced by Mainland Chinese students studying in Hong Kong. The first level is a consequence of having a habitus fashioned in mainland Chinese HE which made it difficult for students to mobilise resources available in the Hong Kong HE field in the same way their Hong Kong peers were able to. The second level of disjuncture Xu's analysis reveals is that the students' Hong Kong education credential', the institutionalised cultural capital they had acquired, had become an added layer to their original habitus. But this new layer constituted a degree of deficit in so far as it bestowed on them the identity of being 'educated locally' whilst also implying a critical 'absence' from mainland China. The chapter is also an important example of an increasing number of research studies that transport Bourdieu's conceptual toolkit from the traditional location of Bourdieusian studies, that of Europe and North America, to more distant locales. What becomes evident, in the reflexive and sustained analysis, is that the concern of critics that Bourdieu's concepts are not transferable to unfamiliar settings is unwarranted as long as a rigorous reflexivity is maintained.

Taking a Bourdieusian approach to educational research is to recognise the importance of context and resources, and to always include both in the analysis of data. In 'The power of one? Conditions which challenge managerial professional development practices', Ian Hardy offers a cautionary note in relation to working with the concept of habitus without a recognition of the field it is located in. He also provides an illuminating example of a familiar theme in educational research that works with Bourdieu – analyses that contest and challenge dominant, often taken-for-granted, mainstream practices. Based on the professional development practices of one teacher in the UK, the paper works with concepts of habitus, capital and field to develop an in-depth analysis of the socially situated teacher, engaged by and engaging in an alternative politics to those associated with more managerial conceptions of teacher learning. As with many of the other papers in this collection, the findings operate as a provocation to dominant understandings of the heroic individual overcoming adverse circumstances, but rather underline that access to resources and the possibilities (and barriers) provided by the context are always crucial.

'Violent youth or violent schools? A critical incident analysis of symbolic violence' attempts to capture the mechanisms of symbolic violence. The chapter works with Bourdieu's 'law of conservation of violence' (Bourdieu 1998: 40) as a powerful explanatory tool for understanding the continuum – from symbolic to physical forms – of violence that exists in schools. The research explains how violence is generated symbolically within schools, reproducing larger systems of structural violence and producing local instances of emotional and physical violence. Through the analysis of a number of critical incidents symbolic violence is revealed to be inflicted on students often by well-meaning, capable, caring teachers. But we also see the generative way in which one teacher is able to interrupt symbolic violence, causing ripples that initiate interruptions across micro, meso and macro levels of schooling. As in the Hardy paper in this collection, there is a questioning of mainstream assumptions of the agentic subject, in this instance in relation to working-class students who are seen to have higher levels of motivation and achievement and thus automatically are viewed as being more competitive in what is presumed to be a legitimate, meritocratic system. As James argues in relation to the concept of misrecognition, Herr and Anderson assert that by leaving such assumptions unexamined, social and cultural analysis in education can itself become a form of symbolic violence.

Rajani Naidoo's 'Fields and institutional strategy: Bourdieu on the relationship between higher education, inequality and society' is a critical exploration of the concept of 'field'. The paper illustrates the centrality of contestation and conflict within Bourdieusian analyses. Bourdieu's theoretical constructs therefore make a significant contribution to understanding, first, the relationship between macro-sociopolitical forces and universities and, second, why institutions within the same system develop divergent strategic responses to external pressures. As in all Bourdieusian analyses power is pivotal to understanding. As Naidoo makes clear, relationships in the field are primarily relationships of power. The chapter concludes that field, together with concepts of capital, and in particular academic capital, provides a conceptual apparatus through which macro forces and institutional practices can be analytically related.

Conclusion

> Bourdieu's sociological imagination, was an extraordinarily fertile source of hypotheses, concepts and schemas, almost all of which could be reused in the service of empirically relevant theories. (Jean-Claude Passeron quoted in Truong and Weill 2012)

These papers in a rich variety of ways implicitly, and sometimes explicitly, make the case for a Bourdieusian analysis of education. The vital lesson from Bourdieu's scholarship they all adopt, through one means or another, is that empirical research can be a powerful tool for breaking through the taken-for-granted, everyday assumptions about the purposes and practices of education. At the core of all these papers is the attempt to achieve a truer knowledge of how education works, the ways power operates in and through the educational system and whose interests it serves. Despite doing this in very different ways, and drawing on diverse aspects of Bourdieu's conceptual framework, what they all clearly illustrate is that Bourdieu is extremely useful for thinking with.

References

Atkinson, W. (2011) From sociological fictions to social fictions: Some Bourdieusian reflections on the concepts of 'institutional habitus' and 'family habitus', *British Journal of Sociology of Education*, 32, 331–347.

Bourdieu, P. (1985a) The genesis of the concepts of habitus and of field, *Sociocriticism*, 2, 11–24.

Bourdieu, P. (1985b) From rules to strategies: An interview with Pierre Bourdieu, *Cultural Anthropology*, 1, 110–120.

Bourdieu, P (1990) *In other words: Essays towards a reflexive sociology*. Stanford University Press.

Bourdieu, P. (1992) Thinking about limits. *Theory, Culture and Society*, 9, 37–49.

Bourdieu, P. (1993) Concluding remarks: For a sociogenetic understanding of intellectual works, In: C. Calhoun, E. Lipuma & M. Postone (Eds) *Bourdieu: Critical perspectives*. Cambridge: Polity Press.

Bourdieu, P. (1998) *Acts of resistance*. Cambridge: Polity.

Bourdieu, P. (2004) *Esquisse pour une auto-analyse [Sketch for Self Analysis]*. Paris: Raisons d'Agir.

Bourdieu, P. (2010) For a scholarship with commitment, In: G Sapiro (Ed) *Sociology is a martial art: Political writings by Pierre Bourdieu*. New York, NY: The New Press.

Bourdieu, P. & Wacquant, L. (1992) *An invitation to reflexive sociology*. Chicago, IL: University of Chicago Press.

Calhoun, C. (2002) Pierre Bourdieu, the centrality of the social, and the possibility of politics paper presented at University of Pennsylvania Ethnohistory Workshop, 11 April 2002, University of Pennsylvania.

Frangie, S. (2009) Bourdieu's reflexive politics socio-analysis, biography and self-creation, *European Journal of Social Theory*, 12(2), 213–229.

Jenkins, R. (1982) Pierre Bourdieu and the Reproduction of Determinism, *Sociology*, 31, 270–281.

Jenkins, R. (1992) *Pierre Bourdieu: Key sociologists*. London: Routledge.

King, A. (2000) Thinking with Bourdieu against Bourdieu: A 'practical' critique of the habitus, *Sociological Theory*, 18(3), 417–433.

Mahar, C. (1990) Pierre Bourdieu: The intellectual project, In: R. Harker, C. Mahar & C. Wilkes (Eds) *An introduction to the work of Pierre Bourdieu: The practice of theory*. London: MacMillan.

Medvetz, T. & Sallaz, J. (2018) Introduction: Pierre Bourdieu, a twentieth century life, In: T. Medvetz & J. Sallaz (Eds) *The Oxford handbook of Pierre Bourdieu*. Oxford: Oxford University Press, 1–21.

Reay, D (2004) 'It's all becoming a habitus': Beyond the habitual use of Pierre Bourdieu's concept of habitus in educational research Special Issue of *British Journal of Sociology of Education* on Pierre Bourdieu 25(4), 431–444.

Robbins, D. (2006) *On Bourdieu, education and society*. London: The Bardwell Press.

Stich, A. (2012) *Access to inequality: Reconsidering class, knowledge, and capital in higher education*. Plymouth: Lexington Books.

Thatcher, J., Ingram, N., Burke, C. & Abrahams, J. (2015) *Bourdieu: The next generation*. Abingdon: Routledge.

Truong, N. & Weill, N. (2012) A decade after his death, French sociologist Pierre Bourdieu stands tall, *The Guardian*, 21st February 2012.

Wacquant, L. (1992) The Structure and Logic of Bourdieu's Sociology, In: Bourdieu and Wacquant (Eds) *An invitation to reflexive sociology*. Chicago, IL: University of Chicago Press.

The Practical Importance of Bourdieu's Analyses of Higher Education

DEREK ROBBINS

ABSTRACT *The paper issues a warning about interpreting any one strand of Bourdieu's work in isolation from the other strands but, nevertheless, attempts to effect a functional disaggregation in order to explore the practical implications for contemporary higher education of the educational research undertaken by Bourdieu and his collaborators over the last 30 years. The paper proceeds to represent the main features of that research—concentrating on the three emphases which correspond historically with the 1960s, the 1970s, and the 1980s. The account of Bourdieu's work is, therefore, historical rather than thematic. This reflects Bourdieu's own contention that there is a continuously reciprocal relationship between theory and practice, interpretation and implementation. It does not at all preclude the possibility that Bourdieu's work might acquire cumulatively a relevance which is practically important in the present. By both describing and prescribing social events during the last 30 years, Bourdieu's work—now seen as a corpus of research—has contrived to accommodate and transcend those events in such a way that it now offers a perspective on current developments which escapes the self-fulfilling character of educational research which is solely the product of present concerns and problem definitions. The paper tries to use the detachment which has been constructed in this way out of historical involvement to reflect, within Bourdieu's conceptual framework, on some of the prevailing features of current thought and practice in higher education including, for instance, the practice of accrediting prior learning. It argues, finally, that the tendency for separate institutions to become socially homogeneous in order to present clearly differentiated corporate identities has implications for the practice of higher education research. It means that researchers must be sensitive about their own institutional position, and it also means that the sociology of education needs to be rethought. The concentration on what happens within institutions of higher education has to be set in the context of a sociology of learning which will be able to analyse the trajectories of individuals in society to assess how they use an extensive range of learning contexts to find their way through the social system.*

Introduction

In a recent book of mine, *The Work of Pierre Bourdieu: recognizing society* (Robbins, 1991), I sought to represent in chronological sequence the full extent of Bourdieu's researches in a number of different disciplines. The intention of that book was to lay before the reader an account of Bourdieu's work so as to encourage people to use that work to make sense of their own situations. My claim was that "we should endeavour to apply his thinking pragmatically" (Robbins, 1991, p. 179). This was an attempt to facilitate the kind of response to the whole of Bourdieu's work that he himself recommended to foreign readers of *Homo Academicus* in the preface to the English edition of that text—that it should "lay the foundations of a self-analysis" (Bourdieu, 1988, p. xv).

This paper tries to isolate those aspects of Bourdieu's work which can be said to be about higher education. This is a problematic task because the strength of Bourdieu's analyses of educational practices lies precisely in the fact that he refuses to remove them, as 'pedagogy', from their social contexts. I attempt, therefore, a functional disaggregation of Bourdieu's work specifically so as to relate his perception of French higher education to my perception of United Kingdom higher education. I am, thereby, seeking to put my own injunction into practice, namely to apply Bourdieu's thinking pragmatically. At the end of this double process of interpretation and application, readers are advised to explore their own responses to Bourdieu's effort to understand the place of higher education in French society in the last 30 years.

I shall first try to represent three main emphases in Bourdieu's educational work. For convenience, these will be suggested developmentally as characteristic of the 1960s, the 1970s, and the 1980s. A composite picture will emerge in this process and I shall then seek to bring that composite picture of Bourdieu's educational work into direct confrontation with some of the issues which seem to me currently to be dominating discussion, practice, and research in United Kingdom higher education.

The Work of the 1960s

The Algerian Background

Bourdieu's first educational research has to be seen as a product of the early anthropological field-work which he had undertaken in Algeria during the War of Independence. Bourdieu was clearly a committed supporter of the Algerian struggle for liberation from the oppression of French colonialism. He saw the collapse of the social solidarity of tribes and tribesmen as they were forcibly resettled and he also saw that modernisation was ensuring that old values and traditions were no longer going to be a viable basis for the social organisation of the independent state of Algeria. He was eager that the activism against the French in Algeria should gradually express itself positively as a social and socialist revolution rather than define itself negatively as a movement of liberation.

He documented the evidence which he found of cultural dislocation precisely so as to provide the Algerians themselves with the raw materials of a self-understanding with which they might construct a nation state by constructing, as a prerequisite, a national identity. He believed that the new state consciousness would need to develop from the bottom upwards if it were to be real rather than notional. A centrally controlled educational system would be a necessary mechanism for facilitating the process of nation creation, but the control should only be operational and not substantive.

In an important passage at the end of *Le Déracinement* (Bourdieu, 1964a), Bourdieu makes it clear that it was his view that state education should not mean the central prescription of a curriculum which would be transmitted undifferentially to all recipients but, instead, the central organisation of a system which would use the pedagogic process as a means of securing a collaborative socialisation whereby pupils and teachers would work together to construct the new social structures by which they would be contractually bound. Bourdieu's hope was that this kind of participatory construction of a social consensus would ensure that obligations would no more be experienced as impositions by the new Algerians than they were by the Kabyle tribesmen by whose social organisation—now destroyed—he had been so impressed. I label this as Bourdieu's 'Algerian vision' of social reconstruction through education.

Les Héritiers (1964): the analysis of the problem of French higher education

Back in France in the early 1960s, Bourdieu saw that the post World War II decline of rural and regional societies had produced a disparity of values between the country and the town and between the provinces and Paris which mirrored the disparity he had seen between the values of the desert tribesmen of Algeria and those of the other immigrant casual labourers of Algiers. The difference was that the French disparities were established elements of the *status quo*. The disparities constituted structural inequalities in a nation state which had already been constructed over many centuries. The state education system in France which had been heavily influenced by the Durkheimian socialism of the Third Republic seemed to have become a mechanism for sustaining these structural inequalities rather than removing them. The research which Bourdieu began, mainly at the University of Lille, which led to the publication of *Les Héritiers* (Bourdieu, 1964b) was an attempt to expose how anti-socialist had become the French socialist system of state education.

Bourdieu knew the statistical data which demonstrated that few 'working-class' students entered higher education. He was philosophically or, perhaps, morally committed to the view that this exclusion from higher education could not be adequately explained in terms of the lesser intelligence or giftedness of the working class. Sociological analysis offered a more adequate explanation. He analysed the performance of students within a selection of French higher education institutions and concluded that working-class students were less successful that middle-class students because the curriculum content was biased in favour of those things with which middle-class students were already ex-curricularly familiar. As is well known, Bourdieu coined the phrase that the working-class students were poorly endowed with 'cultural capital'.

Bourdieu's own findings were based on the responses to questionnaires issued to students of philosophy and social science, but his colleagues confirmed the same explanation in respect of science and technology students. Bourdieu's conclusion seemed to suggest that the working-class students were at an unfair disadvantage and that there was a conspiratorial collusion between middle-class staff and middle-class students which meant that these students received a structurally preferential treatment which was a kind of cheating. The assumption of these findings in respect of the performance of working-class students within the higher education system was that this explained the tacit exclusion or self-exclusion of working-class people from the student population.

Les Héritiers (1964): the proposed solution

Bourdieu had diagnosed the problem sociologically and had, therefore, offered an explanation which challenged the psychological thinking which had lain behind the currency of IQ testing in the previous decade. Nevertheless, he provided a solution which was traditional in assuming that pedagogical reform would be sufficient to secure change. The proposed solution was that the higher education curriculum should be a culture *sui generis* which would, therefore, be accessible to working-class and middle-class students on equal terms.

Bourdieu did not want a form of reverse discrimination which would make the curriculum preferentially amenable to the working class. He discarded this 'populist' solution. He sought to encourage forms of 'rational pedagogy' which would introduce students possessing different amounts of cultural capital to the norms and values of the autonomous discourses enshrined in the curricula of higher education institutions.

In this way, Bourdieu's Algerian vision remained intact. As he tried to argue in 'Systèmes d'enseignement et systèmes de pensée' (Bourdieu, 1967), the system of education of a society determines the system of thinking which is available to it. It was, therefore, precisely by sponsoring within its educational system the notion of curricular autonomy that a state might establish institutional contexts within which otherwise competing cultures might encounter each other to fabricate together a consensus which would endorse the state's authority.

La Reproduction (1970)

The research which was written up in *Les Héritiers* was conducted on students attending state universities. At the same time, Bourdieu's colleagues analysed the nature of the processes obtaining in the more prestigious private institutions within the French educational system. They analysed the *classes préparatoires* and the *grandes écoles*—an institutionalised conveyer belt on which privileged children were carried naturally forward towards privileged occupational positions.

When, therefore, Bourdieu came to rewrite the early Lille researches in the light of subsequent projects undertaken within the Centre de Sociologie Européenne, Paris, it was not surprising that he should focus on the process of 'reproduction' in education and society. *La Reproduction* (Bourdieu, 1970) represented a decisive break with the 'Algerian' view that the encouragement of rational pedagogy within a state controlled education system would in itself create the social solidarity which would confirm the state in its authority. The new recognition, instead, was that any society accommodates a plurality of institutions which perpetuate themselves by educational means. The 'state' constitutes itself by balancing rival interest groups. It does not constitute itself by privileging the self-perpetuation secured educationally within the 'education' system.

The ideas introduced in *La Reproduction* are as well known as that of 'cultural capital' advanced in *Les Héritiers*. Propositions which have the status of mathematical or logical formulae spell out the consequences of the initiating contention that "All pedagogic action (PA) is, objectively, symbolic violence in so far as it is the imposition of a cultural arbitrary by an arbitrary power" (Bourdieu, 1970—English translation, p. 5). Religious instruction and technical training, for instance, are both forms of pedagogic action and both are mechanisms for initiating students into the world views, either theological or technological, which endorse the religious or technical authority of those controlling the respective educational processes.

The effectiveness of pedagogic action can be measured in all contexts in terms of 'pedagogic work', whether enough work has been done to ensure that the students internalise the culturally arbitrary knowledge and values which they receive. The efficiency of the pedagogic process can, in other words, be calculated in terms of the extent to which it functions to enable any interest group to reproduce itself, without reference to any supposed absolute value or truth of the content which is transmitted. Educational processes are just that. They are value free instruments which are equally at the disposal of competing value systems.

In identifying the common features of the pedagogic process or, even more, by implying that all forms of communication possess those same features and can be said to be forms of pedagogy, Bourdieu was accepting that the reproductive practices of the *grandes écoles* are examples of the ways in which all interest groups normally seek to achieve self-perpetuation. Importantly, this recognition applied to 'state' education itself. The providers of 'state' education constituted an interest group seeking to exercise symbolic violence in the same way as any other interest group. In the absence of any (literally) comprehensive system of state education, the state had to secure its authority by accommodating a plurality of pedagogic systems amongst which the system of state sponsored schooling was only one.

The Work of the 1970s

The Analysis of Competing 'Fields'

Given that Bourdieu had claimed that educational processes similarly serve the interests of rival groups within society, it was logical that Bourdieu should next try to analyse the struggle for domination between various self-reproducing systems. The success of the work of the 1970s can be attributed to the productive use Bourdieu made of the concept of 'field' which, by way of Kurt Lewin, he borrowed from physics. The concept was first advanced in 'Intellectual field and creative project' (Bourdieu, 1966), and it was elaborated significantly in 'Genèse et structure du champ religieux' (Bourdieu, 1971a).

The starting point of Bourdieu's analysis is philosophical. 'Fields' can be defined as mutually supporting combinations of intellectual discourses and social institutions. As a thoroughgoing phenomenologist, Bourdieu insists that discourses do not have reference to any realities beyond themselves. They function socially to reinforce social institutions which, equally, have no absolute meaning. Discourses provide the arbitrary content which is pedagogically processed to sustain arbitrary institutions or social groups. Social change is the consequence of the emergence of new fields or of shifting relations between fields. Bourdieu's is a relational functionalism. There is no necessary or unchanging structure of relations between fields or subsystems within society. History is an account of the 'realpolitik' of conflicts between interest groups which are enacted from generation to generation.

To pursue the discussion in respect of the field of religion, Bourdieu's position is predicated on the view that there is nothing in the human condition or in the physical world which should render religious beliefs and religious institutions anything other than socially contingent. The Church is an arbitrary social presence which is sustained by theological discourse which is non-referential. The resolution of internal conflicts in religions—balancing the competing tendencies of prophets and priests or of heresy and orthodoxy—has had the effect of reinforcing the autonomy of the religious field. Prophets have often drawn their inspiration from ideas outside the conceptual framework of dominant modes of religious thinking, but the process by which these ideas have been assimilated by religious institutions and transformed into priestly orthodoxy has served to neutralise the external threat. It has enabled religions to redefine the grounds on which religion is distinguished from non-religion, a distinction which is a *sine qua non* of the survival of the religious field. Whilst the work of the 1960s culminated in *La Reproduction,* the work of the 1970s culminated in *La Distinction* (Bourdieu, 1979).

The Fields of Education and Employment

The position which Bourdieu worked out theoretically in relation to the field of religion transferred readily to other fields. Pedagogical processes were certainly the mechanisms adopted by different interest groups to reproduce themselves, but it became clear to Bourdieu that the motivation for reproduction was that of sustaining the pre-existing distinctions between culturally arbitrary groups. Autonomous fields strategically assimilate aspects of other fields in order to strengthen their resistance to the absolute threat which other fields might pose.

In practical terms, Bourdieu particularly examined the nature of the changing relations between the fields of education and employment. His work devastatingly exposed the weakness of a crude functionalist understanding of the relations between the two fields. Bourdieu showed that educational institutions do not manufacture students as products who possess universally valid—and validly graded—qualifications which offer correspondingly appropriate opportunities for employment in the job market. On the contrary, occupational opportunity is the main place of conflict in the struggle between the field of education which has traditionally attempted to sustain an institutional and ideological independence from other fields and the field of employment in which employers in commerce and industry might wish to use their own criteria for selection and develop their own internal mechanisms for reproducing and differentiating themselves.

Just as in the conflict between the religious and the secular, that between education and employment takes the form of strategic and reciprocal appropriation: the field of employment seeks to appropriate the values of education whilst the field of education seeks to accommodate the field of employment. On the one hand, for instance, institutions which were established specifically to meet the perceived needs of industry and commerce such as business or management schools have sought to acquire educational status by asserting the scientificity of business or management education. On the other hand, traditional universities have sought to accommodate the field of employment by introducing work-experience and work-based learning into the curriculum.

The Hidden Agenda of the Competition between Fields

Bourdieu's view is that these appropriations are devices adopted by those who posses power in society to ensure that their power is retained. Just as conflict within religion strengthens its autonomy, so the conflict between fields in society is equally contrived. Adopting an historical perspective, Bourdieu suggests that cultural status and economic power are the joint keystones of class domination but that they can only function jointly if they collude in concealing that they are mutually dependent. Although the dominance of 'high' culture and high intellectual achievement is a function of the wealth which gives it distinction, it is in the interest of those in possession of high cultural and intellectual status to assert that these are expressions of intrinsic taste or intelligence. Those who owe their cultural status to inherited wealth and position wish to conceal the vulgarity of its origin whilst those who acquire wealth by vulgar means also immediately aspire to the cultural status which will conceal that they are *nouveaux riches.*

In 'La défense du corps' (Bourdieu, 1971b) and 'Le titre et le poste' (Bourdieu, 1975), Bourdieu viewed this complicity from the perspective of the teaching staff within the field of education, whilst in 'Les stratégies de reconversion' (Bourdieu, 1973) and 'Le patronat' (Bourdieu, 1978) he examined the ways in which employers deployed educational qualifications to legitimate non-educational forms of patronage. The conclusion from both perspectives was the same: educational qualifications do not have an absolute value within the employment market but only have the value which the market assigns to them at any time. The 'same' qualification at different times does not possess the same value, and the variations in valuation and in supply and demand are regulated by those who have inherited power and intend to retain it.

Summary of the 1960s and the 1970s

In the terms developed by Bourdieu in *La Reproduction, Les Héritiers* had produced evidence of the incidence of 'symbolic violence'. There was a cultural mismatch between staff and some students which resulted in the failure of those students. However, *La Reproduction* did not seek to develop a 'rational pedagogy' which would counteract this state of affairs. Instead, it analysed the pedagogical process by which all kinds of different groups, subcultures, institutions or fields produce and reproduce their differences. Yet there was, in the work of the 1960s, still the sense that Bourdieu was talking about a plurality of subsystems within an educational system which still possessed a distinct relationship with the field of employment. To put the matter another way, there was still the sense that he was seeking to describe the competition between rival groups within an intellectual field which still retained its autonomy.

The work of the 1970s removed that comfortable prop because employers were now seen to be rival producers and reproducers within the social system, sustaining and communicating values which competed with those traditionally transmitted within an educational system that still belonged within the intellectual field. Bourdieu perceived that it was decreasingly the case that education could be thought to be carrying out a process of reproduction which was *prior* to employment or *distinct* from it.

The combination of the eclipse of the notion of 'rational pedagogy' in the 1960s and the exploration of the solely relational character of the educational field in the 1970s had important consequences for the work of the 1980s. In effect, *La Reproduction* assigned to pedagogy exclusively a homogenising function. The success of pedagogic work in every specific context could be measured in terms of the degree of identification established between individuals and institutions. Pedagogy was transformed from an instrument of instruction to one of socialisation. Not only was the possibility that teachers might convey to students what they were not already predisposed to know subverted by this reduction of pedagogy but, even more, the possibility that the separate identity of individuals could be developed through education was much diminished. In theory, the goal of every pedagogic action should be to make its authority totalitarian.

Because of the intrinsic indeterminacy of educational institutions—their lack of absolute value or adherence to absolute values—they could themselves, like pedagogy before them, become the instruments for a more widespread homogenisation. Although the intellectual content of what was transmitted within the educational sphere might be devalued or rendered impotent in subordination to the process of socialisation, nevertheless the status of the traditional values of education might be appropriated to legitimate quite different values.

The Work of the 1980s

Individuals and Institutions

In presenting his analysis of the career patterns of the 'patrons' of 200 leading industrial companies in 'Le patronat' (1978), Bourdieu was already aware of the fallacy of attempting to carry out the analysis as if the identities of those 'patrons' could be distinguished from their company image. At the same time, he was becoming reflexively interested in the relationship between his intellectual or attitudinal position and his social or institutional position. This interest was heightened by his appointment in 1982 to the Chair of Sociology at the Collège de France, Paris, a position which was already socially invested with a distinctive institutional meaning. In his inaugural lecture, *Leçon sur la leçon* (Bourdieu, 1982a), Bourdieu wrestled with the paradox that he owed his new identification with the institutional image of the College to the reputation he had acquired from relentlessly exposing the ways in which institutional images are socially constituted. He was clear that it was a question of whether he was appropriating the Collège more than it was appropriating him.

Homo Academicus (1984)

The educational works which he has published in the 1980s are not derived from new researches. He has re-used the research undertaken in the late 1960s and has imposed a gloss which reflects his new concern with the relationship between individuals and institutions. *Homo Academicus* (Bourdieu, 1984) offers a sociology of intellectual discourses in the Paris of the late 1960s, a sociology of the trajectories of the individual producers of these discourses, and a sociology of the relative positions of the higher education institutions. Crucially, these three kinds of sociology all involve an analysis of the competing claims of intellectual and institutional autonomy on the one hand and of market-led economic forces on the other. Crucially, also, these three kinds of sociology are shown to be fundamentally one and the same. Intellectual positions are used to consolidate social ones and individual social trajectories cannot be dissociated from the structural location of institutions. Bourdieu assumes a process of convergent coherence whereby, ultimately, the separate analysis of any of the component parts of the whole—discourses, individuals, institutions—necessarily generates an analysis of the whole.

It is typical of Bourdieu, however, that he is always anxious to demonstrate that what can be *analysed* as a necessary convergence is not a necessary *occurrence.* The structural affinities which we perceive are constructed by the human agents acting within the process of convergence. Indeed, of course, Bourdieu makes clear reflexively that his subjective perception of convergence plays a part (with what effect depends on the power of his individual/institutional position) in realising an objective convergence. This is because, in his own terms, to describe is to prescribe to an extent which is measurable as a function of the personal or institutional power that can be harnessed in support of the description. (See *Ce que parler veut dire* [Bourdieu, 1982b].)

La Noblesse d'état (1989)

Bourdieu's most recent full text, *La Noblesse d'état* (Bourdieu, 1989), again uses research undertaken in the late 1960s to demonstrate the procedures adopted in the particular case of the *grandes écoles* by which the dispositions of individual applicants, curriculum content, and institutional ethos are moulded together to constitute a marketable commodity. It would be a mistake to see this simply as an old-style left-wing critique of the pernicious system of privilege in operation in French society. That would be to read *La Noblesse d'état* in terms of *Les Héritiers.* Rather it should be read in terms of *La Reproduction.* The exposure of the self-validating procedures of the *grandes écoles* serves to illustrate the mechanism which is in operation in the plurality of self- validating systems which are in competition within society—whether they are 'élitist' or 'alternative'.

The Composite Picture

For Bourdieu, all scientific endeavour requires the active construction of discourses and institutions which constitute just such self-validating systems. It is only in this way, for instance, that social scientific analysis can create the power base to challenge, perhaps, the conceptions of society communicated in the tabloid press or, equally, official government statistics. To think 'scientifically' about society does not involve taking refuge in any ready-made personal or institutional detachment. It involves creating the conditions which will mean that thinking will be taken to be scientific. To acquire the aura of scientificity for thinking is, for Bourdieu, to generate ideological support for a particular fiction—the fiction of the detached observer. It is, nevertheless, a fiction that we need to cultivate in order to stimulate as many alternative perceptions of reality as possible. Bourdieu's overall position stands Rousseau's contention on its head. It is not that we are born free but are everywhere in chains. On the contrary, we are born in chains and constantly strive to construct the functional fiction that we are free.

I have shown that in the last 30 years Bourdieu has engaged analytically with the French higher education system in different ways. It has been a process of continuous involvement and detachment. He does not accept the notion of 'participant observation' but he would argue, instead, that he has tried to offer 'participant objectification'. It has been the case that the analyses of one decade have been superseded by those of the subsequent decade. The main characteristic of Bourdieu's recent work is that he has overtly accommodated this supersession. He would argue that his recent work surpasses what went before without invalidating it.

The work of the 1960s involved an analysis of the process of transmission from teachers to learners. From this analysis, Bourdieu concluded that this was primarily a self-fulfilling process with the result that he was compelled to analyse, instead, the competing values of the competing contexts in which the transmission process was located. This was the thrust of the work of the 1970s. But there developed the danger that Bourdieu might be thought to be charting a static structure of relationships between competing channels of value communication. He has always wanted to support the fiction of free human agency—arguing that the freedom to act is dependent on a clear recognition of the constraints which circumscribe the scope of action. As a result, the work of the 1980s has wanted to suggest that there is scope for individuals to modify the institutions by which they are partly constrained. Hence the constructivist structuralism of *La Noblesse d'état.*

The problem with *La Noblesse d'état,* however, is that the analysis of the way the institution's structural position is constructed by human agents seems, in the end, to reinforce the view that individual agents, such as admissions tutors, are automatically operationalising a predetermined affinity between student intake and institutional ethos. It could be thought, therefore, that Bourdieu's analysis unwittingly gives support to an interpretation which might claim that individual agents are impotently subordinate instruments of institutional intentions. It could be thought, in other words, that Bourdieu's socialism, like so many socialisms, has been appropriated by the market economy and that his analyses have colluded in their own neutralisation.

The concept of 'habitus' has always been crucial in all of Bourdieu's thinking. It means the disposition to act which individuals acquire in the earliest stages of socialisation and which they consolidate by their subsequent choices in life. Bourdieu's conviction that individuals inevitably 'live out' in some sense the 'habitus' that is their inheritance means that, vestigially, he is able to retain the notion that individuals do have a point of reference which enables them to withstand market pressures if they hang on to the will to be authentic persons. The values which individuals inherit are held to pre-date those which are current in society even though it is admitted that these inherited values are the product of the ways in which the previous generation reconciled their 'habitus' with the values of their society. Maintaining the influence of all our personal 'habitus' must, for Bourdieu, be the last hope for ensuring that agents control systems or, to put this in terms used by Habermas, to ensure that the 'Life-world' prevails over the 'System-world'. Recognising the realities of class differentiation and of transmitted deprivations must be the last hope for mounting a critique of the ideology of classless consumerism.

The Pragmatic Response

Bourdieu's *The Political Ontology of Martin Heidegger* (Bourdieu, 1991) is such an important and relevant book because he there gives an account of the way in which institutionalised academic philosophy in Germany in the 1930s came to acquiesce in the discourse which fostered the rise to power of the Nazis. It documents, therefore, the betrayal by intellectuals of the inherited moral attitudes on the basis of which they might have used their institutional autonomy to launch a critique of the developments which gradually enveloped them.

Culminating in *La Noblesse d'état,* I have suggested that Bourdieu's analyses of higher education have become ambivalent precisely because the reciprocity between description and prescription has meant, perhaps, that his work has come close to being appropriated by the system which it describes. My pragmatic response, therefore, takes two forms. First of all, I try to indicate those points where I believe that Bourdieu's analyses illuminate the current condition of higher education. Given, then, that Bourdieu's composite picture adequately represents a general reality, I try, secondly, to derive an analytical stance from his work which might now help to insert, as science, into that reality some grounds for changing it.

The Current Condition of Higher Education

My point of reference is United Kingdom higher education since 1970 and, in particular, my own institution—the Polytechnic of East London (formerly North-east London Polytechnic)—but there are undoubtedly resonances for international higher education during the last 20 years. Like many of the polytechnics established in the United Kingdom in 1969/70, my institution from inception was committed to the view that courses should be designed to meet the needs of students who were 'likely to benefit' and to prepare these students to satisfy the demands of employers. This dual commitment seemed to be satisfied by varying forms of 'rational pedagogy' designed to help students to learn on the one hand and, on the other, by involvement with employers, to secure the relevance to the world of work of the studies undertaken within the educational institution. There was the stable sense that the institution was located in the public sector and was part of the system of state education. There was also the assurance that the validation procedures of the Council for National Academic Awards would ensure that courses which were designed in response to local needs—both of students and employers—would not simply reflect those needs but would retain a national currency. The institution sought to preserve a vocational orientation and to resist any tendency towards 'academic drift' in imitation of established universities, but there was confidence that the aim was to render academic knowledge instrumental—to apply it to problems so that the values of intellectual enquiry would be placed at the disposal of industrial and commercial practice.

In the late 1970s, the vocationalism which had inspired the new polytechnics was taken over by the 'new' vocationalism that has been associated with the 'Thatcherite' label. The attempt of the Conservative Government to bring about economic reform was closely associated with the attempt to create an 'enterprise culture'. Keat (1991) has suggested that there have been two strands to this venture: first, the attempt to remodel all institutions as commercial enterprises, and, second, the attempt to encourage personality traits, such as independence or self-reliance. In the field of higher education, these mutually supporting strands have been in evidence.

The Government has withdrawn polytechnics from the control of local authorities so as to enable them to compete as institutions in an open market. Through measures adopted by the Manpower Services Commission, the Training Agency and, most recently, the Training and Education Division of the Department of Employment, it has sought to diminish the autonomy of the higher education system *vis-à-vis,* in particular, the field of employment. Although this was achieved by financial incentives, the crude economic manipulation was euphemised by the insidious deployment of a new educational terminology or rhetoric. The new goals of education—the acquisition of skills and competencies—were indicative of the appropriation of the field of education by the field of employment.

The old anti-academic vocationalism had been a product of post World War II socialism (see Robbins, 1988). The orientation had been to teach those who might benefit, normally perceived to be the local, disadvantaged working-class. In opposition to the entrepreneurial ideology of the new Conservatism, a new socialism emerged—mainly associated with the Greater London Council—which emphasised the rights of access to higher education institutions of newly classified social groups. Social class background ('habitus') ceased to be the dominant basis for the classification of students. Generic classifications were constructed— such as, for instance, in terms of gender, ethnicity, and age—and these gave rise to curricula specifically designed to meet the needs of women, ethnic minority, or mature students.

These tendencies of the late 1970s—apparently inspired from opposite extremes of the political spectrum—have amalgamated interestingly to constitute our present situation. Higher education institutions now have to market themselves as institutions. They have to attract students and they need to benefit from the financial sponsorship of business and industry. Market forces operate at the level of corporate images, public relations, prospectuses and logos.

The consequence of the market differentiation of institutions is the phenomenon observed by Bourdieu in *La Noblesse d'état:* there is a growing homogenisation of individuals and their institutions without reference to curricular content. The rationale for the accreditation of prior learning and the recognition of experiential learning, for instance, is that these selection procedures widen access to the institution's provision. Instead, however, the notion that 'experience' is equivalent to formal educational qualification reduces the cognitive to the affective and accelerates the diminution of the autonomy of the educational field. The consequence of this reduction in the importance of the assessment of objective levels of attainment as a basis for entry into higher education is that, often unconsciously, students are selected as acceptable 'persons'. Similarly, the growing trend towards self-assessment or to forms of peer assessment encourages a process of cultural self-endorsement since the members of socially homogeneous groups have no extraneous criteria by which to judge each other's performances.

The erosion of the norm of objectivity at the point of admission and at the point of assessment means that staff are not called upon to embark upon the transactions which would encourage students to confront what they do not know. Staff who are experts in their fields and do, therefore, potentially represent those fields to their students, find themselves increasingly redundant and irrelevant in the process of producing accredited products. At the other extreme, the process of 'distance learning' where students may have no sense of belonging to an institution at all, is further confirmation of the irrelevance of the face-to-face communication traditionally associated with tutorials and of the autonomous input of the institutional ethos.

Without entering into further close detail, there is, I think, much evidence to suggest that Bourdieu's analyses help us to understand what is currently happening in higher education. It seems correct to observe that the autonomy of higher education institutions is extremely weak; that the boom in accreditation is in inverse proportion to the quality of what is accredited in spite of the huge smoke-screen of quality auditing; and that the consumer control of students over their studies in fact neutralises the possibility that they might acquire knowledge which would enable them to question the directions being taken by the societies to which they belong.

For a Sociology of Learning

Much of this attempt to confirm Bourdieu's perception of things has amounted to little more than assertion. The pragmatic use of Bourdieu's work must involve a process of testing these assertions. What is needed, I submit, is a concerted attempt to re-insert the consideration of course or cognitive content into the analysis of the teaching and learning process. We need to examine what happens within higher education in order to articulate the *differences* between the cultural capital of staff and students. We need to accept that educational institutions have lost their autonomy and we need, therefore, to analyse the trajectories of learners in society in terms of what they acquire from different institutional contexts. We need to analyse how this learning modifies the 'habitus' which people have inherited. All of this means that the sociology of learning in society need only partially be concerned with the ways in which higher education institutions seek to privilege some learning above other kinds. Such a sociological endeavour would involve an assessment of the function of information derived from the media, attitudes derived from religious affiliation, or skills obtained in employment in determining the amelioration of the life-chances of individuals. It would restore to the sociology of education the possibility that the transference of values and knowledge in encounters between different people might be analysed.

It will be argued, of course, that this is a socialist, humanist, existentialist, or, even, sociologistic fantasy. So be it. The assumption of the argument would be that it is, equally, an old-fashioned fantasy. Bourdieu's sociology, however, undermines the notion of the anachronistic. The fantasy cannot be put down by reference to some supposed historical progress which invalidates it. Timing is beside the point. Whether the fantastic becomes actual is a question of value and of the competition between values.

REFERENCES

Bourdieu, Pierre (1964a) *Le Déracinement, la crise de l'agriculture traditionnelle en Algérie* (Paris, Editions de Minuit) (with A. Sayad).

Bourdieu, Pierre (1964b) *Les Héritiers, les étudiants et la culture* (Paris, Editions de Minuit) (with J. C. Passeron). Translated by R. Nice as *The Inheritors, French Students and their Relation to Culture* (1979) (Chicago London, University of Chicago Press).

Bourdieu, Pierre (1966) Intellectual field and creative project in: M. F. D. Young (Ed.) (1971) *Knowledge and Control: new directions for the sociology of education* pp. 161–188. (London, Collier-Macmillan).

Bourdieu, Pierre (1967) *Systèmes d'enseignement et systèmes de pensée, Revue internationale des sciences sociales,* XIX(3), pp. 367–388. Translated as: Systems of education and systems of thought, in: M. F. D. Young (Ed.) (1971) *Knowledge and Control: new directions for the sociology of education* pp. 189–207 (London, Collier-Macmillan).

Bourdieu, Pierre (1970) *La Reproduction. Eléments pour une théorie du système d'enseignement* (Paris, Editions de Minuit) (with J. C. Passeron). Translated by R. Nice as *Reproduction in Education, Society, and Culture* (1977) (Second edition, 1990, with a new preface by Bourdieu.) (London Beverley Hills, Sage Publications).

bourdieu, Pierre (1971a) *Genèse et structure du champ religieux, Revue française de sociologie,* XII(3), pp. 295–334.

Bourdieu, Pierre (1971b) *La défense du corps, Information sur les sciences sociales,* X(4), pp. 45–86 (with L. Boltanski & P. Maldidier).

Bourdieu, Pierre (1973) *Les stratégies de reconversion. Les classes sociales et le système d'enseignement. Information sur les sciences sociales,* XII(5), pp. 61–113 (with L. Boltanski & M. de Saint Martin). Translated as Changes in social structure and changes in the demand for education, in: S. Giner & M. Scotford-Archer (Eds) (1977) *Contemporary Europe, Social Structures and Cultural Patterns* pp. 197–227. (London, Routledge & Kegan Paul).

Bourdieu, Pierre (1975) *Le titre et le poste. Rapports entre le système de production et le système de reproduction, Actes de la recherche en sciences sociales,* 2, pp. 95–107 (with L. Boltanski). Translated by R. Nice as Formal qualifications and occupational hierarchies: the relationship between the production system and the reproduction system, *Reorganizing Education,* 1, 1977, pp. 61–69.

Bourdieu, Pierre (1978) *Le Patronat, Actes de la recherche en sciences sociales* 20, pp. 3–82 (with M. de Saint Martin).

Bourdieu, Pierre (1979) *La Distinction. Critique sociale du jugement* (Paris, Editions de Minuit). Translated by R. Nice as *Distinction. A Social Critique of the Judgement of Taste* (Cambridge, MA, Harvard University Press, 1984, and, in paperback, London, New York, Routledge & Kegan Paul, 1986).

Bourdieu, Pierre (1982a) *Leçon sur la leçon* (Paris, Editions de Minuit). Translated in P. Bourdieu (1990) *In Other Words* (Oxford, Polity Press).

Bourdieu, Pierre (1982b) *Ce que parler veut dire. L'économie des échanges linguistiques* (Paris, Fayard). Partly translated in *Language and Symbolic Power* (Oxford, Polity Press, 1991).

Bourdieu, Pierre (1984) *Homo Academicus,* (Paris, Éditions de Minuit) Translated by P. Collier (Oxford, Polity Press).

Bourdieu, Pierre (1989) *La Noblesse d'état, Grandes écoles et esprit de corps* (Paris, Editions de Minuit).

Bourdieu, Pierre (1991) *The Political Ontology of Martin Heidegger* (Oxford, Polity Press).

Keat, Russell (1991) Introduction: Starship Britain or Universal Enterprise? in: R. Keat & N. Abercrombie *Enterprise Culture,* pp. 1–17 (London, Routledge).

Robbins, Derek (1988) *The Rise of Independent Study—the politics and the philosophy of an educational innovation, 1970–87* (Buckingham, Society for Research into Higher Education & Open University Press).

Robbins, Derek (1991) *The Work of Pierre Bourdieu: recognizing society* (Milton Keynes, Open University Press).

How Bourdieu bites back: recognising misrecognition in education and educational research

David James

Having noted that some use of Bourdieusian concepts in educational research is superficial, this paper offers a view of the distinctiveness of Bourdieu's concepts via the example of misrecognition, which is differentiated from the concept with the same name in Fraser's work. An account is given of a recent research project on white middle-class identity and school choice, which suggests that whilst parents avoided a common misrecognition (regarding school quality), they were nevertheless reliant on other forms of misrecognition (regarding the qualities of their children) that are equally important in the relationship between social class and educational inequalities. Finally, the paper suggests that educational understandings, including some educational research, are predisposed to misrecognise Bourdieusian concepts, and four areas of tension are identified. The paper argues against 'light usage' of Bourdieu whilst acknowledging that the approach can produce a pessimistic account that is at odds with some educational values.

Introduction

Many educational researchers find Bourdieu's concepts attractive and useful, though there is great variability in what we might call 'depth in use'. Undoubtedly, some usage remains at the level of what Reay described as 'the habitual use of Habitus' (Reay, 2004), or what Hey (2003) termed 'intellectual hairspray'. This paper sets out an argument that, at least in the case of educational research, the superficial use of Bourdieusian tools is likely to be due to (a) the apparent similarity of other concepts with similar names, and (b) important tensions between a Bourdieusian approach and some key characteristics of educational practice, policy and research

To do this, the paper begins with a comparison of the concept of *misrecognition* as this appears in the hands of Nancy Fraser and Pierre Bourdieu, respectively, arguing that the first is more readily understood than the second, and that whilst the concepts overlap they are crucially different. It then looks at the concept of misrecognition as this applies to the analysis of some of the data in a research project entitled 'Identities, Educational Choice and the White Urban Middle Classes', which studied 125 families in three English cities to investigate motives, experiences and outcomes where families made 'against the grain' choices of secondary school.

© 2015 The Author(s).
This is an Open Access article distributed under the terms of the Creative Commons Attribution License http://creativecommons.org/licenses/by/3.0/, which permits unrestricted use, distribution, and reproduction in any medium, provided the original work is properly cited.

The argument here is that the families concerned identified and avoided one very common and powerful form of misrecognition, but that other forms of misrecognition remained key in their engagements with education. Finally, having identified areas of tension, I argue that whilst it is understandable, 'light usage' of Bourdieu is of little value and that the tendency to pessimism in Bourdieusian social theory presents particular difficulties to educationists.

Misrecognition: Fraser and Bourdieu

It is tempting to illustrate the potential confusion between Bourdieusian concepts and other similar-sounding concepts with the example of social capital: When Puttnam's concept with the same name was taken up and used widely by some national governments and international organisations in the early 2000s, many of those wishing to use Bourdieu's concept often found themselves explaining the contrast with Puttnam and Coleman (see for example Blackshaw & Long, 2005). Here, my focus is on misrecognition, a term central to the work of both Nancy Fraser and Pierre Bourdieu in the sets of ideas they each provide that can help in the task of investigating, understanding and ameliorating aspects of the social world. The philosophical relationship between Fraser's and Bourdieu's thinking is helpfully explored in an edited collection (Lovell, 2007), inspired by an exchange between Honneth and Fraser in which Bourdieu was 'a tacit third party' (Lovell, 2007, p. 67). Whilst the detail of Lovell's account is beyond the scope of the current paper, it is worth noting Lovell's strong implication that there is both an affinity and a useful complementarity:

> Fraser holds the place ... for participatory parity, dialogics and agency in normative social transformation. Bourdieu, on the other hand, holds the place for the powers that thwart these processes and that condition and shape agency.... He is a pessimist rather than a determinist, and his pessimism is sometimes salutary. (Lovell, 2007, p. 7)

This complementarity might lead one to expect that *misrecognition*, a prominent term in the work of both theorists, refers to a similar set of concerns. However, whilst they are related, the concepts of misrecognition in the work of each actually refer to different processes.

In Fraser's hands, the concept of misrecognition refers to one of two 'distinct species of injustice':

> (T)he most general meaning of justice is parity of participation. According to this radical-democratic interpretation of the principle of equal moral worth, justice requires social arrangements that permit all to participate as peers in social life. Overcoming injustice means dismantling institutionalized obstacles that prevent some people from participating on a par with others, as full partners in social interaction. Previously, I have analysed two distinct kinds of obstacles to participatory parity, which correspond to two distinct species of injustice ... On the one hand, people can be impeded from full participation by economic structures that deny them the resources they need in order to interact with others as peers; in that case they suffer from distributive injustice or maldistribution. On the other hand, people can also be prevented from interacting on terms of parity by institutionalized hierarchies of cultural value that deny them the requisite standing; in that case they suffer from status inequality or misrecognition. (Fraser, 2007, p. 20)

As in Weber's sociology, these 'class structure' and 'status order' dimensions have a degree of autonomy and do not neatly mirror each other in modern capitalist societies. They can interact in a causal way, but neither can be collapsed into the other. This dual framework for looking at and thinking about social justice is now widely known and appreciated. Fraser has, however, augmented it in later work, taking into account the limitations of considering justice issues mainly or only within a particular concept of the territorial state. Globalisation makes us question the previously largely unexamined assumptions that justice itself was to be understood within what Fraser calls the 'Keynesian-Westphalian frame'.

> The third dimension of justice is the *political*. Of course, distribution and recognition are themselves political.... But I mean political in a more specific, constitutive sense ... (which) furnishes the stage on which struggles over distribution and recognition are played out. Establishing criteria of social belonging, and thus determining who counts as a member, the political dimension of justice specifies the reach of those other dimensions: it tells us who is included, and who excluded, from the circle of those entitled to a just distribution and reciprocal recognition. (Fraser, 2007, pp. 20–21)

The Keynesian-Westphalian frame is now firmly part of the problem – 'as it partitions political space in ways that block many who are poor and despised from challenging the forces that oppress them ... this frame insulates offshore powers from critique and control' (Fraser, 2007, p. 23).

For Fraser, then, misrecognition includes the denial of common humanity or citizenship, and the equal worth that flows from that (see Lister, 2007, p. 164). Her concepts of recognition and misrecognition include but are not confined to questions of identity, group identity and the psychological damage to individual selves that might follow denigration of a group. Her 'status model' is primarily about material conditions – whether or not people have 'participatory parity' – that is, whether or not they are full partners in social interaction (for Lister, Fraser underplays the psychic harm that flows from misrecognition, and she gives an example from Adair's work on poverty to illustrate – see ibid., p. 165). In Fraser's developed model, the 'economic realm' concepts (maldistribution/redistribution) and those of the 'cultural realm' (recognition/misrecognition) are augmented with those pertaining to the political realm, that is, inclusion, exclusion and marginalisation. Together these offer a means to explore and understand injustice, whether it is that following from the denial of 'voice' to certain social groups, for example that suffered by workers in garment factories supplying consumer markets in the West, or that produced by the operation of categories of citizen, immigrant, migrant worker, refugee or asylum-seeker. One particularly interesting application of this framework uses it to examine post-1944 education policy in England, illustrating a shift through policies that focus on redistribution, then recognition, then representation (Power, 2012). There is a strong resonance between Fraser's three realms and Bourdieu's concept of *field*, specifically that persons are differentially positioned in fields by virtue of the capitals to which they have access. A good example here might be a well-qualified professional who settles in a new country and finds that his/her standing and qualifications are not recognised in the new setting.

However, Bourdieu's concept of misrecognition is different, and it arises from his central concern with social practices in social spaces or fields. In Bourdieu's view, social fields produce knowledge, and knowledge is a form of capital, associated with prestige or power. Crucially, 'knowledge' here is a translation of the French word '*connaissance*', so does not only refer to knowledge of facts or knowledge about things, as usually implied in phrases like 'knowledge is power' or 'the knowledge economy': it also means being familiar in an implicit or tacit way, and knowing how to do things, such as how to act or how to engage in different social situations or in relation to different orthodoxies. The close connection with 'habitus' is clear, in the sense given in that most well-known of all Bourdieu quotes: 'when the habitus encounters a social world of which it is the product, it finds itself "as a fish in water", it does not feel the weight of water and takes the world about itself for granted' (Bourdieu, 1989, p. 43). It is only through appreciating this meaning of 'knowledge' that we can fully grasp the related terms, namely '*reconnaissance*' (knowing again – recognition) and '*meconnaissance*' (misrecognition). The latter term is not about recognition or the lack of it in Fraser's terms, but rather refers to a social practice of individual or collective misattribution:

> Misrecognition relates to the ways ... (that) underlying processes and generating structures of fields are not consciously acknowledged in terms of the social differentiation they perpetuate, often in the name of democracy and equality.... As a translation of *meconnaissance*, however, *misrecognition* does not quite place the necessary emphasis on how a practice might be made "...invisible through a displacement of understanding and a reconstrual as part of other aspects of the habitus that 'go without saying'" (Mahar et al., 1990, p. 19). Such misrecognition operates in the education system, Bourdieu argues, through an arbitrary curriculum that is "naturalised" so that social classifications are transformed into academic ones. The result is that instead of being experienced for what they are (i.e. partial and technical hierarchies), such social classifications become "total" hierarchies, experienced as if they were grounded in nature. (Grenfell & James, 1998, pp. 23–24)

For Bourdieu, then, misrecognition refers to an everyday and dynamic social process where one thing (say, a situation, process, or action) is not recognised for what it is because it was not previously 'cognised' within the range of dispositions and propensities of the habitus of the person(s) confronting it (see Bourdieu, 2000). Instead the thing is attributed to another available realm of meaning, and, in the process, interests, inequities or other effects may be maintained whilst they remain concealed. An everyday example of this would be the contemporary use of supermarket and retail loyalty cards. These are deliberately presented (and conventionally regarded) as a system for rewarding repeat custom through the accumulation of points that represent cash value. However, they are also (one might say *really*) a system for harvesting detailed information about consumption that enables new forms of individually targeted marketing. Customers are likely to attribute actions around loyalty cards to the realm of customer loyalty, whereas it could be argued that they are selling detailed information on their purchasing habits to a group of retailers, who are then in a much better position to secure further profit from the same individuals. Another everyday example is the way that most mobile phone use is carried out without much awareness that it generates a vast amount of detailed data that has high value to those able to generate new forms of profitable business. As both examples illustrate, the concept of misrecognition is linked to Bourdieu's rejection of any simple distinction between the conscious and unconscious: Many people half know that something else is going on with their loyalty card, but that is not the same thing as saying that this vague awareness comes to the surface in conscious and calculated decisions about how to act, such as whether or not to use their loyalty card. The example also illustrates another important point: that misrecognition is 'functional' rather than simply aberrant or some sort of unintended by-product. Bourdieu would describe it thus:

> In an economy which is defined by the refusal to recognise the 'objective' truth of 'economic' practices, that is, the law of 'naked self-interest' and egoistic calculation, even 'economic' capital cannot act unless it succeeds in being recognized through a conversion that can render unrecognizable the true principle of its efficacy. Symbolic capital is thus denied capital, recognized as legitimate, that is, misrecognised as capital.... (Bourdieu, 1990, p. 118)

The classic example of educational misrecognition refers to the general relationship of educational success to social advantage. The common-sense assumption here is rather like traditional functionalist sociology – that social background does affect educational progress and achievement, but that the fact it does so is an unfortunate anomaly, an aberration or dysfunctional feature of an otherwise largely benign and socially neutral process. Common sense has it that education should not really generate social inequality and that it doesn't *have* to, and that action to overcome this effect is about identifying and then removing the 'barriers', or perhaps 'raising standards for all'. Bourdieu explicitly counters this view:

> Misrecognition of the social determinants of the educational career – and therefore of the social trajectory it helps to determine – gives the educational certificate the value of a natural right and makes the educational system one of the fundamental agencies of the maintenance of the social order. (Bourdieu, 1984, p. 387)

Here, the 'social order' includes ongoing social inequality, within which certain forms of a lack of recognition (misrecognition in the Fraser sense) will play a large part. Clearly, both Fraser and Bourdieu are concerned with social inequalities and how they may be understood, challenged, reduced or overcome, yet their distinct concepts of misrecognition also point to different starting-points and projects. In one sense Fraser's concept of misrecognition is close to Bourdieu's *symbolic violence*, because those excluded or without a voice are denied part of what it is to be fully human, and this appears at least psychologically abusive. However, the concept of symbolic violence, and that of symbolic capital, represents an important part of Bourdieu's break with Marxism (for a good account of this, and of the various theoretical traditions brought together by Bourdieu, see Swartz, 1997). For Bourdieu, most domination in advanced societies is now symbolic rather than achieved by force and, furthermore, the process is not one of simply 'duping' people or flooding them with propaganda, or even persuading them. Domination usually involves at least some sense of largely below-conscious complicity on the part of those subjugated, and processes of misrecognition are what make this possible: 'symbolic violence is that form of violence which only acts on social agents with their complicity' (Poupeau, 2000, p. 71).

Putting Bourdieu's concept of misrecognition to work

Given its centrality in Bourdieu's theoretical tools, it is at first surprising to find that the concept of misrecognition is not as widely used as concepts like cultural and social capital in contemporary educational research. A notable exception would be Thompson's recent critique of the notion of 'scaling up' (Thomson, 2014). Misrecognition was, however, central to the UK Economic and Social Research Council (ESRC)-funded project 'Identity, Educational Choice and the White Urban Middle Classes' (Award reference RES-148-25-0023), which investigated a cross-section of 'against the grain' examples of school choice, where white urban middle-class families in England eschewed more apparently dependable state and private alternatives available to them and instead chose ordinary state comprehensive secondary schools for their children. The purposes of the study included attempting to understand school choice practices and processes in terms of orientations and motivations, and ethnicity and class, and it aimed to investigate how such practices were related to identity and identification in the light of contemporary conceptions of the middle-class self. The investigation included interviewing parents and children in 125 white middle-class households in London and two provincial cities in England, 'Riverton' in the South West and 'Norton' in the North East.[1] These families had all made a positive choice in favour of a state secondary school that was performing at or below the England average according to conventional examination league-tables. The study began in mid-2005 and covered a 30-month period, concluding in 2007, and was part of the ESRC Identities and Social Action Programme. The outcomes of the study are extensively reported elsewhere (e.g. Crozier et al., 2008; James et al., 2010; Reay et al., 2007; Reay et al., 2008; Reay et al., 2011 [2013]): Here, some brief details are given to contextualise the discussion, but the main purpose is to consider how Bourdieu's concept of misrecognition was put to work in the study, and to give some consideration of how this illuminates a tension between a Bourdieu-inspired approach and some common values and understandings that run through the world of education.

One of the most striking findings was that surprisingly few of the 'against-the-grain' school choices could be attributed to strong commitments to the welfare state or a strong communitarian, egalitarian political position. Instead, a widespread motivation was a wish for children to have an educational experience that would prepare them for a globalised, socially diverse, multicultural world. Sometimes this was linked to parents' active dislike for privileged educational routes on the grounds that they were socially divisive, and their wish to avoid contributing to social division. Often the higher-achieving secondary schools available to them were, in their view, insufficiently socially and ethnically diverse and could not provide the sort of 'real world' environment that would help realise a broad educational project and develop their child in particular, valued directions.

The analysis differentiates between first-generation, second-generation and established middle-class families, as family history played a prominent role in school choice and across these groups there were some important differences in the rationales given. However, taken as one group the parents concerned were distinctive in a number of respects. A high proportion were educated to degree level (83%) and around a quarter of these also held some kind of postgraduate qualification. Most (69%) were recent 'incomers' to the area in which they lived. In 70% of families, at least one parent worked in the public sector. The parents in the study were strongly represented on school governing bodies: There were 11 chairs of governors in the sample, and in 57% of the London families at least one parent was currently serving or had served as a school governor. Riverton and Norton figures were lower but still substantial, at 43% and 22% respectively. In most cases, becoming a school governor was rooted in a desire to make a civic contribution, though as we found with the many other explicit connections with schools (friendships with teachers or the Head, or professional links with education), being a school governor was at the same time a way of monitoring and intervening in schooling. In turn, schools seemed especially responsive to the wishes and concerns of white middle-class parents and their children, and in part of the analysis of the project we argue that there was a particular mutual affinity between the accountability needs of the school and the wishes of this particular group of parents, a point returned to below.

An important strand in UK policy for the last 15 years or so has sought to place schools at the heart of initiatives to realise greater social inclusion and to build a greater sense of community: the Extended Schools initiative was one prominent example of this (Cummings et al., 2007). Partly in the light of such policies, we were interested to see whether 'against the grain' school choice made a positive contribution to social mixing and, therefore, potentially, to social cohesion. We found segregation *within* schools with white middle-class children clustered in top sets, in most cases benefiting from 'Gifted and Talented' schemes,[2] and little interaction with children from other backgrounds. The children rarely had working-class friends and their few minority ethnic friends were predominantly from middle-class backgrounds. Overall, there was some evidence of *social mix* but little evidence of *social mixing*. Parents often declared their hopes that their children would make friends across ethnic groups, and sometimes they intervened to facilitate this, but on the whole friends were other white middle-class children. Both parents' and children's attitudes to classed and ethnic others sometimes displayed a perception of cultural and intellectual superiority that would work against social cohesion and the development of common ground and common understandings. For many of the parents in the study (and especially in London) the wish for their children to have a multicultural educational experience was closely connected to how they identified as white. The data suggest that their own identity was constructed in opposition to that of both white working-class people and those white middle-class people making more conventional choices of secondary school. Rather, these parents saw themselves as part of a more culturally tolerant and even anti-racist white middle class (see Reay et al., 2007).

Against-the-grain school choice was for the most part experienced as a risky strategy, and it generated considerable anxiety that we found was linked to parents' attempts to monitor and manage the process (see Crozier et al., 2008). The accounts of many of the parents suggested immense difficulties in acting ethically in an unethical context. At the same time, however, we were surprised by the extent to which both the specificity of school choice and more general issues of inequality were seen in individualised, instrumental terms. Once under way, school experiences were very closely monitored and managed, and some parents described how they could and would 'pull out' if things did not go well, suggesting they saw school choice as remaining provisional, and the school as a service provider and themselves as consumers who could keep the choice of provider under review. Schooling was seen as one element (albeit the largest element) in a broader educational project, and this led us to suggest that the metaphor of a 'risky investment' was apposite. The school choices made could and did produce high gains, but parents exercised high levels of vigilance and often engaged in close monitoring through roles and relationships that gave them close proximity to schooling.

Refusal of a mainstream misrecognition

In 'mainstream choosing', the measurement and comparison of a specific set of secondary school examination results, together with published Inspection outcomes, is intended by policy-makers to provide the information needed in a market in which people will make informed choices. Middle-class parents appear to be the ideal consumers here because they are likely to be in a position to make choices that will place their children in the best situation for academic achievement.[3] General strategies may include moving home before the date used by the local authority to define place of residence, with the purpose of being nearer to (or further away from) a particular school. Some families move house well ahead of the period in which they are required to 'choose', which when the day comes makes the choice appear uncomplicated (in Bourdieusian tems, 'natural'). Others will fight hard for places in specific, high-performing schools, and as well as house purchase and moving home this may include renting an extra address, paying for private schooling, renewing religious allegiances and so forth. The stakes are sufficiently high for some families to resort to fraud or deception, such as using a false address so that they appear to live closer to a desired school (BBC, 2008; Harvey, 2008).

In contrast to such strategies of 'mainstream choosing', the families in our sample were on the whole highly suspicious and/or critical of the main indicators via which schools are compared, and of the associated league tables. Many felt that dominant, conventional measures of school quality (particular groupings of the results of General Certificate of Secondary Education [GCSE] examinations) were invalid as indicators of the quality of education on offer in any particular school, since they would mainly depend on the school's intake rather than on educational processes. As one put it, they were interested in what their own child would achieve, not what the class or year group would achieve. Our analysis here led us to suggest that the policies designed to engender 'choice' and 'markets' operated with too crude a conception of choice. In other words, they treat schooling as if it were the same as buying a washing machine, and imply that all schools can be arranged, ultimately, on a single continuum from best to worst. By contrast, the parents in our study appeared to see schooling in *much* broader terms, as something more akin to their only real shot, beyond the home, of shaping their child's fundamental dispositions, or habitus. We found Andrew Sayer's distinction between *preferences* and *commitments* (Sayer, 2005) especially useful in trying to grasp this gulf between policy assumptions and actual practices in the realm of school choice:

> What we have termed parental managerialism … sees parents putting great efforts into constructing a broad educational project in which actual school choice is just one element, albeit the most important single feature. Such parents have a *commitment* to particular notions of society and to particular kinds of socialisation: Their choices make sense in relation to their commitments. (Reay, Crozier, & James, 2011, pp. 70–71)

The 'particular kinds of socialisation' are a frequent feature of the interview data, and strongly linked to the parents' own educational experiences. Examples include parents describing their wishes thus:

> I don't want my children to think you know, that everybody's got a holiday house in Sardinia, and everyone's daddy drives a four by four … and everyone you know can go to tennis club and squash club and blah, blah, blah, have holidays skiing and this that and the other. You know, they've got to realise that … not everyone does that, we're not all the same … and I just think, God, if everybody would just go to state schools it would be so much better, but a lot of people don't. (Audrey)[4]

> There is definitely something about producing a different kind of middle-class child. This is a speculation but I think there is definitely something about not being arrogant or not appearing arrogant. There is some kind of modesty that some people might see as them not being confident. You are not being educated to be a woman of the world; you are being educated to take your part, a place. And I think there is an understanding

> of others you can only have if you are sort of with them all the time. It is something to learn of other cultures, but to actually learn with other cultures, of other cultures, it is a completely different thing. (Avril)

The interviews are peppered with examples that speak of a much greater educational project than that signalled by examination outcomes, and a common element of this was a desire to avoid the perceived (and, often, formerly experienced) social homogeneity of more selective school settings so as to create a more resilient, socially fluent young person equipped to thrive in a multicultural society. There was also disdain for those other parents who appeared driven by league table position in their choice of secondary school. In sum, then, these parents are 'seeing through' the myth of the market, refusing to reduce something as complex as an educational process to the dominant single indicator of quality, and acting in accordance with some strongly held values and conceptions of the educational project.

The persistence of misrecognition

However, our analysis also suggests that, in the convoluted relationship between social class, education and inequality, the attempt to act ethically in unethical circumstances produces social practices characterised by other forms of misrecognition. In one interview, we had been talking about whether, in retrospect, the choice of school had been a good one to have made:

> *Father*: I feel vindicated...
> *Mother*: Yes, I do (too)
> *Father*: ... in that because our feeling is that we're not interested in results, we're not interested in percentages of A–Cs, what we're interested in is what our own children are going to achieve. So it could be that a year group do appallingly, but if the teachers have given our children *the opportunity to rise to their natural place* and get the qualifications that they're capable of, a good teacher will work with children and if they have *one bright child* in that class they should be able to take them *where they need to go*. (Tom & Trudy – emphases added)

The interviews with parents contained many mentions of 'bright' and 'brightness', plus a number of close synonyms including having something 'extra' or being 'special'. This was linked to certainty about capability and key elements of the child's future trajectory, and also sometimes to denigration of the white working class, and a contrasting admiration for the 'bright and ambitious' amongst some minority ethnic children. Middle-class 'brightness' was the main way in which middle-class distinction was characterised and expressed:

> Across 251 interview transcripts there were a staggering 256 references to brightness, made by parents, and to a lesser extent their children, without prompting by the interviewers. We would argue that such discourses, which position middle-class brightness as both normative and a justification for middle-class privilege, are one of the main means through which the middle classes defensively use their own investments in class hierarchies to distinguish themselves as superior to others.... Brightness then becomes a rationalisation for holding on to more: educationally, socially and economically. Furthermore, investment in brightness defends against the fear of failure. For the white middle classes educational failure is often intolerable and needs to be projected elsewhere. (Reay, Crozier, & James, 2011, pp. 117–118)

It would not be unreasonable to say that, collectively, most of these 'against the grain' choosers were *so confident* about the brightness of their children that they felt justified in making the riskier investment in the average or lower-performing secondary school. This may be described using the Freudian notion of 'splitting' (in which information that challenges the integrity of the ego is dealt with by disavowal: so any responsibility for inequalities, being shameful, is projected onto subordinate groups). On the other hand (or as well) it can be understood as a form of *misrecognition*, a regular feature of educational processes, in which the institutional welcome, nurturance and certification of certain sets of dispositions (relative to others) is reinterpreted as the result of natural difference rather than socially maintained difference. In other words, in the right circumstances, children will 'rise to their natural place'.

This theme is closely linked to another, which we called the mutual affinity apparent between the relatively isolated white-middle class child in many of the schools, and the needs of the schools in highly performative conditions. To put it crudely, head teachers wanted middle-class kids and would go to great lengths to attract and keep them. Meanwhile, parents were quite demanding of teachers and head teachers, and many of their demands were met: they got a particularly good 'service', often bolstered, as mentioned earlier, with the extra resources coming through the 'Gifted and Talented' scheme. Both parents and schools were acting – at least indirectly - with knowledge derived from social science concerning the relationship of social class and educational outcomes.

The concept of misrecognition, then, helps us to unpack a series of partially shared rationales amongst the parents and families, in which they rejected GCSE results, a mainstream indicator of quality of secondary schooling, because of its poor compass in relation to what they valued about schooling. At the same time, the concept of misrecognition enabled an exploration of other senses in which parents' perceptions of the young person and engagements with the school (and education more generally) appeared to serve their interests well beyond those that were immediately apparent. This suggests it would be a mistake to see parents like those in the study who have rejected 'league table thinking' as *simply* more enlightened than their mainstream-chooser counterparts. There may well be a complex array of other types of misrecognition at stake in the relationship between middle-class families and schools. To put this another way, it may take more than a rejection of 'league table thinking' to challenge or even disturb the intricate and convoluted processes by which, from a Bourdieusian perspective, social difference is converted through educational action so that it appears naturally-occurring and thoroughly explicable via reference to individual differences in motivation and intelligence. As some earlier work in Finland demonstrated, notions of intelligence are a fundamental building-block in educational discourse and representations of educability (see Raty & Snellman, 1998).

Reflexivity and recognising tensions

As a team conducting the above project we commented that the project had been:

> ... a difficult, sometimes painful process. Many of the research team could be described as white, urban-dwelling, first-generation middle class. Researching the white middle classes was often like holding a mirror to the self. We were confronted with our own culpability, failings, conceits and self-deceptions. (Reay, Crozier, & James, 2011, p. 167)

This kind of reflexivity is important and, in Bourdieusian terms, central to achieving any kind of scientific insight (Grenfell & James, 1998). What does it really mean to be sociologically reflexive if one is deeply engaged in educational activities? I want to suggest that there is a fundamental dissonance between a Bourdieusian approach and some widely held values and goals of educational endeavour (and some educational research), and that these can be articulated as four 'areas of tension'.

First, there are tensions around *interest and proximity*. In educational research, many are accustomed to regarding personal or professional proximity to educational processes as a bonus, albeit one that needs careful handling. The whole 'teacher as researcher' tradition, and much of the work collectively known as 'action research' in the educational community, relies heavily on the longstanding methodological pivot of dealing with familiarity by making it strange (see for example Atkinson, et al., 2003; Sikes, 2003, 2006). However, in Bourdieu's social theory, this is not enough. To do social science, we need to achieve an analysis of our own position vis-à-vis the object of study. This means recognising that as, say, teachers we have *interests* that limit what we (and a good number of other teachers) can easily see. The same point can be made in respect of parents, children, policy-makers, politicians, civil servants and indeed researchers. There is a need, one might say, to make the strange familiar. Where someone is accustomed to seeing their daily and strenuous efforts as an educator in generally positive terms, it will seem difficult and quite possibly perverse to be asking in what sense they are part of a system that generates inequalities.

Second, there are tensions around *the unit of analysis*. In education, although people usually do things in groups, we are accustomed to dealing with individuals, who are the prime unit of nurturing, encouragement, achievement, reward, celebration, accountability and so forth. This is partly an observation about Anglo-Saxon culture, but we should note that the growth of psychology (and especially educational psychology and, within this, psychometrics) is roughly conterminous with the rise of state educational provision, and there is a longstanding interweaving of psychological concepts, measurements and conceptions of the person in educational policy, especially in assessment. This is probably one reason that individualistic conceptions of the self, which are axiomatic in neo-liberal thinking, appear to be accepted in many educational settings. This is not to say Bourdieu was uninterested in individuals: he put enormous amounts of effort into emancipatory projects that sought to improve the lives of many people. Rather, it is to make a more mundane but crucial point, which is that individuals are not the primary unit of analysis for Bourdieu. As he once put it:

> The socialized body (what is called the individual or the person) is not opposed to society: it is one of its forms of existence. (Bourdieu, 1993, p. 15)

Those dealing mainly in educational practice and policy may object to knowledge and insight that refers to people not as individuals *qua* individuals, but for their part in social practices which are indicative of fields, capitals, positions, relationships or tendencies. Following Mey (1972), I would liken this perspectival 'shift to the relational' to that between Newtonian and Einsteinian physics. However, some in education will find it disrespectful or otherwise objectionable that social researchers do not always take the testimony of participants at face value, or impute motives that people themselves do not directly express, acknowledge or even recognise. Thus, practices that appear self-evidently good or 'the way things are' in an educational setting might, from another perspective, show themselves to both respond to and reproduce structural inequalities.

Third, and related to the above, there are tensions around *compass* or *scale*. Whilst a sociological account drawing on Bourdieu may attempt to theorise how aspects of home background give advantages to some students and disadvantages to others, the boundaries of the issue will need to be more tightly drawn where it is considered as a problem for educational practice or policy. To put this another way, even if practitioners and policy-makers accept the Bourdieusian account, what elements of the complex array of practices, structures and relationships would they consider are in their purview? What are the excellent teachers in a relatively low-attaining school to take from an account that shows that their efforts can amount to so little in mainstream terms? For all its practical derivation and relevance, the *compass* of a Bourdieusian analysis is not, in this instance at least, likely to lend itself to 'reading off' recipes for action.

This brings us to the fourth – and arguably most important – tension between an analysis derived from Bourdieu's theoretical tools, and the worlds of education, educational practitioners and to some extent educational researchers. I will call this a tension around *tenor*, and it centres on a deceptively simple distinction between optimism and pessimism. Whilst many working in education have become highly disillusioned, many others have not, and both popular and academic literatures on teaching and leadership continue to underline the importance of enthusiasm and other forms of positivity. In addition, a diverse range of initiatives bear witness to a seemingly inexhaustible appetite for innovation. Some initiatives are large scale and 'top down' (e.g. policies like Every Child Matters, and Extended Schools in the UK) whilst others are more local and 'bottom up' (e.g. the Royal Society of Arts' Area Based Curriculum in the UK – see James, 2012). Yet others are best understood as the 'bottom up' invention and performance of 'top down' requirements (see for example Jones and Thomson's excellent analysis of the now-terminated Creative Partnerships scheme in England – Jones & Thomson, 2008). Perhaps due to the absence of shared purposes at the system level (Pring et al., 2009), an endemic reluctance to engage in problematising the ends of education or a tendency to prioritise technical over cultural aspects in collecting and using evidence of 'what works' (Biesta, 2007), these movements often encapsulate a collective imagination of what education could be or should be. For a time they appear to hold out the possibility of great change for the better in schooling, and/or solutions to problems that go well beyond the normal functions of schooling. For some of those involved, such educational visions are congenitally, sometimes infectiously, optimistic about what is possible and achievable through educational processes.

Through a Bourdieusian lens, such movements continually overestimate the capacity to act to bring about genuine change. Arguably, this tells us as much about Bourdieu's social theory as it does about the interests, values and world-views of educationists. Bourdieu's approach is largely a sociology of domination, bringing with it a strong concept of power, and whilst there is plenty of scope for agency it also illustrates limits and tends towards pessimism. This has been noted many times, by both critics and advocates of Bourdieu's approach. An early example of the former would be Paul Willis, for whom Bourdieu 'presents, finally, a gloomy, enclosed Weberian world of no-escape. There is no theoretical basis for a politics of change, for the production of alternatives or radical consciousness' (Willis, 1983, p. 121) (though as Walker argues, this overstates the case and Willis's own grounds for optimism can be shown to rely on an unwarranted romantic view of a particular form of working-class culture – see Walker, 2007). Even one of the most positive accounts of Bourdieu's work notes 'an element of fatalism or, perhaps of reluctant cosmic conservatism' (Robbins, 1991, p. 175). Yet whilst there can be little doubt that Bourdieu represents a tendency to pessimism, it would be wrong to see this a some kind of theoretical fatal flaw, for three reasons. First, until we have firmer grounds for optimism, the tendency may be warranted (cf. Walker, 2007); second, the tendency does not of itself prevent change-for-the better; and third, to position it as a 'flaw' would suggest a banal and mistaken view of the nature of Bourdieusian theory. Many (including Bourdieu himself) have pointed out that the work does not offer a grand theoretical system, but rather it is a set of related theoretical tools (albeit an 'impressively consistent' one – Calhoun, 2014) developed over time via empirical work.

Conclusion

I started by indicating that, when it comes to Bourdieu, there is great variety in 'depth-in-use', and that some connections that are made with Bourdieu's concepts in educational research are superficial. Such usage probably helps to sustain suspicions – outside and sometimes inside academic institutions – that when it comes to educational matters, theory is some kind of optional, ultimately dispensable, gloss. However, 'light' usage may not always indicate a lack of application or seriousness on the part of the researcher. First, it may be a product of the ease with which Bourdieusian concepts can be confused with others that sound similar, a point I have illustrated with the concept of misrecognition. Second, and as indicated by the four potential areas of tension identified, there is much scope for the misrecognition (in the true Bourdieusian sense) of this especially strong form of sociological reasoning when it clashes with elements of the *doxa* of the educational field, including many firmly held values. When educationists become critical social researchers, they must find ways of reconciling or living with such tensions; they must begin to subject themselves and their educational assumptions to new forms of scrutiny, to take steps to 'dislodge their thinking' (Stich, 2012). The task here is so much more than the conventionally understood one of trying to minimise the distorting effects of one's values (Greenbank, 2003) and its difficulty cannot be overstated, as many a former or current teacher on an education-related Doctoral programme would testify. There is evidence that it is worth the struggle and the end results can be distinctive, practical and worthwhile (see e.g. Anyon et al., 2009; James, 2010).

It would appear that there is no such thing as a convincing 'light' adoption of Bourdieusian tools. They cannot be used as if we were ignorant or unconcerned about how, in schools and other settings, educational processes naturalise social differences. Their use entails acknowledgement that people working in education may be unwitting (or perhaps, semi-witting) agents of inequality, whatever their motives and despite what else their actions achieve. Furthermore, a Bourdieusian perspective includes considering how, like other professionals, educationists (and educational researchers) will have collective interests that include maintaining certain arrangements and a demand for their services. Whilst the approach can provide great insight, its tendency to produce pessimism may dampen some of the enthusiasm that is so often a fundamental constituent of educational endeavour, whether at classroom or policy level. For such reasons, even the most reflexive educational professional and the most broad-minded educational policy-maker are likely to find Bourdieusian research difficult to 'do' and difficult to 'hear', regardless of how ultimately practical or useful it might actually be.

Acknowledgements

The author is grateful to the UK Economic and Social Research Council for their funding of Identities, Educational Choice and the White Urban Middle Classes (ESRC Reference RES-148-25-0023), the research project he co-directed with Reay and Crozier on which this paper draws. He would also like to thank guest editors Trevor Gale and Bob Lingard for their comments, all of which led to improvements in the paper.

Notes

1. Both 'Riverton' and 'Norton' are pseudonyms.
2. Described at the time of the study on the UK Government Department for Children, Schools and Families 'Standards' website thus: 'Gifted and talented children are those who have one or more abilities developed to a level significantly ahead of their year group (or with the potential to develop these abilities). In England the term "gifted" refers to those pupils who are capable of excelling in academic subjects such as English or History. "Talented" refers to those pupils who may excel in areas requiring visio-spatial skills or practical abilities, such as in games and PE, drama, or art'. *The Guidance Note Identifying Gifted and Talented Learners – getting started* was revised in 2008 and is now available at https://www.education.gov.uk/publications/eOrderingDownload/Getting%20StartedWR.pdf (accessed January 11, 2014).
3. The system in England combines choice and entitlement. See https://www.gov.uk/government/uploads/system/uploads/attachment_data/file/203,221/Schools_Choice_Framework.pdf (accessed January 11, 2014).
4. All participants are given pseudonyms.

References

Anyon, J., with Dumas, M., Linville, D., Nolan, K., Perez, M., Tuck, E., & Weiss, J. (2009). *Theory and educational research: Toward critical social explanation*. London: Routledge.

Atkinson, P., Coffey, A., & Delamont, S. (2003). *Key themes in qualitative research*. Walnut Creek, CA: Alta Mira Press.

BBC. (2008, March 19). More parents lie to get schools. *BBC News Online*. Retrieved June 2009, from http://news.bbc.co.uk/1/hi/education/7304588.stm

Biesta, G. J. J. (2007). Why 'what works' won't work. Evidence-based practice and the democratic deficit of educational research. *Educational Theory, 57*(1), 1–22.

Blackshaw, T., & Long, J. (2005). What's the big idea? A critical exploration of the concept of social capital and its incorporation into leisure policy discourse. *Leisure Studies, 24*, 239–258.

Bourdieu, P. (1984). *Distinction: A social critique of the judgement of taste*. (R. Nice, Trans.). Cambridge, MA: Harvard University Press.

Bourdieu, P. (1989). In L. Wacquant Towards a reflexive sociology: A workshop with Pierre Bourdieu. *Sociological Theory, 7*, 26–63.

Bourdieu, P. (1990). *The logic of practice*. (R. Nice, Trans.). Oxford: Polity Press.

Bourdieu, P. (1993). *Sociology in question*. (R. Nice, Trans.). London: Sage.

Bourdieu, P. (2000). *Pascalian meditations*. (R. Nice, Trans.). Cambridge: Polity Press.

Calhoun, C. (2014). *Pierre Bourdieu in context*. New York University. Retrieved April 28, from www.nyu.edu/classes/bkg/objects/calhoun.doc

Crozier, G., Reay, D., James, D., Jamieson, F., Beedell, P., Hollingworth, S., & Williams, K. (2008). White middle class parents, identities, educational choice and the urban comprehensive school: Dilemmas, ambivalence and moral ambiguity. *British Journal of Sociology of Education, 29*, 261–272.

Cummings, C., Todd, L., & Dyson, A. (2007). 'Towards extended schools? How education and other professionals understand community-oriented schooling'. *Children and Society, 21*, 189–200.

Fraser, N. (2007). Re-framing justice in a globalizing world. In T. Lovell (Ed.), *(Mis)recognition, social inequality and social justice: Nancy Fraser and Pierre Bourdieu* (pp. 17–35). Abingdon: Routledge.

Greenbank, P. (2003). The role of values in educational research: The case for reflexivity. *British Educational Research Journal, 29*, 791–801.

Grenfell, M., & James, D. (with Reay, D., Hodkinson, P., & Robbins, D.) (1998). *Bourdieu and education – Acts of practical theory.* London: Falmer Press.

Harvey, M. (2008, April 29). Parents who cheat at school. *The Times* Retrieved June 10, from http://women.timesonline.co.uk/tol/life_and_style/women/families/article3840412.ece

Hey, V. (2003). 'Identification and mortification in late modernity: New Labour; alpha femininities and their dis/contents' Keynote address, International Conference on Gender and Education, University of Sheffield.

James, D. (2010). Extended review – Theory and educational research: Toward critical social explanation. *British Journal of Sociology of Education, 31*, 243–248.

James, D. (2012). *The RSA area-based curriculum in Peterborough: An independent evaluation.* London: Royal Society of Arts, Manufactures and Commerce. Retrieved February 10, 2014, from http://www.thersa.org/__data/assets/pdf_file/0015/1000770/RSA_ABC_Peterborough_Independent_evaluation.pdf

James, D., Crozier, G., Reay, D., Beedell, P., Jamieson, F., Williams, K., & Hollingworth, S. (2010). Neoliberal policy and the meaning of counter-intuitive middle class school choices. *Current Sociology, 58*, 623–641.

Jones, K., & Thomson, P. (2008). Policy rhetoric and the renovation of English schooling: The case of creative partnerships. *Journal of Education Policy, 23*, 715–727.

Lister, R. (2007). (Mis)recognition, social inequality and social justice: A critical social policy perspective. In T. Lovell (Ed.), *(Mis)recognition, social inequality and social justice: Nancy Fraser and Pierre Bourdieu* (pp. 157–176). Abingdon: Routledge.

Lovell, T. (Ed.). (2007). *(Mis)recognition, social inequality and social justice: Nancy Fraser and Pierre Bourdieu.* Abingdon: Routledge.

Mahar, C., Harker, R., & Wilkes, C. (1990). The basic theoretical position. In R. Harker, C. Mahar, & C. Wilkes (Eds.), *An introduction to the work of Pierre Bourdieu* (pp. 3–25). Houndmills: Macmillan.

Mey, H. (1972). *Field-theory: A study of its application in the social sciences.* (Trans. Douglas Scott). London: Routledge & Kegan Paul.

Poupeau, F. (2000). Reasons for domination, Bourdieu versus Habermas. In B. Fowler (Ed.), *Reading Bourdieu on society and culture* (pp. 69–87). Oxford: Blackwell.

Power, S. (2012). From Redistribution to recognition to representation: Social injustice and the changing politics of education. *Globalisation, Societies and Education, 10*, 473–492.

Pring, R., Hayward, G., Hodgson, A., Johnson, J., Keep, E., Oancea, A., Rees, G., Spours, K., & Wilde, S. (2009). *Education for all: The future of education and training for 14–19 year olds.* Abingdon: Routledge.

Raty, H., & Snellman, L. (1998). Social representations of educability. *Social Psychology of Education, 1*, 359–373.

Reay, D. (2004). "It's all becoming a habitus": Beyond the habitual use of habitus in educational research. *British Journal of Sociology of Education, 25*, 431–444.

Reay, D., Crozier, G., & James, D. (2011–2013). *White middle class identities and urban schooling.* Basingstoke: Palgrave Macmillan.

Reay, D., Crozier, G., James, D., Hollingworth, S., Williams, K., Jamieson, F., & Beedell, P. (2008). Re-invigorating democracy? White middle class identities and comprehensive schooling. *Sociological Review, 56*, 238–255.

Reay, D., Hollingworth, S., Williams, K., Crozier, G., Jamieson, F., James, D., & Beedell, P. (2007). A darker shade of pale? Whiteness, the middle classes and multi-ethnic inner city schooling. *Sociology, 41*, 1041–1060.

Robbins, D. (1991). *The work of Pierre Bourdieu.* Milton Keynes: Open University Press.

Sayer, A. (2005). *The moral significance of class.* Cambridge: Cambridge University Press.

Sikes, P. (2003). Making the familiar strange: A new look at inequality in education. *British Journal of Sociology of Education, 24*, 243–248.
Sikes, P. (2006). Travel broadens the mind or making the strange familiar: The story of a visiting academic. *Qualitative Inquiry, 12*, 523–540.
Sitch, A. (2012). *Access to inequality: Reconsidering class, knowledge, and capital in higher education*. Plymouth: Lexington Books.
Swartz, D. (1997). *Culture and power – The sociology of Pierre Bourdieu*. Chicago: University of Chicago Press.
Thomson, P. (2014). "Scaling up" educational change: Some musings of misrecognition and doxic challenges. *Critical Studies in Education, 55*, 87–103.
Walker, J. C. (2007). Romanticising resistance, romanticising culture: Problems in Willis's theory of cultural production. In L. Barton (Ed.), *Education and society: 25 years of the British journal of sociology of education* (pp. 19–44). Abingdon: Routledge.
Willis, P. (1983). Cultural production and theories of reproduction. In L. Barton & S. Walker (Eds.), *Race, class and education* (pp. 107–138). London: Croom Helm.

EMOTIONAL CAPITAL AND EDUCATION: THEORETICAL INSIGHTS FROM BOURDIEU

by MICHALINOS ZEMBYLAS

ABSTRACT: This article seeks to explore existing conceptualisations of emotional capital in educational research, and to undertake a critical analysis of these conceptualisations, including a reflection on my own explorations of teachers' and students' emotional practices. Drawing from Bourdieu's work, I offer a theoretical discussion of how emotional capital as a conceptual tool suggests a historically situated analysis of the often unrecognised mechanisms and emotion norms serving to maintain certain 'affective economies'. This point is made in reference to a brief discussion of my ongoing ethnographic work over the last ten years. I conclude the article with outlining some new possibilities of theorising the potentiality and usefulness of the concept of emotional capital in the field of educational research.

1. INTRODUCTION

There is a growing body of literature on the contributions of Pierre Bourdieu's work in education (Allard, 2005; Dika and Singh, 2002; Gillies, 2006; Grenfell, 2004, 2007; Grenfell and James, 1998; McClenaghan, 2000; McLeod, 2005; McNamara Horvat, 2003; Reay, 2000, 2004a, b, c). Bourdieu's writings provide us with powerful conceptual tools to avoid a number of 'debilitating' (Bourdieu, 1990, p. 25) dualisms – such as the subject/object, agency/structure, private/public, and nature/culture dichotomies – pervading educational research for many decades (Shilling, 2004). In his work, Bourdieu develops a conceptual framework that renders these dichotomies meaningless; instead, he emphasises how the embodied agent is shaped by, but also shapes (and often reproduces), society in a more integrated fashion. In particular, his analysis of embodiment as 'practical sense' maps *emotions* onto experiences constituted and displayed by enculturated social actors (Probyn, 2004).

© 2007 The Author

Emotions are increasingly the focus of analysis across a number of disciplines and professional settings, including education (Schutz and Pekrun, 2007; Zembylas, 2005). Although emotions have largely been investigated through a range of scientific, biomedical and psychological discourses that consider emotional phenomena primarily as 'individual' and 'private' (Boler, 1999; Lupton, 1998), there is a growing effort to integrate these ideas with alterative views branching out into the sphere of culture and society (Ahmed, 2004; Lutz and Abu-Lughod, 1990; Williams, 2001). Historical and ethnographical work on emotions in the last decade show how emotions are experienced through social relations and culture, and thus are managed, not merely expressed, in interpersonal communication in conformity with collective social norms (Barbalet, 1998; Lupton, 1998; Reddy, 2001). Also, recent work on theorising affect in terms of relations and encounters involving the capacities and intensities of affecting and being affected (Berlant, 2000; Massumi, 1996; Probyn, 2004; Skeggs, 2004) indicates the implications of understanding affects and emotions as embodied through variable cultural frames. It is against this background of ideas that Bourdieu's non-dualistic views on habitus, field, and capital may provide new insights in educational theory and research around the role of emotions in education and change.

This article seeks to explore existing conceptualisations of *emotional capital* in educational research; to undertake a critical analysis of these conceptualisations, including a reflection on my own explorations of teachers' and students' emotional practices; and finally, to suggest implications for an extended investigation of the concept of emotional capital for research in the field of education. 'Emotional capital', understood in general as 'emotional resources', can provide a more useful conceptual tool to educational researchers for two reasons. First, the use of emotional capital as situated in Bourdieu's work provides a rich account of how emotions-as-resources are circulated, accumulated and exchanged for other forms of capital. The concept of emotional capital offers a tool for thinking about the ways in which emotion practices are regulated within an educational context, based on emotion norms that may change but are also reproduced. In these terms, emotional capital is both generated by and contributes to the generation of the habitus of a particular educational context. Secondly, the notion of emotional capital can help educational researchers understand the importance of teachers' and students' emotion practices as forms of resistance to prevalent emotion norms. Particularly, in light of functionalist and deterministic calls for an optimal exploitation of emotional capital in contemporary

© 2007 The Author

education and the workplace – for instance, the movement to promote 'emotional intelligence' (see Hartley, 2003; Zembylas, 2006; Zembylas and Fendler, 2007 for relevant critiques) – insights from Bourdieu's work can help gain a deeper understanding of such normative ways of socialisation.

This article begins by clarifying the notions of 'emotion' and 'affect' and how they contribute to the social formation of embodiment. Then I briefly discuss Bourdieu's use of the concepts habitus, field, and capital to ground the section that follows in which the focus is on the notion of 'emotional capital' and how it has been used in educational research so far. My interest here is in the meanings and usefulness of emotional capital in understanding how emotions and affects influence educational experiences. Drawing from Bourdieu's work, I offer a theoretical discussion of how emotional capital as a conceptual tool suggests a historically situated analysis of the often unrecognised mechanisms and emotion norms that serve to maintain certain 'affective economies'. This point is made in reference to a brief discussion of my ongoing ethnographic work over the last ten years. I conclude the article with outlining some new possibilities of theorising the potentiality and usefulness of the concept of emotional capital in the field of educational research.

2. Theorising Emotions, Affect and Embodiment

In recent times, several social theorists assert that emotions are simultaneously signs for bodily states and cultural categories (Barbalet, 1998; Williams, 2001). While it is cultural categories that enable individuals to put embodied sensations into words and make them into emotions, the affective experiences that precede these cultural categories cannot be ignored (Lupton, 1998; Massumi, 2002). Thus, it is important to differentiate what is meant by the terms 'emotions' and 'affects' and briefly refer to the social formation of bodies. For this purpose, I turn to ethnographic work across cultures as well as theorisations of the embodied aspects of emotions (Leavitt, 1996; Thrift, 2004). In this literature, affect is defined as something first experienced in the body and then named and re-experienced through social relations and culture. According to this view, for example, the basic affects of anger, fear, disgust and so on are universal and embodied but cultural experiences and social interpretations of the embodiment of emotions allow much variation.

The convergence between embodied experiences of emotions and their cultural understandings takes place around the notion that 'socialised human bodies, bodies that normally exist as groups and

© 2007 The Author

in interaction rather than as isolated entities, have their being in recurrent situations that call forth the meaning/feeling responses we recognise as emotions' (Leavitt, 1996, pp. 524–525). This perspective, argues Leavitt, seems truer to our common, daily life experience of emotion than a vision of emotion as either bodily or simply sociocultural. Emotions cannot be reduced to biology, relations or discourse alone but belong to all these dimensions as they are constituted through ongoing relational practices (Burkitt, 1997). In other words, emotions are not *in* either the individual or the social, but produce the very surfaces and boundaries that allow the 'individual' and the 'social' to be delineated as such (Ahmed, 2004).

Ahmed's (2004) notion of 'affective economies' is another way of arguing that emotions do not reside in a subject but rather circulate involving relations of difference, whereby what is 'moved' and what 'moves' is the effect of affective intensities and energies. In other words, Ahmed acknowledges the significance of corporeality in the constitution of emotional attachments and meanings, that is, how emotions become attached to objects, bodies and signs – a process that is crucial in the constitution of subjectivity. What characterises emotionality, according to Ahmed, is that it functions as an economy; it separates us from others as well as connects us to others. For example, she points to an economic understanding of hate and explains that hate does not reside within an individual but is circulated and draws other bodies together making them members of a group united by their hatred of other groups. This economy of hate works to differentiate some bodies from other bodies, a differentiation that is never over.

Adopting this approach – that is, the mapping of affect onto emotions through variable cultural understandings – Probyn (2004) builds on Bourdieu and theorises emotion as the biographical understanding we attach, through the habitus, to our affective experiences. Thus, habitus – understood as a socially constituted system of dispositions – provides the link between emotions, affect and embodiment, because it works as a practical sense of moving through space, producing the embodied norms of everyday life. The habitus makes up our habitual patterns of understanding and inhabiting the world (McNay, 1999), producing embodied experiences that coincide with objective structures (see Bourdieu, 1990). Therefore, as McNay notes, a social analysis is possible in which affects are filtered through habitus into emotions (as self-perceived) and emotional performances (as displayed by enculturated social actors); in this model, emotions and emotional performances may be redirected by readjusting our habitus.

© 2007 The Author

Finally, it is important to emphasise that the context for habitus is socially and historically constituted. Raymond Williams's (1977) concept of 'structures of feeling' is especially significant to the analysis undertaken here because he too – just like Bourdieu – contributed a needed bridge between social structures and the tendencies to analyse feelings only in terms of their individual and psychological significance (Harding and Pribram, 2004). Williams suggests a mediation between objective structure and lived experience in the study of cultural practice and production calling attention to the importance of locality. Structures of feeling name the simultaneously cultural and discursive dimension of our experience but do not neglect that these experiences are also felt and embodied. Williams's theorising about the 'structures of feeling' provides us with a heuristic speculative and theoretical instrument for illuminating the crucial issues for the development of emotion norms within an educational context and for understanding new challenges to these norms (Zembylas, 2002). Emotion norms, just like other norms, delineate a zone within which certain emotions are permitted and others are not permitted, and can be obeyed or broken, at varying costs; they reflect power relations and thus are techniques for the discipline of habitus in the emotional expression and communication between teachers and students (Zembylas, 2005).

3. Bourdieu's Concepts of Habitus, Field, and Capital

The concept of 'emotional capital' cannot be understood without a brief exploration of some central concepts in Bourdieu's work, namely habitus, field and capital. In his sociological writings, Bourdieu sees emotions as integral aspects of what he terms 'strategies' (Emirbayer and Goldberg, 2005). Strategies are modes of response to and action within the world and are grounded in systems of dispositions which he terms *habitus* (Bourdieu, 1977). Dispositions include a spectrum of cognitive and affective factors and thus the concept of habitus is used to explain how objective structures and subjective perceptions impact upon actions (see also Bourdieu, 1990, 2000; Bourdieu and Wacquant, 1992).

In his earlier work, Bourdieu wrote that the concept of habitus 'is predisposed by its range of historical uses to designate a system of acquired, permanent, generative dispositions' (1990, p. 53). The habitus provides a window to the world – it is 'a product of history [that] produces individual and collective practices ... . [The habitus is] embodied history, internalized as second nature and so forgotten as history' (Bourdieu, 1990, pp. 54, 56). This product of history is

© 2007 The Author

'deposited in each organism in the form of schemes of perception, thought and action' (p. 56). In this way, Bourdieu explains the relations between individual habitus and the social circumstances from which it emerges. It is precisely in this manner that institutions produce real effects on individuals, and these effects are inscribed in individuals' bodily practices. This is why the habitus is also described by Bourdieu as 'practical sense' (1990, p. 57) which constitutes a feeling of 'knowledge in the body' (ibid.); the body becomes an active source in the unfolding of social relations and is permeated everywhere by the historical. An example that exemplifies this point is how the politics of gender in a particular society shape and are revealed in ways of walking, looking, and even standing (Jenkins, 1992).

In his later writings, Bourdieu assigned more plasticity to the habitus (Jenkins, 1992), explaining that it constitutes 'a system of lasting, transposable dispositions which, integrating past experiences, functions at every moment as a matrix of perceptions, appreciations, and actions' (2000, pp. 82–83). 'Transposable' means that the habitus is adaptable enough to reproduce itself as circumstances change (Hoy, 2004). Habitus – just like Williams's notion of 'structures of feeling' – may be seen, then, as a set of embodied practices which are to some extent a product of prior experiences – not in the sense of a cluster of dispositions that are static and unavoidable, but rather as embodied practices that are strongly influenced by historical, social, and cultural contexts.[1] In other words, the concept of habitus is dynamic and *generative* of its own possibilities and thus is not wholly structured (Hoy, 2004; McNay, 1999; Probyn, 2004; Swartz, 1997).

Habitus is formed through the embodied accumulation and effects of dispositions (McLeod, 2005; McNay, 1999) and thus constitutes what Ahmed (2004) calls an 'affective economy' – within which emotional capital, as it is argued in the next part of this article, accumulates, moves and is invested for particular purposes. Consequently, emotionality and embodiment, as expressed in the notion of habitus, are open-ended processes rather than determining structures between an agent and the world. According to Probyn (2004), 'The habitus as a description of lived realities is that which *generates* practices, frames for positioning oneself in the world, and indeed ways of inhabiting the world' (p. 229, added emphasis). This generative view of habitus may constitute a site of transformative emotion practices; that is, while an agent might be predisposed to act in certain ways, the potentiality for innovation and new affective connections with the world is not foreclosed (Emirbayer and Goldberg, 2005; McNay, 1999). For example, kinship dispositions among members of

© 2007 The Author

an ethnic group predispose individuals to select particular forms of conduct with *others* such as avoiding to socialise with them or feeling discomfort to sit next to them; however, this set of dispositions that makes an individual who he or she is adjusts his or her expectations according to social structure and available resources that may eventually be reinforced or modified. There is room for different ways of inhabiting the world, for instance, if individuals stop considering others as threatening and fearsome and instead engage in alterative networks, relations or connections with them.

The habitus is in what Bourdieu calls a *field*. Bourdieu uses the term 'field' to capture the 'rules of the game' (Bourdieu and Wacquant, 1992). A field is a social arena within which networks, relations and struggles over resources take place. Fields are like regions of the world, explains Hoy (2004), such as the political, the religious, the scientific, or the pedagogic fields; there is no way to do science, for instance, outside the scientific field. Fields, therefore, are structured systems of social positions – occupied by individuals or institutions – the nature of which define the situation for their occupants (Jenkins, 1992). However, fields do not completely determine action; norms (e.g. emotion norms), institutions, rituals, conventions and categories structuring a field can always be renegotiated. A field receives its form from power relations and the struggles over *capital*; to put it differently, capital has meaning only in a specific field.

Bourdieu (1977, 1984, 1986) explains the ways in which capital operates as a tool of cultural reproduction and perpetuates unequal educational achievement. He discusses various forms of capital – economic, cultural and social – that exist in conjunction with one another and together constitute the differentiation and distribution of resources in society. Economic capital refers to income and other financial resources, while cultural capital may take various forms, reflecting the modes of thinking, values, dispositions, sets of meaning and qualities of style that are primarily transmitted through the family. These qualities are assigned a particular social status in relation to what the dominant classes label as the most valued cultural capital (Giroux, 1983). Cultural capital can exist in three forms: embodied (dispositions of mind and body), objectified (cultural goods), and institutionalised (educational qualifications). Reay (2004a) and Skeggs (2004) argue for a broad understanding of cultural capital that also recognises its affective aspects such as levels of confidence and empowerment.

Finally, social capital is generated through social processes and exists as social relations and networks (such as contacts and group

© 2007 The Author

memberships). According to Bourdieu, these relationships and memberships add up to potential and actual resources that individuals can mobilise. It is the battle for distinction that gives social capital its qualities. Social capital constitutes then a useful emotional resource for individuals in their social relationships and thus includes certain norms and obligations that are maintained through rewards and punishments (cf. Halpern, 2005). What makes Bourdieu different from other theorists who also talk about social capital is his analysis of social capital as ubiquitous and continually transmitted (e.g. through community norms) and accumulated in ways that may reinforce existing social structures (Blackshaw and Long, 2005; Dika and Singh, 2002; Edwards, 2004).

According to Bourdieu (1993), all capitals are the products of investments and resources to be exploited; each form of capital can be transformed into another. All the kinds of capital constitute the different fractions of the social classes, because through the movement of capital some individuals and groups are included and others are excluded. Thus, the concept of capital helps us explain how particular cultures (e.g. a culture of inequality, a culture of hatred for other ethnic groups) are generated through social, cultural and economic mechanisms and institutions (e.g. schooling). In a sense, then, the various forms of capital mark the different resources and values around which power relations are exercised in a particular field. The struggle for possession of capital thus indicates not only the uneven distribution of available resources but also their circulation. It is in this sense that Bourdieu's argument comes close to Foucault's analysis of power, in other words, the idea that power is not possessed by individuals or institutions but becomes 'coextensive with a complex set of relations between different fields' (McNay, 1999, p. 106). Although social control becomes more insidious and hence more effective in this manner, the potential for subversion arises from the movement and circulation between fields of action (Bourdieu, 1990).

4. Emotional Capital and Education

Bourdieu's notions of habitus, field and capital yield an understanding of society as a differentiated and open structure and provide a framework that conceptualises the uneven ways in which emotional embodiment and capital are realised in relations between groups or individuals. Bourdieu himself never refers explicitly to the concept of *emotional capital* in his theory of social capital. Several sociologists of education, however, have drawn on the work of Bourdieu to theorise the notion of emotional capital and highlight the ways in which

© 2007 The Author

emotional involvement is implicated in social relationships such as parenthood (Gillies, 2006; Reay, 2000) or vocational and childcare education and training (Colley, 2003, 2006; Colley *et al.*, 2003). Diane Reay (2000, 2004b), in particular, has made important contributions in using the concept of emotional capital in education, but she admits that she has utilised the concept more 'as a heuristic device than as an over arching conceptual frame' and thus suggests that 'it requires further refining both theoretically and empirically' (2000, p. 569).

According to Reay (2000, 2004b), Nowotny (1981) was the first to employ the term 'emotional capital'. Nowotny theorised emotional capital as a form of social capital and saw it as the social and cultural resources generated through affective relations, especially in the sphere of the family. As she argued, emotional capital denotes the 'knowledge, contacts and relations as well as access to emotionally valued skills and assets, which hold within any social network characterized at least partly by affective ties' (p. 148). Endorsing Bourdieu's analysis of women as responsible for maintaining social relationships, Nowotny saw emotional capital as a resource women have in greater abundance than men (Reay, 2000, 2004b).

Allatt (1993) built on Nowotny's work and defined emotional capital as 'emotionally valued assets, skills, love and affection, expenditure of time, attention, care and concern' (p. 143). Thus, emotional capital may be understood as the emotional resources – such as support, patience and commitment – built over time particularly within families. Contrary to Nowotny, Allatt did not limit emotional capital solely to women, although she also saw emotional capital as 'more the province of women than men' (Reay, 2000, p. 572).

More recently, Reay (2000, 2004b) has used the term emotional capital as a 'heuristic device' to denote 'the emotional resources passed on from mother to child' (2000, p. 284). Reay's work is focused on mothers' emotional involvement in their children's education and explores the extent to which emotional capital may be understood as a specifically gendered capital. She emphasises the close relationships between educational success, emotional capital and emotional wellbeing in the family. Reay also discusses the importance of viewing emotional capital as an investment in others – thus highlighting the emotional costs of those involved and particularly the costs for mothers. Unlike Nowotny, Reay (2004b) suggests that adverse circumstances such as poverty diminish emotional capital; for this purpose, Manion (2007) criticises Reay in that she does not account for the possibility that conditions of poverty may actually catalyse the development and transfer of specific emotional capital resources between family members. In her study, Manion explores

© 2007 The Author

the concept of emotional capital in the context of women's decision-making in The Gambia and emphasises how emotional capital may be in fact the most abundant resource of marginalised groups.

The common thread of these past few accounts on emotional capital is an effort to describe the emotional resources of individuals within a strictly social – and primarily parental – sphere. Yet while emotional capital is a potentially useful analytic tool, it risks being co-opted into a parenting model for the emotional profit (or cost) generated in families and its repercussions for children. As Gillies (2006) points out correctly, this perspective relies on a value judgment as to what constitutes profit, not only within the restricted sphere of parental involvement but also more generally in the political arena. The question, who profits from spending, exploiting or investing in particular forms of emotional capital, is clearly much more complex than limiting emotional capital to the emotional investments made by parents as part of their desire to promote their children's wellbeing.

Also, Reay's argument about emotional capital as a gendered capital may fall into the trap of traditional emotion discourses in many societies, that is, the notion that women are naturally more nurturing and caring and thus are 'more emotional' than men (Boler, 1999; Zembylas, 2005). Such discourses have been heavily criticised in the last few years for perpetuating traditional gender roles. On the other hand, this criticism would be unfair to Reay's work, if one did not look carefully at the specific context in which she made this argument. Reay does not claim in general that women have more emotional capital than men; she clearly states that it is within the sphere of parental involvement in education that the gendered nature of emotional capital is powerful. This finding indicates once again the great importance of extending the use of emotional capital to other fields besides parental involvement or women's roles.

Some of Colley's recent work on 'vocational habitus' (Colley *et al.*, 2003) and the emotional labour demanded in vocational learning adapted habitus as a way of extending its use in the field of vocational and childcare education and training (Colley, 2003, 2006). Vocational habitus is defined as the combination of idealised and realised dispositions to which students must orient themselves in order to become the 'right person for the job ... It [vocational habitus] operates in disciplinary ways to dictate how one should properly feel, look and act, as well as the values, attitudes and beliefs that one should espouse' (Colley *et al.*, 2003, p. 488). Colley draws on Hochschild's (1983) theory of emotional labour in order to analyse feelings as prescribed and learned in the context of powerful norms. Emotional labour has its roots in Marxist thinking and describes the requirement

© 2007 The Author

to induce or suppress feelings in order to sustain the 'proper' state of mind and behaviour to others. A major tenet of Hochschild's work is that the management of emotions based on social norms requires effort and leads to a commodification, where the organisation controls the worker's emotions; the expression of these social norms, however, differs not only for men and women, but also between classes. Hochschild argues that women typically possess greater emotional resources than men, not least because they tend to have access to fewer of the other forms of capital (Colley, 2006). In patriarchal societies, explains Colley, the oppression of women makes it less likely that their resources can be fully deployed as capital, therefore, emotional capital is not essentially an economistic metaphor, but expresses sets of social relations and inequalities of power.

Colley (2006) critiques Reay's analysis of emotional capital on the basis that this concept locates the exploitation of women's resources in those to whom they devote their emotional work (i.e., children). According to Colley, this assumes that the problem of capitalism and its unequal social relations is a problem of consumption, and that emotions are *goods* generated by women, but consumed by others. Instead of misplacing the root of the problem to gender and class, Colley suggests that available repertoires of feeling are related to the mode of production in any given society, to multiple divisions of labour within it, and to different relationships to the means of production. In other words, emotional labour demands that individuals not only mobilise existing dispositions but also work further on their own feelings and dispositions in learning to labour appropriately (Colley, 2003). The field and the habitus allow emotional resources to count as capital within highly restricted parameters; learning is a process of becoming, yet the possibilities are not boundless.

My own understanding of emotional capital has emerged through a different entry point, particularly the consideration of the dialectics of history, politics and emotions (e.g. see Ahmed, 2004; Lutz and Abu-Lughod, 1990; Reddy, 2001; Stearns, 1994; Stearns and Stearns, 1986). My ethnographic research on emotions in education for the past ten years (e.g. see Zembylas, 2005, 2007a, b; Isenbarger and Zembylas, 2006) and even more so others' research (e.g. see Boler, 1999; Schutz and DeCuir, 2002; Schutz and Pekrun, 2007; Van Veen and Lasky, 2005) is fuelled by evidence of how emotions are a crucial capital in relations among social groups. In my own work, for example, I have documented how emotional capital is built over time within classrooms and schools and contributes to the formation of particular emotion norms and affective economies. In this context, emotional capital – expressed through the circulation of emotional resources

© 2007 The Author

among teachers and students – is systematically transformed into social and cultural capital – such as stronger relations in the classroom and empowered feelings in the school community. It is in this sense that I have argued that emotional capital – although I haven't always used the term explicitly and certainly not in the context of a systematic theoretical frame – reflects particular historical, cultural and social manifestations. Yet, it is important to acknowledge that the exchange and circulation of emotional resources take place within particular affective economies; the possibilities of change, in other words, are not limitless.

For example, in an ongoing ethnographic study that is being conducted in an ethnic conflict setting in Europe, I provide evidence for the politics of resentment and hatred within an ethnic group against a different ethnic group (Zembylas, 2007c,d). In this project, it is shown how negative emotions about the Other draw on past histories of perceived injustice and feed present resentment that things are not fair and that the Other is 'evil'. This analysis explains how various institutional and everyday (e.g. school) practices of encounter and estrangement with the Other work to construct emotional capital that circulates and forms a particular habitus. It is the emotional practices of educators and learners nurtured in schools that work to demarcate differences with the ethnic Other and transform emotional capital to cultural capital or social capital and vice versa; thus it is within this restricted social and political field that dominant national, social and cultural taxonomies are reproduced or occasionally destabilised.

Data from exploring teachers' and students' emotion practices in this study shows how an 'ethnocentric' habitus operates in disciplinary ways to normalise students' and teachers' feelings and actions both in and outside schools. As such, this habitus is affective and embodied and calls upon the need that teachers and students adapt to the emotional demands of the hegemonic culture, given its more powerful economic, social and cultural capital. The field demands that teachers and students further work upon and develop their emotional resources (e.g. love and sacrifice for one's own country and their collective identity; resentment for the injustice others have caused). Yet, the habitus is transformed, not essentialising. The evidence collected in this study suggests that the habitus contains important ambivalence and tension, which students and teachers must negotiate. For instance, it is shown that the emotional capital of hatred is full of contradiction and uncertainty and is not (always) absolute. The argument of hatred as ambivalence enables educators to locate the study of the emotional capital of hate feelings in both

© 2007 The Author

individual human needs and motivations, as well as in social and political struggles. The implication of a relational understanding of hatred is that it shifts attention from the individual to the practices with which hate is socially, historically, culturally and politically constituted. In other words, structure and agency combine to render the process of socialisation far more complex than a passive absorption of the dominant affects that are circulated. Such an analysis of affect enables educators to explore how emotional investments to some ideals (the nation-state, national identity, religion etc.) are experienced, expressed, and circulated, that is, how emotion norms function to constitute socially 'acceptable' and 'unacceptable' beliefs and actions for educators and their students.

The preceding examples underscore the close relationship between various forms of capital and emotional capital and how the circulation of particular affects and emotions between social groups reinforces other forms of capital. For instance, in the earlier example on the ambivalence of hatred it is shown that students and teachers give and withhold emotional resources. However, through this circulation and distribution of emotional resources teachers and students form social relationships and differences, negotiate meanings about one's nation-state and culture, and constitute their subjectivities. What characterises those emotional resources, according to Ahmed (2004), is that they separate 'us' from 'others' as well as connect us to others through circulation and distribution of affects. Under some circumstances, however, as it is shown in this study, the circulation of hatred-as-ambivalence exchanges emotional capital for cultural capital (e.g. the emergence of positive dispositions about 'others') and social capital (e.g. the creation of new relations and networks with 'others'). The ambivalence of hatred is bound up with the positing of an affective relationality between the 'I' and the 'we' (Ahmed, 2004). But the meaning of 'we' is neither fixed nor univocal; in fact, this study documents how some individuals may develop emotional attachment to new meanings of 'we' as they acknowledge the politics of difference. Thus a richer emotional understanding of the Other allows for new relations and dispositions to emerge. The conversion between emotional capital and other forms of capital is certainly an issue that needs deeper investigation. However, I do want to highlight the importance of drawing on a broader definition of emotional capital as emotional investments that have significant social, cultural and economic implications; a definition of emotional capital that is not restricted to the gendered or classed processes which make up involvement in schooling, but is exemplified in the complex manifestations of capital.

© 2007 The Author

5. Future Directions of Theorising Emotional Capital in Educational Research

There are both possibilities and limitations of using the concept of 'emotional capital' in educational research. First, I want to discuss two important dangers. The first danger is relevant to the strong associations of the term with economic theory and the second one is related to existing efforts that the term is co-opted by management and functionalist discourses. These dangers are evident in discussions about emotional intelligence, emotion management, emotional competencies and the optimal exploitation of human capital (e.g. Goleman, 1995, 1998; Thompson, 1998). The equation of emotional intelligence with self-control provides evidence for efforts to instil new forms of morality, utility, efficiency and professionalism both in education and in the workplace (Hartley, 2003; Zembylas, 2006; Zembylas and Fendler, 2007). In this manner, the application of emotional intelligence becomes a technology of schooling and joins other disciplinary technologies that function as modes of normalisation: if you are 'emotionally intelligent', you are more likely to avoid the risks of 'unacceptable' emotional behaviour and enjoy the pleasures of 'normal' emotional expression.

Gendron (2004) refers particularly to the importance of emotional capital as a set of resources (emotional competencies) that are useful for an individual's cognitive, personal, social and economic development. He argues that emotional capital is crucial in knowledge and self-management for companies, schools and organisations in the increasingly complex and competitive global workplace. However, the term is completely stripped of its social and political context, and cultural differences or social hierarchies are not accounted for in the manifestation of emotional practices. The emphasis is on how individuals can 'use' emotional capital, i.e. how it can be valuable in facilitating certain actions. Therefore, an important component of emotional capital, according to Gendron, is its successful management through learning the appropriate emotional competencies – that is, controlling undesirable emotions and acquiring the desirable ones. In this way, emotional capital is used as a component of emotional intelligence and emotion management calls that are directed toward a particular kind of self-policing the affect.

However, such an understanding of emotional capital is precisely the opposite of what Bourdieu's analysis attempted to develop. According to Reay (2004a), Bourdieu viewed the concept of capital as breaking the common assumptions that success or failure is a result of (any kind of) intelligence. Although it may be tempting to

© 2007 The Author

theorise emotional capital in association with emotional intelligence, there are substantial inequalities in the symbolic values accorded to various forms of emotional capital; yet emotional intelligence discourses assume that emotional self-control should be valued highly. Bourdieu's work helps us contextualise the focus on the ways different emotional practices are implicated in the production of unequal forms of emotional capital.

According to the understanding of emotional capital developed here, I want to emphasise the importance of retaining Bourdieu's idea on the interconnections among the various forms of capital and the notion that emotional orientations provide different opportunities for converting emotional capital into other forms of capital (and vice versa). The concept of 'emotional capital' is valuable not only because it illustrates the importance of emotions within a particular habitus, but because of the significance of emotions and affects in the circulation of other forms of capital. Therefore, like the major capitals Bourdieu identified, emotional capital is integrally linked with other resources – e.g. political, cultural and social – and as such it blends with them to facilitate or prevent certain practices and discourses. Conceptualising emotional capital as political, cultural, and social enriches educators' understanding of the power relations involved in affective relations, and illustrates how previously established emotional capital – solidarity, trust, hope, loyalty, enmity and so forth – may influence later practices. Without theorising the transformation of emotional capital and its relation to social and political practices, one is unable to conceptualise power relations, to see how emotional capital is arrayed and operates during particular events, or to see how actors (e.g. administrators, teachers, parents, students) contest or seek to re-channel it.

In addition, Bourdieu's relational concepts of the field and habitus contextualise the notion of emotional capital as sets of emotions or feelings which are not only shared by groups of individuals implicated in social structures and processes, but which are significant in the formation and maintenance of political and social identities and collective behaviour (Barbalet, 1998). Thus collective identity is what enables individuals to feel themselves part of a community as opposed to others that are considered to be outsiders (Melucci, 1996a, 1996b). In this manner, love and hate, faith and fear are all part of a collective body-field and cannot be simply relegated to the domain of individual-level factors. Emotional capital includes emotional patterns which differentiate social groups by virtue of the fact that they are shared by their members and unlikely to be shared with non-members (Barbalet, 1998). Thus emotional capital may be understood as

© 2007 The Author

involving emotional practices that are inextricably linked to the ways individuals and groups form their habitus and perceive themselves and others.

Consequently, Bourdieu's work enables the exploration of how (emotional) investments in some categories (e.g. race, ethnicity, religion etc.) are experienced, expressed, and circulated within or across fields. The implications from the circulation of emotional capital may be seen in the ways that various events (ethnic celebrations, national mourning days, religious events and so on) connect an individual to his or her large group with a profound sense of belonging and constitute a source of collective action: individual identity is subsumed to the group (Petonito, 2000). This rather political understanding of emotional capital draws attention to the ways in which groups establish particular affective economies that actively manipulate emotions for political purposes, and point out how they may use this ability as a form of investment (Svasek, 2002, 2005). That is, as Ahmed (2004) asserts, emotions work to shape the boundaries of individual and collective bodies; emotions do not reside in subjects or objects but are produced, circulated and capitalised on to achieve political purposes such as unity or conflict. An affective economy circulates the use-value of particular affects held by dominant discourses to impose the legitimate mode of feeling and thinking.

The notion of emotional capital – within the context of an extended understanding of Bourdieu's work, however, and not grounded in economic theory – focuses on the situatedness of emotional practices without ignoring the materiality of the body (cf. Shilling, 2004). The movement of emotional capital within a field involves the embodiment of emotion and the fashioning and display of the body and its affects. Bourdieu's work offers the ground for developing links among affects, emotions and bodies that go beyond reproductionist implications (cf. McLeod, 2005). Particularly, in view of the demands for conformity and homogeneity within schools – for example, through the calls for emotional intelligence and emotion management – Bourdieu's framework of ideas provides a powerful analysis of the possibilities for theorising change.

As McLeod (2005) argues, habitus and field are helpful for understanding socialisation reproduction but may be less so for explaining the process of change. McNay (1999) suggests that although Bourdieu's conceptualisation of change is not fully realised in his work, it nevertheless offers ways of doing so because the historicisation of norms is acknowledged. As my own work suggests, to analyse and challenge emotion norms in education, for example, means to reveal their historicity and contingency that have come to define the limits

© 2007 The Author

and possibilities of teachers and students' understandings of themselves, individually and collectively (Zembylas, 2005). By doing so, it is to disturb, destabilise, and subvert these rules, to identify some of the weak points and lines of fracture where new affective connections (as counter-hegemonic) might make a difference.

The analysis provided here makes possible an interpretation of the differential impact of emotional capital on teachers' and students' emotional practices, that is, how, for instance, emotion norms come and go. In making these observations, it seems that teachers' and students' emotional practices are profoundly influenced by their participation in particular affective economies in schools. By making this point, I wish to avoid a suggestion that subordinates the individual to the social (or the subjective dispositions to the objective structures) and loses sight of the reciprocal relation between the two. As I have already emphasised, there is a great deal at stake in the movement of emotional capital that 'governs' the lives of teachers and students. However, professional and classroom communities are able to constitute habituses that have the potential to subvert disciplinary mechanisms and practices.

6. Conclusion

In this article, I have tried to outline the current uses of the notion of 'emotional capital' in educational research and explore its possibilities as a conceptual tool in future empirical work in educational research. I have emphasised the importance of extending both Bourdieu's work in relevance to the notion of emotional capital and the scope of its uses in education. In dialogue with this work, I have argued for a social and political analysis of the (trans-)formation of emotional capital in education and its relationship with habitus and field in ways that change is addressed. Using emotional capital as a conceptual tool ensures not only that emotions and the work of emotions are acknowledged in education, but also that the research focus becomes broader in terms of its socio-political implications.

Extending Bourdieu's work amounts to an intervention in a much larger debate about subjectivities in the classroom, in which concepts of affective elements of consciousness and relationships, community, and reform are slowly being re-examined. These sociopolitical aspects of emotions and affects in education create the difference between possible and real transformation, and it is this difference that constitutes the power of emotional capital as a conceptual tool to challenge our existing conceptions. The need for a deeper conceptualisation of emotional capital and its conversion to other capitals

© 2007 The Author

may guide ethnographic work on emotions in education in whatever locality, informed by a search to understand the possibilities and the limitations of the social and political merits or demerits of emotional capital.

7. Note

[1] As Wouters (1986, 1987, 1991) and Stearns (1994; Stearns and Stearns, 1986) demonstrate, there has been a definite shift in the emotion norms of Western societies from an implicit emphasis on individual control toward a greater concern with group conformity and attunement to peers' reactions. This amounts to what Wouters (1986, 1987, 1992) has called 'a controlled decontrolling of emotions', a key description of 'informalisation' in individual and collective habitus in which emotion norms diminish in favour of a more complex, mutually negotiated series of emotional self-restraints. Thus, emotional self-restraint must be seen as an important force that reshapes various interactions in contemporary relationships.

8. References

AHMED, S. (2004) *The Cultural Politics of Emotion* (Edinburgh, Edinburgh University Press).

ALLARD, A. (2005) Capitalizing on Bourdieu: how useful are concepts of 'social capital' and 'social field' for researching 'marginalized' young women? *Theory and Research in Education,* 3 (1), 63–79.

ALLATT, P. (1993) Becoming privileged: the role of family processes. In I. BATES and G. RISEBOROUGH (Eds) *Youth and Inequality* (Buckingham, Open University Press), 139–159.

BARBALET, J. M. (1998) *Emotion, Social Theory, and Social Structure: A Macrosociological Approach* (Cambridge, Cambridge University Press).

BERLANT, L. (2000) The subject of true feeling: pain, privacy and politics. In S. AHMED, J. KILBY, C. LURY, M. MCNEIL and B. SKEGGS (Eds) *Transformations: Thinking Through Feminism* (London, Routledge), 33–47.

BLACKSHAW, T. and LONG, J. (2005) What's the big idea? A critical exploration of the concept of social capital and its incorporation into leisure policy discourse, *Leisure Studies,* 24 (3), 239–258.

BOLER, M. (1999) *Feeling Power: Emotions and Education* (New York, Routledge).

BOURDIEU, P. (1977) *Outline of a Theory of Practice* (Trans. R. NICE) (Cambridge, Cambridge University Press).

BOURDIEU, P. (1984 [1979]) *Distinction: A Social Critique of the Judgement of Taste* (Trans. R. Nice) (Cambridge, MA, Harvard University Press).

BOURDIEU, P. (1986) The forms of capital. In J. RICHARDSON (Ed.) *Handbook of Theory and Research for the Sociology of Education* (New York, Greenwood), 241–258.

BOURDIEU, P. (1990) *The Logic of Practice* (Cambridge, Polity Press).

BOURDIEU, P. (1993) *Sociology in Question* (London, Sage).

BOURDIEU, P. (2000) *Pascalian Meditations* (Trans. R. Nice) (Stanford, Stanford University Press).

BOURDIEU, P. and WACQUANT, L. (1992) *An Invitation to Reflexive Sociology* (Cambridge, Polity Press).

BURKITT, I. (1997) Social relations and emotions, *Sociology,* 31 (1), 37–56.

© 2007 The Author

COLLEY, H. (2003) 'Children can wind you up!': learning to labour in the nursery. Paper presented at the Gender and Education Association Conference, Revisiting Feminist Perspectives on Gender and Education, University of Sheffield, 14–16 April.

COLLEY, H. (2006) Learning to labour with feeling: class, gender and emotion in childcare education and training, *Contemporary Issues in Early Childhood*, 7 (1), 15–29.

COLLEY, H., JAMES, D., TEDDER, M. and DIMENT, K. (2003) Learning as becoming in vocational education and training: class, gender and the role of vocational habitus, *Journal of Vocational Education and Training*, 55 (4), 471–498.

DIKA, S. and SINGH, K. (2002) Applications of social capital in educational literature: a critical synthesis, *Review of Educational Research*, 72 (1), 31–60.

EDWARDS, R. (2004) Present and absent in troubling ways: families and social capital debates, *The Sociological Review*, 52 (1), 1–21.

EMIRBAYER, M. and GOLDBERG, C. A. (2005) Pragmatism, Bourdieu, and collective emotions in contentious politics, *Theory and Society*, 34 (5/6), 469–518.

GENDRON, B. (2004) Why emotional capital matters in education and in labour? Toward an optimal exploitation of human capital and knowledge management. In *Les Cahiers de la Maison des Sciences Economiques* (Paris, Université Pantheon-Sorbonne) 1–37.

GILLIES, V. (2006) Working class mothers and school life: exploring the role of emotional capital, *Gender and Education*, 18 (3), 281–293.

GIROUX, H. (1983) *Theory and Resistance in Education: a Pedagogy for the Opposition* (South Hadley, MA, Bergin and Garvey).

GOLEMAN, D. (1995) *Emotional Intelligence* (New York, Bantam Books).

GOLEMAN, D. (1998) *Working with Emotional Intelligence* (New York, Bantam Books).

GRENFELL, M. (2004) *Pierre Bourdieu: Agent Provocateur* (London, Continuum).

GRENFELL, M. (in press, 2007) *Bourdieu, Education and Training* (London, Continuum).

GRENFELL, M. and JAMES, D. (1998) *Bourdieu and Education: Acts of Practical Theory* (Lewes, Falmer Press).

HALPERN, D. (2005) *Social Capital* (Cambridge, Polity Press).

HARDING, J. and PRIBRAM, E. D. (2004) Losing our cool? Following Williams and Grossberg on emotions, *Cultural Studies*, 18 (6), 863–883.

HARTLEY, D. (2003) The instrumentalisation of the expressive in education, *British Journal of Educational Studies*, 51 (1), 6–19.

HOCHSCHILD, A. R. (1983) *The Managed Heart: Commercialization of Human Feeling* (Berkeley, CA, University of California Press).

HOY, D. (2004) *Critical Resistance: From Poststructuralism to Post-critique* (Cambridge, MA, The MIT Press).

ISENBARGER, L. and ZEMBYLAS, M. (2006) The emotional labour of caring in teaching, *Teaching and Teacher Education*, 22 (2), 120–134.

JENKINS, R. (1992) *Pierre Bourdieu* (London, Routledge).

LEAVITT, J. (1996) Meaning and feeling in the anthropology of emotions, *American Ethnologist*, 23 (3), 514–519.

LUPTON, D. (1998) *The Emotional Self: a Sociocultural Exploration* (London, Sage).

LUTZ, C. A. and ABU-LUGHOD, L. (Eds) (1990) *Language and the Politics of Emotion* (Cambridge, Cambridge University Press).

MANION, C. (2007) Feeling, thinking, doing: emotional capital, empowerment, and women's education. In I. EPSTEIN (Ed.) *Recapturing the Personal: Essays on Education and Embodied Knowledge in Comparative Perspective* (Charlotte, NC, Information Age Publishing), 87–109.

© 2007 The Author

MASSUMI, B. (1996) The autonomy of affect. In P. PATTON (Ed.) *Deleuze: A Critical Reader* (Oxford, Blackwell), 217–239.
MASSUMI, B. (2002) *Parables for the Virtual: Movement, Affect, Sensation* (Durham and London, Duke University Press).
McCLENAGHAN, P. (2000) Social capital: exploring the theoretical foundations of community development education, *British Educational Research Journal*, 26 (5), 565–582.
McLEOD, J. (2005) Feminists re-reading Bourdieu: old debates and new questions about gender habitus and gender change, *Theory and Research in Education*, 3 (1), 11–30.
McNAMARA HORVAT, E. (2003) The interactive effects of race and class in educational research: theoretical insights from the work of Pierre Bourdieu, *Penn GSE Perspectives on Urban Education*, 2 (1), 1–25.
McNAY, L. (1999) Gender, habitus and the field: Pierre Bourdieu and the limits of reflexivity, *Theory, Culture and Society*, 16 (1), 95–117.
MELUCCI, A. (1996a) *Challenging Codes* (Cambridge, Cambridge University Press).
MELLUCI, A. (1996b) *The Playing Self* (Cambridge, Cambridge University Press).
NOWOTNY, H. (1981) Women in public life in Austria. In C. FUCHS EPSTEIN and R. LAUB COSER (Eds) *Access to Power: Cross-national Studies of Women and Elites* (London, George Allen and Unwin), 147–156.
PETONITO, G. (2000) Racial discourse and enemy construction. In P. G. COY and L. M. WOEHRLE (Eds) *Social Conflicts and Collective Identities* (Oxford, Rowman and Littlefield), 20–40.
PROBYN, E. (2004) Shame in the habitus, *Sociological Review*, 52 (2), 224–248.
REAY, D. (2000) A useful extension of Bourdieu's conceptual framework?: emotional capital as a way of understanding mothers' involvement in their children's education, *The Sociological Review*, 48 (4), 568–585.
REAY, D. (2004a) Education and cultural capital: the implications of changing trends in education policies, *Cultural Trends*, 13 (2), 73–86.
REAY, D. (2004b) Gendering Bourdieu's concept of capitals? Emotional capital, women and social class, *The Sociological Review*, 52 (2), 57–74.
REAY, D. (2004c) 'It's all becoming a habitus': Beyond the habitual use of habitus in educational research, *British Journal of Sociology of Education*, 25 (4), 431–444.
REDDY, W. M. (2001) *The Navigation of Feeling: a Framework for the History of Emotions* (Cambridge, Cambridge University Press).
SHILLING, C. (2004) Physical capital and situated action: A new direction for corporeal sociology, *British Journal of Sociology of Education*, 25 (4), 473–487.
SCHUTZ, P. and DECUIR, J. T. (2002) Inquiry on emotions in education, *Educational Psychologist*, 37 (2), 125–134.
SCHUTZ, P. and PEKRUN, R. (Eds) (2007) *Emotion in Education* (San Diego, Academic Press).
SKEGGS, B. (2004) Exchange, value and affect: Bourdieu and 'the self', *The Sociological Review*, 52 (1), 75–95.
STEARNS, P. N. (1994) *American Cool: Constructing a Twentieth-century Emotional Style* (New York, New York University Press).
STEARNS, C. Z. and STEARNS, P. N. (1986) *Anger: The Struggle for Emotional Control in America's History* (Chicago, University of Chicago Press).
SVAŠEK, M. (2002) The politics of emotions: emotional discourses and displays in post-Cold War contexts, *Focaal-European Journal of Anthropology*, 39 (1), 9–27.
SVAŠEK, M. (2005) The politics of chosen trauma: expellee memories, emotions and identities. In K. MILTON and M. SVAŠEK (Eds) *Mixed Emotions: Anthropological Studies of Feeling* (Oxford, Berg), 195–214.

© 2007 The Author

SWARTZ, D. (1997) *Culture and Power* (Chicago, University of Chicago Press).
THOMPSON, K. (1998) *Emotional Capital: Capturing Hearts and Minds to Create Lasting Business Success* (Oxford, Capstone).
THRIFT, N. (2004) Intensities of feeling: towards a spatial politics of affect, *Geografiska Annaler*, 86 (1), 55–76.
VAN VEEN, K. and LASKY, S. (2005) Emotions as a lens to explore teacher identity and change: different theoretical approaches, *Teaching and Teacher Education*, 21 (8), 895–898.
WILLIAMS, R. (1977) *Marxism and Literature* (Oxford and New York, Oxford University Press).
WILLIAMS, S. (2001) *Emotion and Social Theory* (London, Sage).
WOUTERS, C. (1986) Formalization and informalization: changing tension balances in civilizing processes, *Theory, Culture and Society*, 3 (1), 1–18.
WOUTERS, C. (1987) Developments in the behavioural codes between the sexes: the formalization of informalization in the Netherlands, 1930–85, *Theory, Culture and Society*, 4 (2), 405–427.
WOUTERS, C. (1992) On status competition and emotion management: the study of emotions as a new field, *Theory, Culture and Society*, 9 (1), 229–252.
ZEMBYLAS, M. (2002) 'Structures of feeling' in curriculum and teaching: theorizing the emotional rules, *Educational Theory*, 52 (2), 187–208.
ZEMBYLAS, M. (2005) *Teaching With Emotion: A Postmodern Enactment* (Greenwich, CT, Information Age Publishing).
ZEMBYLAS, M. (2006) Dimensions of a postmodern culture of emotions in education, *Interchange*, 37 (3), 1–25.
ZEMBYLAS, M. (2007a) The power and politics of emotions in teaching. In P. A. SCHUTZ and R. PECKRUN (Eds) *Emotions in Education* (New York, Academic Press), 293–309.
ZEMBYLAS, M. (2007b) Mobilizing anger for social justice in education: the politicization of the emotions in education, *Teaching Education*, 18 (1), 15–28.
ZEMBYLAS, M. (2007c) The politics of trauma: empathy, reconciliation and education, *Journal of Peace Education*, 4 (2), 207–224.
ZEMBYLAS, M. (2007d) The affective politics of hatred in Cyprus: ambivalence and solidarity in education, *Intercultural Education*, 18 (3), 177–192.
ZEMBYLAS, M. and FENDLER, L. (2007) Reframing emotion in education through lenses of *parrhesia* and *care of the self*, *Studies in Philosophy and Education*, 26 (4), 319–333.

© 2007 The Author

The power of one? Conditions which challenge managerial professional development practices

Ian Hardy

This paper draws upon Bourdieu's concepts of habitus, capital and field to better understand and appreciate the conditions which encouraged the productive professional development (PD) practices of one very capable teacher working in a secondary school in the British Midlands. Rather than celebrating this teacher's practices and perspective as evidence of the capacity of the heroic individual to overcome sometimes adverse circumstances, this paper reveals how the experiences of this teacher can be understood as an instance of the socially situated self, engaged by and engaging in an alternative politics to that associated with more managerial conceptions of teacher learning. This research calls for a cautious approach to those renderings of educational practice which construe the creative potential of the habitus, without sufficient regard for the actual conditions which contribute towards this creativity. In this way, this paper is presented not as an example of how one teacher overcame significant barriers to substantive learning practices – as a morality tale for other, individual educators to emulate – but as a provocation to suggest how some teachers' access to professional/community resources helps them sustain a clear focus on substantive learning.

Introduction

This paper provides insights into the conditions which contributed to the teacher professional development (PD) practices of one teacher working in a large, established secondary school in the British Midlands. This teacher's experiences were deemed worthy of further exploration, because in many ways they constitute an alternative to more dominant PD experiences of teachers in the English context. This paper argues that the approach to learning adopted by this teacher tapped into a variety of peculiarly local conditions which enabled his development in a sustained way. Revealing these conditions is important for fostering substantive teacher learning experiences for student learning.

This paper explores this teacher's learning experiences in the context of how PD is typically supported in policy, and undertaken by teachers in schooling settings, with a focus on England. As such, the selected teacher's learning experiences represent alternatives to more dominant, sporadic and sometimes managerial approaches. To make sense of this teacher's socially situated learning practices as contrasting with more sporadic approaches, this paper draws suggestively upon Bourdieu's notion of social practices as undertaken within identifiable, contested social 'fields'. This paper also draws upon Reay's (2004) notion of habitus as productive of creative responses in spite of more detrimental social conditions under which it has been formed. Most importantly, while revealing these agentic possibilities, this paper cautions that it is essential not to lose sight of the nature of the conditions within which habitus is enacted, and how these conditions constitute habitus, and practice more generally.

The literature: understanding current conditions of teacher learning

Teachers' PD,[1] or 'continuing professional development' (CPD) as it is often described in British settings, has been significantly influenced by what Day and Sachs (2004) have described as more 'managerial' influences, as well as more 'democratic' proclivities. More democratic approaches emphasise teachers taking responsibility for their learning, focusing upon more localised needs, and typically working together with school-based colleagues and/or other educators. Managerial approaches typically treat teachers as individuals, and are often construed in terms of compliance with specific government-supported initiatives and bureaucratic conceptions of systemic requirements. Importantly, these authors note that such influences occur concurrently, and that in practice, actual position-takings reflect a variety of stances along a continuum between more extreme 'ideal' types of such phenomena, rather than clearly delineated stances at the boundaries of such continua. At the same time, under current conditions, teacher learning practices have become more reactive in response to managerial demands (Groundwater-Smith & Mockler, 2009).

More managerial approaches can be identified in some of the PD practices of teachers in England. A recent large-scale study into the nature of CPD practices in schools in England (which had 1126 responses) found individual, isolated workshop approaches typify teachers' learning practices, many of which were associated with compliance with specific government priorities (Pedder, Storey, & Opfer, 2008). Similarly, Hustler, McNamara, Jarvis, Londra, and Campbell (2003) reveal how 72% of 2259 survey respondents believed too many PD days in England were driven by national foci. While acknowledging that not all workshops are managerial in nature, more managerial approaches to PD in Western settings are a significant part of the teacher learning landscape, and tend to dominate over what Webster-Wright (2009) describes as more 'authentic learning' approaches involving learners improving practice *in situ*.

Managerial iterations of these more passive approaches to teacher learning reflect changing conceptions of teacher professionalism. Under these circumstances, 'delivery' models often predominate in which teachers become recipients of instances and examples of 'best practice' (Pickering, Daly, & Pachler, 2007, p. 193).

Hodkinson (2009) reports how working in a more managerial context – with an emphasis upon performance management, classroom inspections and schools' rankings on league tables – exacerbates time constraints, encourages PD as an 'add-on' and fosters conditions in which improved standardised test scores are most valued. The result is an emphasis upon testing specific skills (Jacob, 2005) and a general sense in which 'what gets measured gets done' (Wilson, Croxson, & Atkinson, 2006). In the English context, this emphasis upon results currently includes a strong focus upon the proportion of students receiving passing grades (A–C) in the General Certificate of Secondary Education (GCSE; Wilson et al., 2006).

However, teachers do not lack agency under these circumstances. Even under such conditions, research into the micropolitics of teacher and schooling practices reveals teachers' responses to educational reform initiatives with which they disagree, or to which they have little affiliation, result in not only emotional turmoil amongst teachers but also resistance (Kelchtermans, 2005). Hoyle and Wallace (2007) refer to 'principled infidelity' to capture how teachers and principals seek to manage policy and accountability reform and overload, by appearing to respond to policy demands without actually doing so, and, on occasions, to do so would be to disadvantage their students. Kelchtermans and Ballet (2002) argue that incorporating a micropolitical perspective as part of teacher learning is an essential part of understanding teachers' PD. Such a stance reveals that teachers also simultaneously engage in more ongoing, productive and substantive learning initiatives, thereby challenging narrower managerial approaches. In England, for example, a large-scale review of relevant literature found that 11% of teachers undertook university accredited courses (Pedder et al., 2008). Pickering et al. (2007) also reveal how teachers' collaboration in a Master's programme offered through the University of London led to teachers being more readily able to critique their own practices. While teacher agency can be co-opted through, for example, managerial applications of democratic discourses of 'distributed' leadership (Hatcher, 2005), teachers actively interpret these various conditions and the policies which influence their work, and are not simply passive objects of more managerial policy reform (Braun, Maguire, & Ball, 2010).

Consequently, current theorising reveals that while more managerial iterations of teachers' learning exert influence, there is also evidence of alternative practices, and of teachers creating conditions productive of alternatives to managerial approaches, even as they enact and engage in such practices. Shedding further light specifically on how and why some teachers are creative and active in managing more managerial policy conditions, as well as how such foci influence teachers' work, is important for understanding the complexity of resultant practices (Ball, Maguire, Braun, & Hoskins, 2011).

Theoretical resources: comprehending contestation

To better understand how some teachers seem to be able to challenge more reductionist, managerial conditions in the context of the contestation which characterises teachers' PD practices, this paper draws suggestively upon Pierre Bourdieu's (1984) notion of the habitus as actively constituted in contested circumstances, as well as Reay's notion of the habitus as capable of self-scrutiny, self-improvement and creativity (Reay, 2004; Reay, Crozier, & Clayton, 2009). For Bourdieu, social practices are intensely relational; that is, practices are developed *in situ* and only make sense in relation to other possible practices within any given social space or what Bourdieu describes as a 'field'. Fields are 'historically constituted areas of activity with their specific institutions and their own laws of functioning' (Bourdieu, 1990a, p. 87). These specific properties are the result of a process of contestation over the practices considered legitimate at any given time. The practices which come to dominate within fields are both reflective and productive of the particular dispositions of those who occupy them. These dispositions constitute the 'habitus' of individuals and groups which comprise the field, and are responsible for particular characteristics or 'logics' of practice. Consequently, habitus is the product of a long process of socialisation into particular ways of being and reflects the success (or otherwise) of the symbolic violence which attends this process. Habitus is intimately imbricated within the broader social structures within which it is located and influences individuals' and groups' actions.

Individuals and groups are disposed to particular fields and embody a particular habitus as a result of engagement in specific fields, and a consequent process of accumulation of resources or 'capitals' available within those fields. These capitals exist in multiple forms including economic, social and cultural modes (Bourdieu, 1986). The accumulation of particular capitals enables individuals and groups to exercise more or less influence within fields depending upon the capitals most valued. Through this process of capital accumulation, habitus is produced which reflects prior experiences; 'The habitus, a product of history, produces individual and collective practices – more history – in accordance with the schemes generated by history' (Bourdieu, 1990b, p. 54).

Importantly, and at the same time, the dispositions of those who occupy any given field are not static. Rather, through a process of socio-analysis – analysis of the particular circumstances on the part of those influenced by them – actors seek to understand, critique and alter their practices (Bourdieu & Wacquant, 1992). Bourdieu's articulation of habitus was in contrast with conceptions of 'habit', and ensured a focus upon a 'generative (if not creative) capacity inscribed in the system of dispositions as an *art*, in the strongest sense of practical mastery, and in particular as an *ars inveniendi*' (Bourdieu & Wacquant, 1992, p. 122; emphasis original). There is also a sense in which the habitus is not fully regulated, even as it is influenced by previous experiences; 'the habitus goes hand in glove with vagueness and indeterminacy' (Bourdieu, 1990a, p. 77). Such a process always occurs *in situ*, cannot be readily predicted and may not unfold in ways hoped for or anticipated by those engaging in it. At the same time, it is important to acknowledge that Bourdieu's notion of habitus has been critiqued as being overly deterministic, and not sufficiently agentic in orientation (Jenkins, 2002). Some theorists are even more critical, arguing that Bourdieu's efforts to overcome the structure/agency divide are inherently incoherent (LiPuma, 1993). Specific concerns have also been expressed about the way in which habitus has been operationalised in educational research (Nash, 1999); Reay (2004) has described how the notions of habitus have been operationalised in superficial ways in some educational research, often 'overlaid' in research analyses rather than being employed in relation to data and empirical settings (Reay, 2004).

Nevertheless, notions of habitus 'can be made to work' (Reay 2004, p. 431) in educational research in relation to redressing mind/body and structure/agency dualisms, and as a mechanism for productive change through a more socio-analytical process. In the context of teachers' PD, this more productive stance could include an active and positive disposition towards teachers' learning even under conditions which do not institutionally support such a stance. In their research on working-class students in elite universities, for example, Reay et al. (2009) revealed how many of these 'successful' students constantly worked on themselves even under broader social circumstances which might not readily lend themselves to challenging more dominant class dispositions. This self-conscious reflexivity entails a process in which 'self-awareness and a propensity for self-improvement become incorporated into the habitus' (p. 1105). The result is a habitus which is permeable and subject to change as a result of new experiences. This is an active process, aided and abetted by the more agentic, socio-analytic disposition of individual actors. As Reay (2004) argues, 'while habitus reflects the social position in which it was constructed, it also carries with it the genesis of new creative responses that are capable of transcending the social conditions in which it was produced' (pp. 434–435). Such a stance implies an agentic position on the part of individuals as they actively seek alternatives to and potentially challenge prevailing conditions. It is the nature and extent of this capacity for change which is of interest in this paper and which is drawn upon to make sense of the PD practices of a particular teacher whose learning practices seemed at odds with the broader field of PD practices more generally. However, this argument is made on the clear understanding that the conditions within which this teacher undertook his work were themselves productive of the successes experienced. In this way, actual practice is construed as the product of the agentic capacities of the *conditioned* habitus not the heroic individual acting alone.

Teacher learning in context: teaching and learning at Midlands High

This paper draws upon the experiences of a full-time teacher, 'Andrew', working in a secondary school and languages college, referred to in this paper as 'Midlands High' and located in a medium-sized city in the British Midlands.[2] Midlands High is an established school with approximately 1700 students, 150 staff and a long history of academic success, including as a designated languages college. At the time of the interview, the school was engaging in a multitude of PD practices, ranging from individual workshops at the start of the year, through to an ongoing action research initiative, involving several teachers from across the school site, and focusing upon school and classroom-specific issues. These teachers volunteered to participate and met over a series of weekends to engage with one another to reflect upon their work and findings.

An experienced and well-regarded teacher, Andrew had worked at the school for 14 years including 9 years as Head of Chemistry. At the time of the interview, Andrew recently relinquished this role to take up a part-time position as a 'Teaching Fellow' at a neighbouring university. This involved facilitating school student involvement in university-oriented chemistry, PD of teachers and improving connections between A-level school chemistry teachers and students and undergraduate chemistry staff.

Methods and methodology

The data which informs the research were drawn from a broader project into the teacher learning practices at this school site. Data collection involved hour-long, intensive interviews with 18 teachers from across the school's principal faculties – English, Mathematics, Sciences, Social Sciences, the Arts and Languages. Interviewees volunteered and were asked a series of questions designed to elicit their experiences of teachers' learning and CPD under current policy conditions. This included recent PD in which they were involved or aware, the impact of current national policy upon PD practices, the influence of standardised testing, and testing more generally upon teacher and student learning, and the influence of performance management practices on teacher learning. All interviews were transcribed remotely, key themes distilled through repeated reading of transcripts and responses analysed in the light of Bourdieu's understandings of habitus as socially and creatively constituted.

Of all participants, Andrew provided the most detailed elaborations of productive, context-relevant and robust teacher learning. These responses were considered worthy of further and closer scrutiny for what they could reveal about the conditions conducive to improved teacher learning. In this way, the research is an example of what Yin (2009) describes as an 'embedded case study design' – an inquiry into a specific subunit (a particular teacher) which helps to shed light upon a broader phenomenon under investigation (PD practices under current policy conditions, in a specific school site). Such an approach helps to provide a level of detail not otherwise possible in more holistic case study approaches (Yin, 2009). In this case, this detail refers to the agentic potential and capacities of teacher habitus and particularly the specific conditions which contribute to these capacities.

Andrew's comments help shed light onto the field of PD practices, how individuals within the field make decisions in relation to the field and the conditions productive of more authentic, student-centred teacher learning practices. In a sense, such comments also help to construct the field of PD practices differently from how it is construed from a more dominant viewpoint. In this way, this particular participant's responses reflect a stance which challenges more dominant practices, providing evidence of the field of PD practices as contested, but still enabling more progressive, educative PD. Consequently, this particular individual's comments are illustrative of Bourdieu's concepts at the same time as they provide the clearest account of any of the participants of how PD can be 'done' differently and the conditions which contribute to these practices.

Findings: PD in practice

Three broad themes were elicited from the data, and related to: first, Andrew's disposition towards PD, and how his own learning shifted and changed over time; second, the way in which Andrew recognised and valued the learning which occurred in his own faculty and school; and third, recognition of, and responses to, more managerial demands. These themes are delineated in more detail below and then analysed in the subsequent discussion section for what they reveal about the conditions conducive to more productive learning.

Broadening horizons: learning to learn

By his own admission, Andrew had not always conceptualised PD as beneficial. This was particularly the case as a neophyte teacher when PD was construed as something remote from more immediate concerns:

> I used to have a sinking feeling when CPD was mentioned … [I] was really more concerned with the day to day workings of my job … Now obviously CPD should help make you do the job you're doing better, but I felt that I was really wanting to spend all my energy getting my behaviour sorted out in classrooms.

A more conservative habitus was evident, forged from PD experiences which were not sufficiently connected to more immediate, everyday concerns.

However, it was Andrew's exposure to PD experiences as a member of a broader professional body, the Royal Society of Chemistry, which further shaped and shifted this initial disposition:

> But because I became involved in a wide array of Chemistry through Royal Society of Chemistry, I've realised what CPD can actually be, and that it can be really beneficial to teachers. So through the RSC, I'm involved in delivering CPD, which is a slight irony, and I realise now the value that has … It leaves people feeling empowered to do their job.

PD was no longer construed as simply a problematic practice irrelevant to immediate concerns. A more active disposition was evident which valued involvement in a diverse array of activities within the broader field of PD practices.

This broader valuing of PD could also be attributed to a habitus forged from experiences of working part-time at a neighbouring university which, in turn, contributed to teacher learning within his own Chemistry Department:

> My being at the university has created a conduit of information, equipment, facts and all that kind of stuff which the fellas at the school say have been really, really useful. I tell them all the time about undergraduate admissions and things that are required. One of our Chemists is a Head of Year in Sixth Form, so he picks up a lot of useful facts about the latest views on admissions. So it's a lot of CPD beneath the radar.

A habitus which valued professional growth and learning was evident in Andrew's decision to relinquish his role as Head of Chemistry to take on a broader professional learning role with the university:

> I resigned as Head of Chemistry last year to free me up to do more Chemistry-related outreach outside of school. One day a week I work for City University as a School Teacher Fellow. This involves me typically working with a group of 16–18 year olds conducting experimental work in a university Chemistry laboratory setting. I also work with a wide age-range of students from 10 year olds up to adults. Another aspect of my role is to advise the academic Chemistry staff on changes in school education.

However, not all PD were construed favourably. The field of PD practices remained heavily influenced by more traditional and managerial modes of PD, and, at times, Andrew accommodated such modes:

> And some of the stuff we have done that's been offered internally has been good, but sometimes you get – maybe it's the cynic in me – but sometimes you feel that it is being wedged in as 'filler', or to 'tick a box'. And I'd like to think I'm wrong there. Like, that's terrible to think. I'm sure the person who delivered it, didn't feel that it was that, but as the recipient, I often think, 'Yeah, let's just tick the box and then I can get some books marked'.

Conceptions of PD contrasted with other learning experiences supported by the school. For example, a trip to the USA as part of an international exchange programme was seen as useful for encouraging a more reflective and reflexive stance on teaching science:

> We have partnerships with schools all around the world. And taking kids to another country and meeting staff over there, I would argue, is another very good example of CPD… I took kids to America to a school in Georgia, and on a couple of occasions, I lived with the teachers over there … And so our kids and staff were in a totally different education environment – in the 'bible belt'. As different as you can imagine! And, actually, I learned a lot about teaching … by being in an environment where some of the teachers don't believe in evolution and stuff like that. So for me as a science teacher, I developed greatly …

PD was recognised as occurring in a multiplicity of situations and often in ways contrary to more dominant logics within the field of PD practices.

Valuing the local, the situated

For Andrew, some of the most effective PD he experienced was that which occurred during interactions with members of the Chemistry Department in his school. These teachers had a strong knowledge base:

> We feel as a Department that most of our professional development occurs really within, between ourselves. I'd say we're very tight knit. There are six 'A level' Chemistry teachers within our Chemistry Department, and a Chemistry technician who is a PhD chemist in his 50s. And between the seven of us, we talk about Chemistry a lot, and learn a lot from each other.

A discipline-specific habitus was forged through opportunities to learn *in situ*.

There was also institutional support within the school for PD in general, albeit often of a more traditional ilk:

> I've really been encouraged to put in 'pink forms' ever since I've joined – which is basically if you've got something that you'd like to go and do, you're encouraged to go and do it... I've actually been on quite a few of these things. I went on a 'Teaching the Talented and Gifted Chemistry' course ... The school certainly does talk about it, and encourage people to get involved in it.

However, these more traditional logics were also challenged by approaches to teachers' learning which were inclusive of not just students, but support staff and students:

> We also encourage staff and students to go to the university when lectures are on to listen – so try and go in with our technician ...

The 'we' of this particular community was not a 'dangerous pronoun' (Sennett, 1998), perhaps synonymous with exclusion as much as inclusion, but instead embraced a sense of plurality not typically associated with learning logics within the field of PD practices.

While not directly involved, a more learning-oriented disposition was evident in Andrew's support for a Master's programme which had been developed jointly between staff at the school and staff from another universities in the city:

> [Technology University] are the main deliverer, and I think it's delivered in 30 and 60 credit modules, so I think if people do it, it's going to be over a few years ... Which, again, gives me the feeling that this is not about 'gathering letters'. It's about genuine professional development.

While considered valuable, time pressures and a positive engagement with discipline-related PD activities made it difficult to be involved in the Master's programme:

> I don't have the time to do that [Masters], because I've invested my time in other things, like being a Chartered Chemist and a Charted Scientist... which is taking time [to collect] evidence ... So I think it's been useful.

However, for those teachers involved in the Master's programme, there were tangible benefits from participating:

> Yeah, absolutely, and I think it's opened quite a few people's eyes. They're trying things with kids and then telling people about it, so I think it seems to have gone quite well.

In this way, more localised PD logics, in a myriad of formats, were evident and valued within the field of PD practices, and there was at least anecdotal evidence of changes in teaching practices as a result.

Appropriating and mediating external pressures

A more productively conditioned habitus was also evident in how more managerial pressures were imposed. These were associated with the advent of league tables, pressure to perform in response to Ofsted inspections and rearticulated to serve a useful learning function. However, such pressures were also recognised as changing teaching practices in potentially problematic ways:

> I know, as Head of Chemistry for quite a few years, that getting good results out of kids for league table reasons – and obviously knock-on effects in the way Ofsted treated us based on our results – has had a positive effect, in some ways, in that teachers are much more anxious to deliver stuff well. The down-side, which, I think really is a significant one, is that we 'teach to the test' more than we've ever done before.

Such a stance also resonates with notions of 'principled infidelity' (Hoyle & Wallace, 2007) in so far as concerns were expressed about the problematic effects of current policy pressures, although more 'principled' responses are themselves in strong tension with practices of 'teaching to the test'.

Nevertheless, even as pressure for improved test results exerted considerable influence, a learning-focused habitus was evident which valued genuine learning opportunities for teachers:

> Well I hope stuff like 'Chemistry for Non-Specialists' does allow those teachers to deliver a more rounded approach to Chemistry rather than ['teaching to the test']. I'm an intelligent person. I know what's on the exam paper. I can groom them [students] to just answer the questions! I think with the greater depth of knowledge, the teachers can give a much more robust reason [to engage with ideas presented in Chemistry than simply to do well on tests] … So I think that type of CPD to empower teachers is really useful.

Such a stance accords with Watkins (2010) research revealing how learning about learning in the context of strong performance pressures is crucial to fostering substantive student learning and leads to improvements in genuine student learning, as well as improvements in more standardised measures. Substantive PD helped forge a more confident disposition amongst teachers; this enabled them to challenge managerial logics associated with testing and to provide more substantive learning opportunities for their students.

This is not to downplay the focus on testing. As with Watkins' (2010) findings, more test-centric logics continued to dominate the field:

> There have been [PD events] to do with performance of particular cohorts. So we have targets within school, and we issue those targets for Key Stage 4/Key Stage 5 performance things. Like the percentage 'As to Cs', including maths and science. It's a real big one now. So you may have an objective that fits with the school's target in terms of a results-based objective.

In this way, more managerial logics continued to exert influence, and were recognised as doing so, even as alternative practices were enacted, and pressure to 'teach to the test' resisted.

Discussion: powerful PD and the conditions which challenge managerial practices

The way in which this teacher challenged his own and others' practices, and narrowly conceived PD practices more generally, reveals a habitus which both values and is forged from engagement with substantive learning opportunities. Significantly, these opportunities were a product of specific social conditions which contributed to Andrew's adopting an active stance towards his learning. In part, a more creative, responsive habitus (Reay, 2004) focused upon self-improvement (Reay et al., 2009) is evident which challenges more entrenched logics within the broader field of PD practices. PD improved this teacher's own disciplinary understandings and teaching practices, and empowered other teachers. Importantly, the PD this teacher found most beneficial is multifaceted in nature, often in contrast with more traditional approaches to teachers' learning. This teacher was a knowledgeable participant within a broader field of PD practices characterised by competing and, at times, contradictory logics, but also assisted by his location within a field of schooling practices which affords greater autonomy to science teachers than other members of the field.

These more learning-focused logics occur under broader conditions in which more traditional and managerial PD logics dominate. Andrew's concerns about the value of some whole-school PD reveals the field of PD practices as a site in which individualistic workshop approaches continue to act as a default position. Reservations about whether some whole-school PD was simply designed to 'tick-the-box' reveal how managerial logics exert influence and how pressures for compliance to immediate demands can constitute a key part of the PD in which teachers currently engage (Groundwater-Smith & Mockler, 2009). That this teacher was conflicted about the nature of his own reservations also reveals a habitus disposed to learning from all manner of PD experiences, even those which appear, or genuinely are, problematic. Such a disposition was also evident in how he construed pressure to do well on league tables as serving as an impetus to encourage teachers 'to deliver stuff well' more generally. Even as external pressures for improved results on league tables are evidence of managerial logics, demands around teaching and teacher standards more generally can be appropriated by educators for educative purposes (Mayer, Mitchell, Macdonald, & Bell, 2005). However, there is also clear recognition that such conditions are also productive of a culture of 'teaching to the test', and of improved test results as the capitals most valued.

However, these conditions are not the only influences. Instances when Andrew critiqued more short-term practices are in keeping with a more socio-analytical approach to sedimented social practices – practices reflective of more typical, immediate, reactive approaches to teachers' learning undertaken in schooling contexts (Choy, Chen, & Bugarin, 2006; Pedder et al., 2008). Rather than being dominated by more traditional logics, or managerial pressures, alternative conditions enabled Andrew to critique instances of more superficial PD. As a result, instead of becoming transfixed by pressures associated with testing, he endorsed and enacted a broader set of learning experiences – a significant response on the part of dedicated teachers in a broader context in which there is an increasing emphasis upon test-specific skills (Jacob, 2005). Arguably, again, this capacity for critique is also likely enabled by his location in a more dominant fraction of the field of schooling as a chemistry/science teacher. This is not a straightforward process, however, and Andrew did not always critique more limited educational stances himself, as evident in the accepting way he described how individual objectives could be linked to school targets around improving the number of A's to C's in science and maths. As in other English school settings (Wilson et al., 2006), a strong focus upon improving the proportion of students receiving passing grades (A to C) in the GCSE commanded attention. Under these circumstances, the logics evident within the field of PD practices are those oriented towards managing and manipulating teachers to achieve improved test scores.

In their more critical, proactive instantiations, Andrew's responses can be interpreted as more than simply those of a heroic individual under less than desirable circumstances. Andrew's open and fervent support for ongoing professional conversations with his colleagues in the Chemistry Department and his acknowledgement of these conversations as the most valuable form of PD in which he engaged, reveals evidence of the power and influence of the social capital accrued as a member of this particular group, and again, a field position relatively high in autonomy. As in other settings and circumstances (cf. Choy et al., 2006), collaboration with colleagues on instructional issues was valued and valuable. As a result of such substantive collegiality, an inquiry-oriented habitus seems to have been cultivated within this department. In large measure, a strong sense of disciplinarity has been developed amongst a group of teachers with considerable experience and a lab assistant with a Ph.D. in chemistry. The embodied cultural capital (Bourdieu, 1986) cultivated and accumulated within the group constitute members of the chemistry team as favourably disposed to ongoing interaction with one another. In short, the social conditions in which this teacher worked contributed to a more agentic stance.

That he valued the Master's programme within the school, even though he was not formally involved in it himself, further reveals that the influence of a habitus reflective and productive of conditions different from those akin to more dominant and managerial logics. Exposure to this programme, and colleagues who seemed positively disposed to it, and whose practices had changed as a result of this involvement, forged a habitus respectful of formal, site-relevant study. Although involving only a small number of teachers, the opportunity to engage in formal study was seen as conducive to improved understanding of practice. In this way, more dominant logics are challenged by conditions which enable participation in formal study, and by teachers, such as Andrew, supportive of such learning.

The conditions productive of a habitus disposed to learning also include exposure to alternative learning settings and situations. Andrew saw his involvement in the Chemistry Department of a neighbouring university as an opportunity for professional growth. Again, the social capital made possible through this work was seen as having benefits for not only his own learning but that of colleagues in his school. This support by his colleagues as a strong 'community of practice' further supports the relative dominance of these teachers within the field of schooling practices. Representing a variation on the productive learning practices which can arise from formalised interactions between university and school-based staff (cf. Groundwater-Smith & Mockler, 2009), this contact was construed as valuable by Andrew's colleagues, who recognised and valued the knowledge and learning they experienced as a result of the contacts he had cultivated, and the symbolic capital associated with Andrew's work at the university. This also led to 'incidental' learning amongst colleagues within his department with other responsibilities in the school (e.g., the Sixth Form year coordinator). Andrew's exposure to a broader network of colleagues interested in science education/chemistry and his status as a Chartered Chemist/Scientist were productive of the social, cultural and symbolic capital necessary to contest more limited and limiting PD logics. That he relinquished his former more administrative role as Head of Chemistry reveals how more genuinely educative logics can dominate over more management-focused logics.

Finally, participation in an overseas exchange programme constitutes another set of conditions which can contribute towards a more reflective habitus. Having contact with teachers and students whose religious beliefs influenced their approach to science teaching led to consideration and reflection upon this teacher's own values and understandings of science in ways which would not have occurred without such contact. Recognition of such experience as valuable PD does reveal the socio-analytic capacities of a creative, responsive teacher habitus (Reay et al., 2009) not in keeping with more traditional logics. Importantly, however, this response is the product of partnerships between this school and other schools throughout the world, and did not simply transpire in response to individual capacity or desire alone. Again, the conditions within which teachers work and learn are important enabling features.

Conclusion

Active involvement in a variety of initiatives, within and beyond this teacher's school, served as a crucial stimulus to this teacher's learning. However, this learning did not simply arise in a context-free way. Rather, teacher learning of most value is closely associated with exposure to particular experiences and influences in the immediate and extended environment. This suggests that teacher PD is deeply influenced by opportunities for educators to engage with others within individual school settings and professional networks beyond these settings. Teachers' learning does not occur in a vacuum, devoid of contact with colleagues or others. Rather, teachers' learning is facilitated by rich sets of social experiences and opportunities which foster deep thought about everyday practices.

For this reason, it is important to be cognisant of the nature of conditions which enhance teacher learning, and the broader pressures and demands which can limit such learning. Many of the learning practices undertaken by Andrew do not conform to 'typical' PD. A focused inquiry into the practices of an overtly learning-focused teacher reveals effective PD is not simply a product of the individual acting alone, of a creative, responsive teacher habitus in isolation (Reay, 2004). While, as in study by Reay et al. (2009), the individual was indeed working on him/herself, a proactive work environment in which PD was valued in general, in which institutional support was provided for teachers to engage in substantive PD – including teacher exchanges, and flexible working arrangements – contributed to productive PD practices. Working in a context which overtly valued academic work, being a member of the Royal Society of Chemistry, having access to a university Chemistry Department (and a working environment supportive of his work at the university), and having the opportunity to experience very different approaches to teaching his discipline all contributed to substantive PD practices. The findings also suggest chemistry teachers more generally may possess a strong collective identity or 'community of practice'. This contributes to the relatively strong positioning of science in the field of schooling (and secondary education more generally); in Bourdieuian terms, this teacher has a field position which (so long as basic exam results are 'delivered') is high in autonomy. Collectively, such position-taking further reinforces that an overemphasis upon individual agency under limiting conditions does not readily capture the complexity of the structures and supports which contribute to teachers' productive practices. In light of the research reported, such conditions clearly contribute to the production of habitus able to resist the cruder forms of managerialism and maintain an alternative vision of PD.

While certainly not the only means of interpreting this teacher's practices, and while acknowledging the limitations of critiquing approaches to teachers as monadic actors on the basis of a single teacher's practices, a Bourdieuian analysis does enable a focus upon the social conditions which help shape individual and collective action, and as a contribution to efforts to redress Cartesian dualisms of mind/body. Even as recognising the limitations of making claims on the basis of individual teachers' practices, developing better understandings of the economic, social and cultural conditions productive of such instances of a more educative habitus contributes, at least symbolically, towards challenging more managerial logics. Productive PD is not simply the product of individual actions, of the 'power of one', but is an intrinsically social process requiring considered support and development.

Notes

1. I acknowledge that the term 'professional development' is deeply contested. Well-recognised bodies of literature exist which challenge more traditional conceptions of teacher PD as a set of formalised experiences undertaken in schooling settings, typically at the instigation of individual schools and education systems. This paper adopts a broad-based rather than narrow approach to the term, employing it to refer to all instances and experiences in which learning is undertaken by teachers. This is akin to Muijs, Day, Harris, and Lindsay's (2004) understanding of PD as more than 'in-service' or 'on-the-job' learning, which are seen as narrowly focused upon specific workplaces, and the much broader term 'lifelong learning', but as encompassing a wide variety of learning approaches and settings throughout a lifetime. The term 'professional development' is also used interchangeably with the term 'continuing professional development' – the more common term for PD in England.
2. All names are pseudonyms.

References

Ball, S. J., Maguire, M., Braun, A., & Hoskins, K. (2011). Policy actors: Doing policy work in schools. *Discourse: Studies in the Cultural Politics of Education*, *32*, 625–639. doi:10.1080/01596306.2011.601565

Bourdieu, P. (1984). *Distinction: A social critique of the judgement of taste*. Cambridge, MA: Harvard University Press.

Bourdieu, P. (1986). The forms of capital. In J. E. Richardson (Ed.), *Handbook of theory of research for the sociology of education* (pp. 241–258). New York, NY: Greenwood Press.

Bourdieu, P. (1990a). *In other words: Essays towards a reflexive sociology*. Stanford, CA: Stanford University Press.

Bourdieu, P. (1990b). *The logic of practice*. Stanford, CA: Stanford University Press.

Bourdieu, P., & Wacquant, L. (1992). *An invitation to reflexive sociology*. Chicago, IL: University of Chicago Press.

Braun, A., Maguire, M., & Ball, S. J. (2010). Policy enactments in the UK secondary school: Examining policy, practice and school positioning. *Journal of Education Policy*, *25*, 547–560. doi:10.1080/02680931003698544

Choy, S., Chen, X., & Bugarin, R. (2006). *Teacher professional development in 1999–2000: What teachers, principals and district staff report* (NCES 2006-305). Washington, DC: National Centre for Education Statistics.

Day, C., & Sachs, J. (2004). Professionalism, performativity and empowerment: Discourses in the politics, policies and purposes of continuing professional development. In C. Day & J. Sachs (Eds.), *International handbook on the continuing professional development of teachers* (pp. 3–32). Maidenhead: Open University Press.

Groundwater-Smith, S., & Mockler, N. (2009). *Teacher professional learning in an age of compliance: Mind the gap*. Dordrecht: Springer.

Hatcher, R. (2005). The distribution of leadership and power in schools. *British Journal of Sociology of Education*, *26*, 253–267. doi:10.1080/0142569042000294200

Hodkinson, H. (2009). Improving schoolteachers' workplace learning. In S. Gewirtz, P. Mahony, I. Hextall, & A. Cribb (Eds.), *Changing teacher professionalism: International trends, challenges and ways forward* (pp. 157–169). London: Routledge.

Hoyle, E., & Wallace, M. (2007). Educational reform: An ironic perspective. *Educational Management Administration and Leadership*, *35*(1), 9–25. doi:10.1177/1741143207071383

Hustler, D., McNamara, O., Jarvis, J., Londra, M., & Campbell, A. (2003). *Teachers' perceptions of continuing professional development*. Norwich: Department for Education and Skills.

Jacob, B. A. (2005). Accountability, incentives and behaviour: The impact of high-stakes testing in the Chicago Public Schools. *Journal of Public Economics*, *89*, 761–796. doi:10.1016/j.jpubeco.2004.08.004

Jenkins, R. (2002). *Pierre Bourdieu*. London: Routledge.

Kelchtermans, G. (2005). Teachers' emotions in educational reforms: Self-understanding, vulnerable commitment and micro-political literacy. *Teaching and Teacher Education*, *21*, 995–1006. doi:10.1016/j.tate.2005.06.009

Kelchtermans, G., & Ballet, K. (2002). Micropolitical literacy: Reconstructing a neglected dimension in teacher development. *International Journal of Educational Research, 37*, 755–767. doi:10.1016/S0883-0355(03)00069-7

LiPuma, E. (1993). Culture and the concept of culture in a theory of practice. In C. Calhoun, E. LiPuma, & M. Postone (Eds.), *Bourdieu: Critical perspectives* (pp. 14–34). Chicago, IL: The University of Chicago Press.

Mayer, D., Mitchell, J., Macdonald, D., & Bell, R. (2005). Professional standards for teachers: A case study of professional learning. *Asia-Pacific Journal of Teacher Education, 33*, 159–179. doi:10.1080/13598660500121977

Muijs, D., Day, C., Harris, A., & Lindsay, G. (2004). Evaluating CPD: An overview. In C. Day, & J. Sachs (Eds.), *International handbook on the continuing professional development of teachers* (pp. 291–310). Maidenhead: Open University Press.

Nash, R. (1999). Bourdieu, habitus and educational research: Is it all worth the candle? *British Journal of Sociology of Education, 20*, 175–187. doi:10.1080/01425699995399

Pedder, D., Storey, A., & Opfer, D. (2008). *Synthesis report: Schools and continuing professional development (CPD) in England – State of the Nation research project* (T34718). London: Teacher Development Agency.

Pickering, J., Daly, C., & Pachler, N. (Eds.). (2007). *New designs for teachers' professional learning*. London: Institute of Education, University of London.

Reay, D. (2004). 'It's all becoming a habitus': Beyond the habitual use of habitus in educational research. *British Journal of Sociology of Education, 25*, 431–444. doi:10.1080/0142569042000236934

Reay, D., Crozier, G., & Clayton, J. (2009). 'Strangers in paradise?' Working-class students in elite universities. *Sociology, 43*, 1103–1121. doi:10.1177/0038038509345700

Sennett, R. (1998). *The corrosion of character: The personal consequence of work in the new capitalism*. New York, NY: W.W. Norton.

Watkins, C. (2010). *Research matters: Learning, performance and improvement*. London: Institute of Education, University of London.

Webster-Wright, A. (2009). Reframing professional development through understanding authentic professional learning. *Review of Educational Research, 79*, 702–739. doi:10.3102/0034654308330970

Wilson, D., Croxson, B., & Atkinson, A. (2006). 'What gets measured gets done': Headteachers' responses to the English secondary school performance management system. *Policy Studies, 27*, 153–171. doi:10.1080/01442870600637995

Yin, R. (2009). *Case study research: Design and methods* (4th ed.). Los Angeles, CA: SAGE.

Using Bourdieu in practice? Urban secondary teachers' and students' experiences of a Bourdieusian-inspired pedagogical approach

Louise Archer, Emily Dawson, Jennifer DeWitt, Spela Godec, Heather King, Ada Mau, Effrosyni Nomikou and Amy Seakins

ABSTRACT

This article discusses an attempt at a Bourdieusian-inspired form of praxis, developed and implemented in collaboration with nine London teachers, aimed at developing a socially just approach to engaging students with science. Data are discussed from nine months of classroom observations of nine secondary science classes from six inner London schools (approximately 200 students, aged 11–15), interviews and workshop data from the nine teachers and 13 discussion groups conducted with 59 students. The approach resulted in noticeable changes in practice, which were perceived by teachers and students to improve student engagement, cultivate a range of science-related dispositions and promote wider student participation and 'voice' in classes. Issues, limitations and possibilities for sociology of education are discussed.

Sociology of education – beyond the critical secretary?

It has been proposed that a key role for sociology of education is that of the 'critical secretary' of society, speaking truth to power (or as Bourdieu [1990, 16] terms it, 'shining a spotlight on the blinkers'), recording both injustices and progressive/counter-hegemonic practices (Apple 2005, 2013). As Apple discusses, the sociology of education has made major contributions to understanding the reproduction of inequalities in education, with the majority of research in the field fitting this remit.

Yet, at the same time, this role has attracted frustration from both within and outside the discipline. Concerns have been expressed that critical work 'can feel removed from everyday reality' (Rowley 2014, 51) and that, while necessary, critical work can also be 'depressing', revealing issues that cannot be easily 'solved' (Gunter and Willmott 2002). It is arguably also difficult to see any substantive impact of sociology of education theory within current educational policy-making.

In this article, we share our experience of an attempt at praxis – that is, the enactment of theoretical reflection and action (in this case, on classroom practice) – with the hope of lending ballast to efforts aimed at more closely intertwining sociology of education theory and practice. We discuss the development and pilot of a Bourdieusian-informed pedagogical approach in London with teachers and students that aimed to foster more equitable participation and engagement with science among urban, socially disadvantaged students.

Our approach combines sociological critique with a commitment to 'making a difference' within the 'here and now' of everyday classroom contexts. We worked with teachers to collaboratively engineer an approach that might enable Others to speak (Spivak 1988), supporting more inclusive relations of representation and forms of subjectivity. Our attempt at praxis sought to work both within and against the pervasive dominant educational culture of neoliberalism and performativity (for example, Ball 2003), because by working with 'how things are' we hoped to develop a critical pedagogical approach that might have the potential to be both useful and achievable. In other words, we sought to follow Apple's claim that, as sociologists of education, there is value and importance in showing that 'there are things we can do right now' (2013, 164).

'Bourdieu doesn't make for good bullet points' – or does he? The possibilities for praxis

> Bourdieu doesn't make for good bullet points. ('David Megabland' from 'Interview with David Betterman'; FAAB 2003)

In a satirical skit performed by the FAAB collective (a feminist sociology group of education academics and activists who staged performance interventions from 2003 to 2007), New Labour parody politician 'David Megabland' replies to accusations by his interviewer that policy fails to engage with academic research (and is not evidence based) by complaining that sociology of education theory (as epitomised by Bourdieu) operates in an incompatible register from policy.

As Apple (2013) reminds us, critical sociology of education needs to be able to work in different registers – just as neoliberalism does. Apple usefully discusses this in the context of ensuring that sociology can talk with the dispossessed/oppressed. In the interest of disrupting and shaping dominant practices and power relations, we would extend this argument further to argue that it is also important for the sociology of education to be able to talk in registers that can dialogue with policy and practice. Often the 'recommendations' arising from sociology of education work (our own work included!) includes calls to change (or radically overhaul) social power relations and 'change society' in fundamental ways. But what would this actually look like in practice? Also, does this necessarily mean we cannot seek to change policy and practice in the immediate, while acknowledging that substantial, longer-term change is a future goal?

A key tool here is the notion of praxis; that is, the enactment of theory in practice, combining both critical reflection and action. Freire ([1970] 1993, 33) defines praxis as 'reflection and action upon the world in order to transform it', arguing that 'through praxis, oppressed people can acquire a critical awareness of their own condition, and, with their allies, struggle for liberation'. While Freire concentrates on the liberatory potential for the dispossessed to develop critical awareness to precipitate action to change societal relations and inequalities, in this article we explore a broader approach to praxis – as theoretically informed, collaborative, reflective dialogue between researchers and teachers to produce action/change that disrupts some dominant power relations and structures within science classrooms – opening up more inclusive possibilities for students in science (for example, Calabrese Barton, Tan, and Rivet 2008) and building non-dominant students' capital (see Bourdieu and Passerson 1979).

Putting Bourdieu to work in the science classroom

Science classrooms provide an apt context for the study of inequalities. As a myriad of evidence attests, across most western nations there are stark and persistent inequalities in post-compulsory science participation, particularly in the physical sciences and engineering, where women, working-class and/or Black students remain persistently and starkly under-represented (for example, American Association of University Women 2010; Smith 2011). Critique has long been levelled at the dominant white, male, middle-class culture of science (for example, Harding 1998) and attention has been drawn to the ways in which dominant, 'celebrated' practices and identity performances within science classrooms tend to be organised around prototypically masculine and middle-class ways of being (for example, Archer et al. forthcoming; Carlone, Haun-Frank, and Webb 2011; Lemke 1990). Whereas our previous work has focused on identifying and unpicking the intersectional ways in which injustices and power operate within science, to produce patterns of oppression and exclusion (for example, Archer and DeWitt 2016; Archer, DeWitt, and Willis 2014; Archer et al. forthcoming), in this article we reflect on possibilities for change.

Our attempt at praxis is informed by Bourdieu's theory of practice (for example, Bourdieu 1977). From this perspective we understand 'student engagement with science' as occurring at the interface of encounters between habitus, capital and field. That is, we treat student engagement with science as a form of practice that is produced through a dialectical relationship between dispositions, capital and field, and which plays out through students' 'strategic improvisations ... against a background of doxa that ultimately limits them' (Parkin 1997, 376). For instance, we might expect quite different experiences of engagement between a student whose dominant group habitus and capital aligns with, and is recognised and valued by, the field of science education – allowing them to move 'as a fish in water' within the science classroom – compared with a student whose habitus and capital are misrecognised and denigrated (see also Calabrese Barton and Tan 2010; Calabrese Barton, Tan, and Rivet 2008).

Students who possess greater amounts of science capital (but notably those forms with exchange value) are statistically more likely to plan to continue with post-16 science (for example, Archer et al. 2015) and articulate (and be recognised by others as having) a 'science identity' (Carlone and Johnson 2007). Previously, we identified a set of dimensions within science capital which relate most closely to exchange-value outcomes relating to planned post-16 progression and science identity (Archer et al. 2015). Following Bourdieu and Passeron (1977), we thus were led to wonder whether there might be any potential for a social justice-orientated intervention, aimed at 'building' the science capital of students from non-dominant backgrounds (i.e. sharing out dominant/privileged forms of capital)?

Designing a Bourdieusian-inspired teaching approach

From the outset, we were unable to identify any work that had undertaken a similar venture – perhaps because Bourdieu has widely been interpreted as deeply pessimistic, offering no scope for social change. However, in line with conceptual challenges of the inherent pessimism of Bourdieu's work (James 2015), we wanted to explore the potential for using Bourdieusian theory to inform the development of a teaching approach that uses an understanding of the reproduction of inequality in order to challenge the status quo.

Conceptually, we focused on changing the field, rather than the individual student per se (the latter being more common within human capital-orientated approaches, which tend to predominate in science education[1]), because 'it is misleading to isolate factors from the system of relations in which they appear' (Krarup and Munk 2016, 768). Field ascribes the value of capital and is key to the re/production of unequal power relations: field thus determines the 'value' (or lack of) of a student's capital and the relationship between a student's habitus and field will shape the extent to which they experience science as being 'for me', or not (Archer and DeWitt 2016; Archer et al. 2012). Focusing on field thus enables us to understand 'how groups, individuals, and institutions are not so much defined by their objective attributes in themselves, as by their position in the structure of attributes' (Krarup and Munk 2016, 767).

We treated the science classroom as a field – a socially and historically constructed social–spatial arena, imbued with 'rules', within which differently positioned social actors struggle for the control of a range of (cultural, social and symbolic) resources. The science classroom is what Bourdieu would term as a space of positions and position-taking and contains its own logic of practice. That is:

> A field is a structured social space, a field of forces, a force field. It contains people who dominate and others who are dominated. (Bourdieu 2010, 37)

Of course, we were not expecting to radically transform the field; rather, we wanted to explore whether it might be possible to shift some of the contributing and constituting aspects of the field, namely some of the 'rules of the game' and 'exchange rate', teacher–student relations and teacher–student relative positionality. Hence we sought to engage teachers in reflective collaboration to change their practice in relation to these key constituting aspects. Through these shifts, we sought to enable: a closer alignment between student habitus and the field of classroom science education, particularly for students from non-dominant communities; and a broader eliciting and valuing, and translation of non-dominant students' ideas, experiences and use-value capital within the science classroom. The former recognises the importance of respecting and representing the world views of minoritised communities within education (for example, Freire [1970] 1993). The latter draws on a body of US work on 'funds of knowledge' approaches (Moll et al. 1992), which have been proposed as an equity-orientated, non-deficit approach to working with students from minoritised communities and which, as Rios-Aguilar et al. (2011) discuss, aligns closely with a Bourdieusian understanding of capital.

Over nine months, we worked collaboratively with teachers through group sessions, regular lesson observations and one-to-one reflection meetings between researchers and teachers (in which we discussed lesson observations and lesson plans). Two whole-day workshop sessions (one at the start of the year and one mid-way through) provided teachers with the conceptual framework and opportunities to discuss and refine the approach. Outside these sessions we supported teachers to 'tweak' and annotate their lesson plans in order to: maximise opportunities to elicit, value and then link students' ideas, experiences and cultural knowledges to the science content (for instance, in one London school with a predominantly African Caribbean student profile, a Year 8 lesson on sound might foreground eliciting students' experiences of sound systems and vibration at Notting Hill

Carnival as a starting point – and would build in time/scope to elicit any other personally meaningful experiences of sound/vibration, which the teacher reinforces and values as exemplars); address specific dimensions of science capital (for instance, lesson plans might seek to identify apt points to show how the science knowledge and skills being covered can be useful for a wide range of jobs both in and beyond science); personalise and localise science content for students (e.g. lesson plans are adapted to facilitate linking topics to students' own identities and interests – such as when one teacher used his predominantly South Asian Muslim students' knowledge and love of cooking curry within a topic on compounds and molecules); and broaden representations of science and recognise more diverse ways of 'doing science' (e.g. foregrounding more women and non-western scientists within the curriculum and valuing a wider range of student contributions in class, beyond the usual ways of 'talking science through muscular intellect'; Archer et al. forthcoming). The approach also involved providing teachers with regular spaces and support to reflect on their practice with researchers and colleagues.

The approach thus aimed to reduce the 'gap' between student habitus and the science education field and support the potential for translation of use-value capital into exchange-value capital (e.g. scientific literacy, particular scientific dispositions and practices). We were interested to see whether it is possible to alter the 'exchange rate' within science classrooms (Rios-Aguilar et al. 2011, 177) regarding which forms of capital are recognised and legitimated. Of course within this task we recognise the inherent limitations (being mindful that 'it is unlikely that such intervention can match the comprehensive structure of benefits enjoyed in more advantaged positions'; Krarup and Munk 2016, 766). By welcoming and valuing more diverse ways of 'doing science' within the classroom (e.g. what 'counts' as science, valued ways of performing scientifically), we hoped that the intervention might help (partially) reconfigure the dominant culture of science within these nine teachers' particular classroom spaces, opening up more inclusive ways for students to identify with and participate in science, reworking the dominant cultural arbitrary of science.

In this article we reflect on the affordances (or otherwise) of our Bourdieusian-inspired, pedagogic approach ('the intervention'), asking specifically:

- How did participants experience the intervention's impact on student engagement (in terms of interactions of student habitus, capital and field)?
- What is the emancipatory potential? How was the intervention perceived to affect student 'voice' and participation?

Methods

The data reported in this article come from a nine-month research and development project that was conducted with nine teachers from six inner London schools as part of a longer, five year the Enterprising Science study. Three of the participating schools (Coleville, Mareton and Northfields) were approached on the basis of being state-run, co-educational and within ±20% of the GCSE[2] results of other schools within their local area, with high proportions of students eligible for free school meals, reflecting the aims of the wider project to understand engagement with science education among students from minoritised (non-dominant) communities. In each of these schools, two Key Stage 3/4 (students aged 11–16) science teachers were invited to volunteer to take part in the study (i.e. teachers who

Table 1. Details of participant teachers and their observed classes.

Teacher	School	Class
Ms Dennis, Black British woman	Coleville	Year 10, bottom-set science class. Students from a wide diversity of minority ethnic and/or working-class communities
Ms Randel, South Asian woman	Coleville	Year 9, top-set science class. Students from a wide diversity of minority ethnic and/or working-class communities
Ms de Luca, White European woman	Mareton	Year 8, bottom-set science class. Students from a wide diversity of minority ethnic and/or working-class communities
Ms Chuckwu, Black British woman	Mareton	Year 10, bottom-set science class. Students from a wide diversity of minority ethnic and/or working-class communities
Mr Okello, Black British man	Northfields	Year 8, middle-set science class. Students from a wide diversity of minority ethnic and/or working-class communities
Ms. Arkwright, White British woman	Northfields	Year 9, top-set science class. Students from a wide diversity of minority ethnic and/or working-class communities
Mr Hobbes, Hong Kong Chinese man	East End	Year 7, middle-set science class. Students predominantly from South Asian Muslim communities
Ms Smith, White British woman	St Mark's	Year 8, top-set science class. Students from White and some minority ethnic, affluent professional families
Mr Sharma, South Asian man	Metropolitan	Year 9, bottom-set science class. Students predominantly from South Asian Muslim communities

teach at least one class in the 11–16 age range). The remaining three participating teachers (who taught at a further three different schools, two co-educational and one single-sex) had previously taken part in a professional development course that had been conducted in an earlier phase of the project (see King et al. 2015) and were invited to participate because they had expressed an interest in being involved with future project phases. Details of the participating teachers and their classes are presented in Table 1.

As detailed in Table 1, our sample comprised a spread of year groups (one Year 7 class, three Year 8 classes, three Year 9 classes and two Year 10 classes) and set groupings (four bottom sets, 2 two middle sets and three top sets). With the exception of students in Ms Smith's school, students came predominantly from working-class backgrounds and a range of ethnic backgrounds. Urdu/Bengali, Turkish, Polish and Portuguese were the most frequently spoken community languages among the students.

The core data drawn on in this article come from field notes of classroom observations, a teacher workshop, teacher interviews and discussion groups with students.

Observations

Each class was observed by one or two researchers over the nine-month period (September–June). Researchers attended classes approximately every three weeks over this time period. Researchers usually sat at the back or the side of the classroom and recorded field notes either by hand (pen and paper) or on a laptop computer or iPad. Observations followed an ethnographic approach, using a framework developed and agreed by the research team, including student behaviour, tasks, discourse, interactions, engagement and so on. We also noted group dynamics (relations of power).

Student discussion groups

In April/May we conducted 13 discussion groups with 59 students (see Table 2) aimed at eliciting students' experiences of the intervention. Discussion groups were conducted in a quiet space (usually an empty classroom) during class time and varied in length between

Table 2. Details of discussion groups.

School	Discussion groups
Coleville	One group of Year 10 girls (*n* = 5), one group of Year 9 boys (*n* = 5)
East End	Three groups of Year 7 boys (*n* = 13), one group of Year 7 girls (*n* = 4)
Mareton	Two groups of Year 10 (one girls, one boys) (*n* = 7)
Metropolitan	One group of Year 9 mixed boys and girls (*n* = 7)
Northfields	One group of Year 8 girls (*n* = 4), one group of Year 8 boys (*n* = 3), one group of Year 9 girls (*n* = 6), one group of Year 9 boys (*n* = 5)

20 minutes and one hour, depending on the time available. Potential student discussion group participants were identified and grouped by teachers, dependent on parental consent to participate.

Teacher workshops and interviews

Teachers took part in two day-long Saturday workshops, one in early Autumn at the start of the project (covering the study scope and approach) and one mid-way through (in February). The workshops supported teachers to share their experiences, raise issues, collaboratively design and refine their approaches and reflect on emergent themes and data presented by the researchers. Topics covered included understanding the conceptual framework; group reflection exercises on identifying and critiquing dominant 'celebrated' student identities and ways of being in science, and practical sessions in which researchers and teachers collaboratively annotated and 'tweaked' lesson plans and shared their insights and reflections with one another. Workshops were audio-recorded and observed by three members of the research team, who made extensive field notes on what was said and the interactions between teachers during both small group and whole group discussions. All of the participating teachers attended. Teachers were also interviewed (audio-recorded) at the beginning and end of the year.

Ethics

Consent was obtained from teachers and school managers. Parental and student consent was obtained to report and use the data for participating students.

Findings

Our observations recorded substantial and prolonged change in teachers' practice over the course of the academic year. For instance, teachers increasingly 'tweaked' their usual lesson plans and schemes of work to incorporate ideas for fostering student attitudes and dispositions (e.g. that 'science is everywhere'), inviting a broader range of ways of 'talking science' (Lemke 1990) and eliciting regular and sustained links between science content and students' everyday lives in and out of school. In interviews, all teachers described substantial changes in their personal development and practice. As Ms Smith put it: 'that's been a best part you know, it really has changed how I teach'. The majority of students in the discussion groups also reported discernible changes in practice that were enacted consistently over time and which involved a more contextualised approach to science teaching that went beyond the 'usual' content coverage and drew on students' use-value capital (e.g. 'she teaches you based on what you know').

RQ1. How did participants experience the intervention's impact on student engagement (interactions of student habitus, capital and field)?

We begin by reflecting on teachers' and students' accounts of the impact of the intervention on student engagement (i.e. how the intervention shaped the students' experiences at the interface of habitus, capital and field) before moving on to consider more specific shifts in habitus and capital – and whether the intervention might be considered as 'building' student capital, or not.

Perceived influence on student engagement

As discussed earlier, we understand 'student engagement' as a form of practice that is produced at the interface of habitus, capital and field and which involves students' 'invention and improvisation' (Bourdieu 1990, 13), albeit within the constraints of structure. All of the teachers felt that the intervention had made a positive impact on student engagement (e.g. 'I think they're much more engaged with the science'; Ms Arkwright) and articulated a range of practices that they felt had shifted. These changes were associated with increased student 'excitement', 'interest', 'focus', 'attention' and 'active' classroom participation (indicators of engagement that are recognised in the wider literature; for example, Ainley and Ainley 2011), as noted through researcher observations and in the views of participating teachers and students.

For instance, teachers and students commonly described how the intervention had increased their interest in and enjoyment of science lessons, because students experienced science classes as being more 'fun', 'enjoyable', 'creative', 'lively' and 'interesting':

> The boys have really enjoyed it, yeah. I've really enjoyed it. (Ms Smith)
>
> It makes the lessons fun. (Tanisha, Mr Hobbes' class)
>
> I think that makes the lessons more lively. (Fawaad, Ms Arkwright's class)
>
> Like, it's really creative, like the lesson plans that she gives us, which like make it more enjoyable. (Amya, Ms Arkwright's class)

Some students also explicitly articulated how specific aspects of the approach (e.g. linking to particular dimensions of science capital) were key to this increased interest and enjoyment. As Hendrix (Ms Randel's class) put it: 'like she's linking it [science] to jobs that we can have, that was quite interesting'.

As discussed further later, teachers also noted increased student attention, motivation and focus ('on task' behaviours), and described how students were more actively involved in lessons as a result of the intervention – a point that was also borne out by our observations, which recorded students participating more and showing more active attention when teachers were using the approach. As Ms de Luca explained:

> So [Year 10 bottom set] are a very challenging group of students [...] Through the year what I've noticed is when [I use the approach] I can see it their eyes ... they kind of ... like a meerkat, they pop up and you can see the engagement and you can see that they talk about it a bit more.

We suggest that these 'meerkat' moments, when students sit up and take an interest in the class and participate more actively, might be understood as generated by students' experiences of a closer alignment between their habitus (identities and dispositions) and field and through the field's increased valuing of their use-value capital. As the following quote from Mr Okello illustrates, this may be because the approach provides students with more legitimate spaces and opportunities to 'express themselves or their ideas'. This in turn was felt to inflect dispositions, for example, leading students to 'value science' more:

> The big difference has been their engagement and their interaction with the lesson … especially if kids can talk about their experience, express themselves or their ideas – I find they're far more engaged and they value it a lot more. (Mr Okello)

Mr Okello felt that the intervention contributed to producing practices which are inflected with agency and traces of pride (later describing his students as 'eager to share … eager to show'), hinting at a potential closer alignment between habitus, capital and field.

Perceived gains in capital: improved competence and understanding

Analysis identified two main forms of exchange-value capital that were 'built' through the intervention: student 'understanding' and 'attainment'.

The majority of students and teachers felt that the approach increased student understanding of science. Teachers described how the approach helped students to grasp concepts and ideas more quickly and retain information for longer. Across the board, the main benefit identified by discussion group students was that it helped students to better understand, make sense of and remember lesson content – or as Fatima (Year 7 girl, Mr Hobbes' class) put it, 'so it stays in our head even more':

> Yeah I think it has increased their understanding. Like with the lesson today, like I wouldn't be able to repeat things that I've taught before to them because it would be like 'Huh? I don't actually understand this'. (Mr Hobbes)

> Yeah, it's a better way to make us remember things. Like it's not like a boring way of like just reading and then trying to get it into our heads. (Tahir, Ms Enoh's class)

Increased understanding was seen as due to the linking of science content with students' own lives, which students felt enabled them to both understand concepts and meaningfully connect with the content (which we could interpret as reducing dissonance with the habitus), making topics more 'memorable':

> So it kind of like lets us relate to what she's actually talking about … so we can understand it more. (Rohan, Ms Randel's class)

> I think it's like quite cool, 'cos then you like think about it and then you're like, 'oh yeah, that's related to like everyday life' and you're like, 'I'll remember that now'. (Christopher, Mr Okello's class)

> Yeah, I feel like we get a better understanding because we can relate to what she's teaching us. (Alfie, Ms Arkwright's class)

We suggest that student 'understanding' of science can be understood as a form of exchange-value cultural capital in that it is form of scientific literacy – a high-status form of knowledge and/or competency that can have many applications, including translation into formal qualifications. The students' accounts suggest that linking science with their lives enhanced and improved their engagement, which we interpret as due to a reduction in the 'distance' between science content and student habitus.

Attainment

Whereas teachers and students were largely in agreement as regards the benefits of the approach for student understanding of science, views were much more divergent regarding whether it raised attainment. Because of the differences between schools, year groups and curricula, we were not able to deduce a common measure of attainment that would make sense across the participating classes. Instead, we asked teachers for their judgement (based on their intuition and data available to them) as to whether there had been any attainment gains, or not. Only two teachers felt that it had generated concrete improvements:

> It has been better than the target, they've been given like D to E targets but now I'm expecting at least 50% of the class grade C [...] I think it did have some impact because we started off expecting, you know, very poor grades from this group, and I'm really surprised that they have done extremely well over the year when I looked at their overall result ... much better than we've actually predicted. (Ms Dennis)

> I think if you think about this statistically compared to your other classes, I was quite proud of them because they made ... numerically they made really good progress. (Mr Hobbes)

The other teachers were more ambivalent. For instance, Mr Okello felt that the approach did not increase test score attainment – although he also felt that summative assessment does not necessarily represent the wider range of understanding and skills that students might develop:

> The way we assess students with our summative tests, I think science capital doesn't necessarily make them better at that, but it does increase engagement [...] Those tests cater best for kids who can retain a lot of information and grind through a lot of data just before their exam or the test, and I don't think [they] necessarily reflect or show some of the more important skills that we'd like [students] to develop.

Changing student dispositions?

We were also interested in whether the intervention might foster changes in student dispositions associated with symbolic (exchange-value) dimensions of science capital. Teachers and students from across the discussion groups identified such changes, primarily in terms of understanding the presence and value of science in everyday life. For instance:

> At the start of the year I found some of the attitude like really difficult to deal with because some of them did not care [about science]. But as the year progressed they started picking up and some of them actually started showing some interest, yeah. [...] some of them told me 'oh miss, we're really starting to enjoy Science now' [...] I mean the progress that I've seen with some of them is ... I think that's the biggest achievement. (Ms Enoh)

> It's opened their eyes quite a lot ... they're more engaged, they like to be able to think a little bit outside the box and link it to their lives ... and from that they can see the value of it. (Ms Arkwright)

We also noted a widespread expression among the students regarding an increased appreciation of the value of science in everyday life. For instance:

> Its better bringing real life examples into a Science lesson cos it's more interesting. And you can like understand the fact that behind everything in the world there's still science behind it. (Daniel, Ms Enoh's class)

> I think it's helpful because it helps you like see what, why you need to have an x-ray and stuff like that. (Maryam, Mr Sharma's class)

> I think it's more like interesting because you have an idea of where it might come up in your daily lives, whereas in other Science lessons or like in the past, when someone said something, you're like, oh, it's just that, like it won't come to your use. (Shona, Ms Arkwright's class)

A small number of students indicated that there had been a change in some of their out-of-school attitudes and practices, such as more frequent discussion of science with their families. For instance, Ashanti (Ms Dennis' class) described talking with her father about specific topics she had learned in science class. Several of the teachers also reported that students and/or parents had reported back to them that they now talked about science more at home. As Ms Smith explained:

> [They] definitely felt a relevance of what I teaching them to, you know, decisions that their parents had made … [for example] why you shouldn't just use antibiotics all the time. That worked really well. I really do think most of them did have a conversation round the dinner table, you know, yeah … that was really good.

A couple of students also reported changing aspects of their everyday behaviours, in line with something they had learned about in science class which they felt had connected with their daily lives. For instance, after a class on radiation, Kosoko changed how she used her mobile phone:

> Every time I have my phone, like straight away […] Ms Enoh's lesson always comes to mind. I always put it on speaker like, most of the time […] it just comes to mind, so it links to everyday life pretty well.

A few boys from Ms Arkwright's class described watching more science-related media, such as Ted talks, and most students indicated a greater appreciation that science can lead to a wide range of jobs. For instance:

> I think that it's helpful in a way, because not many other lessons like link jobs to the subject, so it like helps you understand. (Shona, Ms Arkwright's class)

A few students also spontaneously mentioned examples of how they now used their school science knowledge and skills within their daily lives. For instance:

> We actually use it [science] in our lives. Compared to other teachers, they just tell us, that's it, we move on, whereas [Ms Arkwright] tells us and then we actually learn from it and implement it in our lives. (Brody)

> I went to Curry's to buy a TV and explained the energy and stuff to my Dad, so now we're saving even more money. (Fawaad, Ms Arkwright's class)

As Bourdieu and Passeron (1977) explain, schools can be socialising agents and can shape student dispositions in various ways. These examples illustrate how this process might also occur at the micro level of the classroom, potentially developing particular attitudes and dispositions relating to perceptions of the value of science in everyday life. Of course, how durable (or not) these changes might be is hard to assess – although we speculate that longer-lasting dispositions would probably require longer-term pedagogic action to embed. For instance, Carlone, Haun-Frank, and Webb (2011) discuss how student science identity and dispositions can vary dramatically from year to year, depending on the class teacher's approach.

Challenging views

The majority of students expressed positive views about the approach, yet a couple were more ambivalent. For instance, despite liking the approach, Joya worried that the real-life contextualisation might mean that they were not covering the 'real' science content:

> Like, half I like it and then half maybe it's a bit of a waste of time [...] I think we miss a lot of the lesson, so most of the time, if he does say his stories, it will take about ... about 20 minutes, something like that, so it kind of takes a lot of time [...] but I quite like it at the same time. (Joya, Mr Sharma's class)

Likewise, Amya reflected: 'it's helpful ... but it sometimes takes your mind off the actual thing that you're actually doing'. We suggest that these students' accounts could be read as signalling how the approach might rub up against the demands of educational performativity, in which the coverage of content and examination preparation is considered the 'real' focus of learning. Moreover, we suggest that these examples highlight how any attempts to challenge and shift prevailing norms about 'how things are' and how learning 'should' be done (doxa), will invariably meet resistance.

RQ2. What is the emancipatory potential? How was the intervention perceived to effect student 'voice' and participation?

The approach aimed to open up spaces for more students to 'do' and participate in science, broadening both 'who speaks' and 'what is spoken about' (whose and what knowledge is valued). Hence we were interested in teachers' and students' views as to whether it had engendered any changes in classroom dynamics and participation – but particularly public oral contributions and the student 'voice' within the classes. This reflects our interest in changing classroom conditions to enable Others to 'speak' (Spivak 1988) and to redistribute capital among non-dominant communities. The approach encouraged teachers to make regular use of student peer discussion and to support a wider range of participation and 'types' of contribution (based on students' own lives). Some teachers were already making use of student discussion, whereas for others, like Ms de Luca, it was a newer departure:

> I know students learn from talking, but usually I kind of ... I'm very strict and I will shut them down very quickly. Whereas now I kind of give them a bit more space to talk because I know that it's helping them to relate and engage more with the topic. (Ms de Luca)

We observed a range of student participation between the different classes, varying from predominantly 'inclusive' classes in which most students spoke in most lessons (e.g. in Ms Arkwright's class) through to classes in which a few students tended to predominate and a few spoke infrequently (e.g. Mr Sharma's class, Mr Hobbes' class). However, across all classes, observations suggested that enactment of the approach encouraged a wider range of students to voice their views in class, particularly among those who were traditionally very quiet and tended not to participate publically. For instance, during a lesson on vibrations Mr Okello elicited students' everyday experiences around the topic, during which Christopher, a very quiet boy who did not normally contribute in class, offered his experience of his grandmother, who is deaf and highly sensitive to vibrations. That is, while the approach did not shift classroom dynamics completely, when enacted it did seem to promote more possibilities for inclusion. Indeed, all of the teachers felt that the approach had helped to broaden and increase the contributions and participation of a wider range of students within their classes, but particularly among 'quieter' and lower attaining students. For instance:

> Yeah, it definitely ... for the boys who didn't want to really talk in class ... that did work. For the boys that got sort of enveloped by other boys. (Ms Smith)

> Generally I think I get overall more participation purely because of science capital, that's what I personally feel. (Mr Okello)

Students in the discussion groups also described how the approach helped foster more inclusive participation in class. For instance, Fawaad felt it created a more 'friendly environment', which he believed also helped his attainment: 'like, I improved more this year, like last year, I wasn't doing as well, but then this year, 'cos I think of the learning environment and the way we're taught, it's improved'. Daniel (Ms Enoh's class) explained how linking of science content to personal experience opened up a wider range of ways for students to participate in and contribute to the class:

> If she's [teacher] explaining something she'll give like an example that everyone could relate to, and everyone's like 'Oh yeah'. And then they'll say something, then someone else will say something. And then quite a few people have something to say. And then it's like 'Oh yeah, so we've experienced it' so yeah.

We interpret these students' accounts as illustrating how the eliciting and valuing of students' use-value capital within the classroom might help promote student 'voice' and participation. This could be particularly valuable within a subject like science that is dominantly associated with bodies of factual knowledge that demands a 'right or wrong' answer and which is popularly associated with public demonstrations of 'braininess' (for example, Archer and DeWitt 2016; Lemke 1990). From a Bourdieusian perspective, these moments might represent a shift in the field, legitimising speech in a wider range of registers and in which use value capital is recognised as a legitimate medium to engage with science. That is, a wider spectrum of students was recognised as authentic contributors and as having 'something to say' (due to the valuing of their lives and experiences as legitimate sources of science-related knowledge and experiences).

Yet, despite these promising moments, wider inequalities and patterns of participation remained and some students still remained scared or shy of participating in class. For instance, Mr Hobbes reflected that although the participation of the girls in his class had improved, they were still 'very quiet'.

Discussion and conclusion

In this article we have discussed our experience of working with nine London teachers to develop and implement a Bourdieusian-inspired attempt at praxis in the context of secondary science education. We did so based on a belief in the value of bringing theory to bear within attempts to engage with (policy and) practice. We thus advocate for a sociology of education that both 'gets its hands dirty' – engaging with the thorny task of how we might (attempt to) improve things on the ground in the here and now – alongside 'higher level' critique. This marrying of theory and practice was something that our teachers also explicitly valued:

> I knew that there's something to this, that there is something that is of value. Because you know sometimes with some research it's a lot of … it's all well and good in theory, but in practice it doesn't always work. So with this when I could see that actually the theory put into practice there is something to it. I thought okay just persevere, keep going with it. (Ms de Luca)

Teachers, and many students, described their experience of the approach in positive terms, suggesting that it enhanced student engagement and participation in a range of ways, but particularly for students from non-dominant communities. The 'funds of knowledge' (use-value capital) aspect of the approach has been advocated by others as a good basis for social justice approaches to re/designing formal education (for example, Basu, Calabrese Barton, and Tan 2011; Zipin 2009). Drawing on Delpit's (1995) two-directional approach for a social justice approach to educating Other (people's) children, Zipin (2009, 317) argues that there are various benefits to employing a Funds of Knowledge (FoK) approach, not least challenging 'the exchange-value power by which competitive academic curriculum selectively privileges cultural capital embodied in elite social-structural positions':

> the *redistribution* impulse is crucial to enable academic success that leads to pathways beyond poverty, ill health and more. Yet the *recognition* impulse is even more vital, both ethically to keep diverse cultures alive, and pragmatically, to *engage* learners through familiar social-cultural resources. (Zipin 2009, 318–319; original emphases)

We also suggest that approaches which, in the words of our teachers, make them 'happier' may hold promise for a range of reasons (see King et al. [forthcoming] for a discussion of the implications of the approach for teacher agency and pushing back against educational performativity).

We thus identified a range of potentially 'hopeful' outcomes, including improving student engagement and understanding, building student science capital, fostering a range of science-related dispositions and practices, and widening classroom participation. However, we also recognise that the potential of the approach is constrained in a number of ways. For instance, following our Bourdieusian framework, we might question how effective attempts at the redistribution of capital and changing relations of representation can actually be when enacted within a system in which wider power inequalities remain intact. The question also arises as to how radical such an approach can be if it does not substantially improve attainment, given that qualifications and examination results can be important levers for social mobility. We acknowledge this point and suggest that – while we cannot discount that improved understanding may lead to raised attainment in future iterations – the more radical promise of the approach lies in its potential for both challenging dominant ways in which science is taught ('prototypical' school science) and enhancing student agency. For instance, a better understanding of scientific concepts and ideas and an improved 'relationship' with science (rather than, say, memorised and later forgotten 'facts' to pass tests) might better support active citizenship among underserved communities than a small attainment gain (e.g. decoding science coverage in the media, supporting family health choices, navigating access to services, etc.). Moreover, as Bourdieu reminds us, dominant social groups are adept at maintaining their positions of privilege – hence we are cautious about too heavy a focus on 'raising attainment'. From a Freirian perspective, the liberatory and 'humanising' potential is also undermined given the lack of social critique within the approach. Moreover, we may question the longer-term impact of the approach if it remains isolated in particular classes, rather than, for instance, being embedded more widely across schools or the education system more generally.

However, we would argue that the alternative – to do nothing and not attempt any form of intervention – is also untenable and maintains the status quo. As Freire ([1970] 1993, 73) reminds us: 'hope … does not consist in crossing one's arms and waiting. In this sense, we argue that there is a value in attempting 'small gains' that might enable minoritised students to play a better 'hand' in the 'game' of educational reproduction, while also speaking truth to power and calling for more radical, 'longer term' visions for a socially just society and education system.

We do not seek to over-claim for our approach – it remains a small-scale, exploratory foray into some possibilities for praxis. The data we discussed focused on teachers' and students' perceptions and experiences of the approach, rather than, for instance, on 'harder' (e.g. quantifiable) measures. We sought to understand participants' experiences of the intervention, because we believe this is useful and valuable both practically and conceptually. This exercise revealed that teachers and students generally saw value in the approach – but it also raises further questions, not least questions of scale-ability, given the relatively long-term nature of the intervention (working individually and collectively with teachers over a nine-month period), especially within the prevailing climate of tight budgets within UK education and the restricted time and money available to support teachers' professional development. This is something that we will continue to think through during the next iterations of the project (being conducted, at the time of writing, in partnership with the National STEM Learning Centre and centres for initial teacher education).

In sum, we hope this article might contribute to further discussion within the sociology of education regarding what might be achievable in the 'here and now' of contemporary UK education in terms of working collaboratively with teachers to improve the experiences and chances of all students. But we also hope the article might add to efforts to demonstrate the wide potential value of sociology of education for policy – as both a critical voice speaking truth to power and as a 'critical partner', offering ideas for how things might be 'done differently' in the ongoing struggle for a more socially just education system.

Notes

1. For instance, approaches commonly focus on trying to improve scientific literacy (e.g. support people to understand and learn more science content/knowledge).
2. GCSEs (General Certificates of Secondary Education) are a series of examinations taken by students in the United Kingdom when they are 16 years old.

Disclosure statement

No potential conflict of interest was reported by the authors.

References

Ainley, M., and J. Ainley. 2011. "Student Engagement with Science in Early Adolescence: The Contribution of Enjoyment To Students' Continuing Interest in Learning about Science." *Contemporary Educational Psychology* 36 (1): 4–12.

American Association of University Women (AAUW). 2010. *AAUW Annual Report*. Washington, DC: AAUW.

Apple, M. W. 2005. *Education and Power*. 2nd ed. New York: Routledge.

Apple, M. W. 2013. *Can Education Change Society?* New York: Routledge.

Archer, L., and J. DeWitt. 2016. *Understanding Young People's Science Aspirations*. London: Routledge.

Archer, L., J. DeWitt, and B. Willis. 2014. "Adolescent Boys' Science Aspirations: Masculinity, Capital and Power." *Journal of Research in Science Teaching* 51 (1): 1–30.

Archer, L., E. Dawson, J. DeWitt, A. Seakins, and B. Wong. 2015. "Science Capital: A Conceptual, Methodological, and Empirical Argument for Extending Bourdieusian Notions of Capital beyond the Arts." *Journal of Research in Science Teaching* 52 (7): 922–948.

Archer, L., J. DeWitt, J. Osborne, J. Dillon, B. Willis, and B. Wong. 2012. "Science Aspirations and Family Habitus: How Families Shape Children's Engagement and Identification with Science." *American Education Research Journal* 49 (5): 881–908.

Archer, L., E. Dawson, J. DeWitt, S. Godec, H. King, A. Mau, E. Nomikou, and A. Seakins. Forthcoming. Killing Curiosity? An Analysis of Celebrated Identity Performances among Teachers and Students in Nine London Secondary Science Classrooms. *Science Education*.

Ball, S. J. 2003. "The Teacher's Soul and the Terrors of Performativity." *Journal of Education Policy* 18 (2): 215–228.

Basu, J., A. Calabrese Barton, and E. Tan, eds. 2011. *Democratic Science Teaching: Building the Expertise to Empower Low-Income Minority Youth in Science*. Rotterdam: Sense.

Bourdieu, P. 1977. *Outline of a Theory of Practice*. Translated from the French by Richard Nice. Cambridge: Cambridge University Press.

Bourdieu, P. 1990. *In Other Words*. Cambridge: Polity.

Bourdieu, P. 2010. *Sociology is a Martial Art*. New York: New Press.

Bourdieu, P., and J. Passeron. 1977. *Reproduction in Education, Culture and Society*. London: Sage.

Bourdieu, P., and J. Passerson. 1979. *The Inheritors: French Students and Their Relation to Culture*. Translated by R. Nice. Chicago, IL: University of Chicago Press.

Calabrese Barton, A., and E. Tan. 2010. "We Be Burnin'! Agency, Identity, and Science Learning." *Journal of the Learning Sciences* 19 (2): 187–229.

Calabrese Barton, A., E. Tan, and A. Rivet. 2008. "Creating Hybrid Spaces for Engaging School Science among Urban Middle School Girls." *American Educational Research Journal* 45 (1): 68–103.

Carlone, H., and A. Johnson. 2007. "Understanding the Science Experiences of Women of Color: Science Identity as an Analytic Lens." *Journal of Research in Science Teaching* 44 (8): 1187–1218.

Carlone, H. B., J. Haun-Frank, and A. Webb. 2011. "Assessing Equity beyond Knowledge- and Skills-Based Outcomes: A Comparative Ethnography of Two Fourth-Grade Reform-Based Science Classrooms." *Journal of Research in Science Teaching* 48 (5): 459–485.

Delpit, L. 1995. *Other Peoples Children: Cultural Conflict in the Classroom*. New York: The New Press.

FAAB Collective. 2003. Performance at the British Educational Research Association Annual Conference 2003, 13th–16th September, Edinburgh.

Freire, P. [1993] 1970. *Pedagogy of the Oppressed*. Translated by M. Bergman Ramos. London: Penguin Books.

Gunter, H. M., and R. Willmott. 2002. "Biting the Bullet." *Management in Education* 15 (5): 35–37.

Harding, S. 1998. "Women, Science, and Society." *Science* 281 (5383): 1599–1600.

James, David. 2015. "How Bourdieu Bites Back: Recognising Misrecognition in Education and Educational Research." *Cambridge Journal of Education* 45 (1): 97–112.

King, H., E. Nomikou, L. Archer, and E. Regan. 2015. "Teachers' Understanding and Operationalisation of 'Science Capital.'" *International Journal of Science Education* 37 (18): 2987–3014. doi:10.1080/09500693.2015.1119331.

King, H., and E. Nomikou. Forthcoming. "Fostering Critical Teacher Agency: The Impact of a Science Capital Professional Development Programme." *Pedagogy, Culture and Society*.

Krarup, T., and M. D. Munk. 2016. "Field Theory in Cultural Capital Studies of Educational Attainment." *BJSE* 37 (5): 761–779.

Lemke, J. L. 1990. *Talking Science: Language, Learning, and Values*. Westport: Ablex Pub. Corp.

Moll, L. C., C. Amanti, D. Neff, and N. Gonzalez. 1992. "Funds of Knowledge for Teaching: Using a Qualitative Approach to Connect Homes and Classrooms." *Theory into Practice* 31 (2): 132–141.

Parkin, R. 1997. "Practice Theory." In *The Dictionary of Anthropology*, edited by T. Barfield, 375–377. Oxford: Blackwell.

Rios-Aguilar, C., J. M. Kiyama, M. Gravitt, and L. Moll. 2011. "Funds of Knowledge for the Poor and Forms of Capital for the Rich? A Capital Approach to Examining Funds of Knowledge." *Theory and Research in Education* 9 (2): 163–184.

Rowley, H. 2014. "Partnerships as a Critical Secretary." In *Education Policy Research: Design and Practice at a Time of Rapid Reform*, edited by H. Gunter, D. Hall, and C. Mills. London: Bloomsbury publishing.

Smith, E. 2011. "Women into Science and Engineering? Gendered Participation in Higher Education STEM Subjects." *British Educational Research Journal* 37 (6): 993–1014.

Spivak, G. A. 1988. "Can the Subaltern Speak?" In *Marxism and the Interpretation of Culture*, edited by Cary Nelson and Lawrence Grossberg, 271–313. Urbana: University of Illinois Press.

Zipin, L. 2009. "Dark Funds of Knowledge, Deep Funds of Pedagogy: Exploring Boundaries between Lifeworlds and Schools." *Discourse: Studies in the Cultural Politics of Education* 30 (3): 317–331.

Education and Cultural Capital: The Implications of Changing Trends in Education Policies

Diane Reay

Within the sociology of education most conceptualizations of cultural capital within empirical research focus on high status cultural participation. A smaller, parallel body of work emphasizes much broader understandings of cultural capital in relation to education. The first part of this article maps different conceptions of cultural capital across the field of educational research before developing a conceptualization that stresses the micro-interactional processes through which individuals comply (or fail to comply) with the evaluative standards of schooling. The article also argues that the growth of policy initiatives that accentuate the role of parents in schooling have made the myriad workings of cultural capital in relation to education more visible. Within government policy parental involvement has become the means whereby schools can tap the cultural capital resources of parents in the drive to raise standards. Economic capital has always had a defining influence, but now it is increasingly possible to see the power of cultural capital especially in relation to the growing emphasis on parental involvement and parental choice, and programmes such as gifted and talented. The second part of the article draws on data from research projects that examine parental choice, gifted and talented programmes, and parental involvement more generally, to illustrate the many ways in which cultural capital operates to reproduce educational advantage. Most of the examples underscore the close relationship between cultural and economic capital and how they work to reinforce each other, but an example is also included to illustrate how cultural capital can operate independently of economic capital. The article concludes that the policy emphasis on parental involvement and initiatives to retain the middle classes within state schooling work to maximize the potential of the already advantaged and are exacerbating class inequalities in education.

Introduction: Bourdieu and Cultural Capital

The term 'capital' is usually associated with a narrowly defined economic category of monetary exchange for profit. As Moore (2004) asserts, Bourdieu's concept of cultural capital is an attempt to expand the category of capital to something more than just the economic and to identify culture as a form of that more general category. Bourdieu includes social capital alongside cultural capital and has also written more generally of symbolic capital and more specifically of linguistic capital (Bourdieu, 1991). However, what all Bourdieu's capitals share is that each requires, and is the product of, an investment of an appropriate kind and each can secure a return on that investment. As with all the other capitals, Bourdieu's concern in relation to cultural capital was with its continual transmission and accumulation in ways that perpetuate social inequalities. He viewed the concept as breaking with the received wisdom that attributes academic success or failure to natural aptitudes, such as intelligence and giftedness. In contrast, Bourdieu explained school success by the amount and type of cultural capital inherited from the family milieu rather than by measures of individual talent or achievement:

> The notion of cultural capital initially presented itself to me, in the course of research, as a theoretical hypothesis which made it possible to explain the unequal scholastic achievement of children originating from different social classes by relating academic success, i.e., the specific profits which children from the different classes and class fractions can obtain in the academic market, to the distribution of cultural capital between the classes and class fractions. (Bourdieu, 1986a, p. 243)

Within the sociology of education most conceptualizations of cultural capital within empirical research have focused on high status cultural participation (Aschaffenburg & Maas, 1996; Dumais, 2002; Ganzeboom, de Graaf & Robert, 1990; Mohr & DiMaggio, 1995; Sullivan, 2001). These studies operationalize cultural capital primarily as knowledge of or competence with highbrow aesthetic culture such as classical music and fine art. For example, in Dumais (2002) cultural capital is defined as the knowledge and competencies belonging to members of the upper classes, while for Sullivan (2001, p. 895) cultural capital is 'familiarity with the dominant culture in the society and especially the ability to use "educated" language'. However, as Lareau and Weininger (2003) argue, such conceptualizations of cultural capital overlook the full potential of cultural capital as a theoretical tool for understanding how inequalities are generated through schooling. They also neglect the full range of dimensions that Bourdieu himself attributed to cultural capital.

For Bourdieu cultural capital encompasses a broad array of linguistic competencies, manners, preferences and orientations, which, Bourdieu terms 'subtle modalities in the relationship to culture and language' (Bourdieu, 1977, p. 82). Bourdieu identifies three variants of cultural capital: first, in the embodied state incorporated in mind and body. The accumulation of cultural capital in its embodied form begins in early childhood. It requires pedagogical action, the investment of time by parents, other family members or hired professionals to sensitize the child to cultural distinctions. Second, cultural capital exists in the institutionalized state, that is existing in institutionalized forms such as educational qualifications, and third, in the objectified state, simply existing as cultural goods such as books, artefacts, dictionaries and paintings (Bourdieu, 1986b). It can be seen here that cultural capital is much more than the high status activities that have traditionally been operationalized in empirical research within education.

Critics of Bourdieu's concepts of cultural capital have either argued that the notion foreshadows a culturalist turn within sociology of education, neglecting the material and the structural, or that Bourdieu's explication of the workings of cultural capital only makes sense in the context of French society. On the first count, as this article demonstrates later, cultural practices can be held in tension with structural and material inequalities. The second criticism can be countered by reference to Bourdieu's writings on method and methodology. Bourdieu viewed his concepts as adaptable to specific empirical contexts rather than as general models or rigid frameworks. He wrote of his concepts, including cultural capital:

> The main thing is that they are not to be conceptualized so much as ideas, on that level, but as a method. The core of my work lies in the method and a way of thinking. To be more precise, my method is a manner of asking questions rather than just ideas. This, I think is a critical point. (Bourdieu, 1985, quoted in Mahar, 1990)

This article is arguing for a broad understanding of cultural capital, one that focuses on qualitative dimensions of cultural capital as well as the measurable, and emphasizes 'the affective aspects of inequality' (Skeggs, 1997, p. 10) such as levels of confidence and entitlement. In research on parental involvement in schooling by the author (Reay, 1998), whilst recognizing more straightforward aspects of cultural capital like educational qualifications and participation in high status activities, the importance of these more subjective aspects was stressed:

> These include confidence, ambivalence or a sense of inadequacy about providing support, the amount of expertise women feel in the educational field, and the extent to which entitlement, assertiveness, aggression or timidity characterize women's approaches to teaching staff. (p. 32)

Although these aspects of cultural capital were related to a specific empirical context, it can be argued that levels of confidence and entitlement are key dimensions of cultural capital across social fields. In their critical assessment of cultural capital in educational research Annette Lareau and Elliot Weininger (2003, p. 2) argue for a conceptualization that focuses on 'micro-interactional processes whereby individuals' strategic use of knowledge, skills and competence comes into contact with institutionalized standards of evaluation'. They also caution that while it is important to have a clear focus on the standards that policy makers, schools and teachers use to evaluate students and their parents, it is also vital to avoid any uncritical acceptance of such standards. Rather, they argue that what is needed is 'a double vision' encompassing both institutional standards and a reflexive consideration of the perspectives and actions of parents and students attempting to comply with them.

Part 1: Cultural Capital in the New Marketized Field of Education

The field of educational policy and especially parental involvement initiatives are particularly generative for illustrating both the salience of cultural capital in the broad sense described above, and how it is mobilized to perpetuate educational inequalities.

Partnership between parents and teachers has become enshrined in educational policy in England (DES, 1985; 1986; 1988; DfEE, 1997). Parents are increasingly encouraged to become not only consumers within education but also 'active partners in the production of educated children' (McNamara *et al.*, 2000, p. 474). During the 1990s parental involvement came to be officially recognized as a key factor in school improvement and effectiveness (Reynolds & Cuttance, 1992), and in 1994 became a requisite part of a school's development plan (Ofsted, 1994). Ofsted guidelines issued the following year (1995, p. 98) encouraged inspectors to explore how well schools help parents to understand the curriculum, the teaching it provides and how this can lead to parents and teachers working together to provide support at home. According to the current Labour Government, parents are children's primary educators (DfEE, 1997).

We have now reached a point at the beginning of the 21st century when parental involvement is no longer optional as parents are increasingly seen to be co-educators alongside their children's teachers. Edwards and Warin (1999) go as far as to argue that collaboration between home and school seems to have been superceded by the colonization of the home by the school. Certainly, schemes like PACT and IMPACT, devised to ensure parents support their children's reading and numeracy development, are widespread (Merttens & Vass, 1993), while in 1999 home-school agreements became a statutory requirement, despite considerable disquiet from both educationalists and parent groups. In 2003 parental involvement was conscripted by the Government's standards agenda and has become a key means by which schooling can tap into the cultural capital resources of parents in the policy drive to raise educational standards (Brain & Reid, 2003)

These policies have been accompanied by an intensification of middle-class anxiety (Beck, 1992) which has both fed into and been fuelled by policy initiatives that prioritize the role of parents in the education of children. 'Leaving children's education to the school' has become 'a thing of the past' or the sign of 'very bad parenting' within both contemporary education policy and middle-class common sense understandings.[1] Whereas before in Bourdieurian terms all that was required was for the school to recognize the cultural capital of its middle-class pupils (Bourdieu & Passeron, 1979), the under-funded, high stakes, standards driven field of state schooling seems to have shifted the rules of the game pushing more and more 'school work' into the home. There is an increasing reliance on, and expectation of, parents acting in relation to their children's education.

Part 2: Cultural Capital as Educational Inequality

This section draws on three very different research projects to show how cultural capital is put to work in education markets, ensuring the continuing advantage of middle-class families. The first two examples underscore the close relationship between cultural and economic capital and how they work to reinforce each other. However, an example from research on social class in the classroom is included to illustrate how cultural capital can operate independently of economic capital to generate educational profits.

In the first research project on mothers' involvement in their children's schooling, cultural capital was employed as a conceptual tool for examining how mothers' activities, despite apparent similarities, add up to significant class differences. Mothers' personal histories and their educational experiences influence their involvement in their children's schooling, particularly their effectiveness in dealing with teachers and such differences are powerfully rooted in cultural capital. Many of the middle-class parents had themselves done very well at school and this educational success translated into self-confidence and a sense of entitlement in relation to parental involvement. As a consequence, the middle-class mothers were far more adept at getting their viewpoint across in dialogue with teachers when there were any disagreements or tensions between home and school, displaying certainty, self-assurance and an ability to counter opposing viewpoints, all aspects of cultural capital. In contrast, the working-class mothers were much more hesitant and apologetic and far more likely to disqualify and, at times, contradict themselves when talking to teachers. As Skeggs (1997, p. 90) asserts in relation to her working-class female respondents, 'they can never have the certainty that they are doing it right which is one of the main signifiers of middle-class dispositions. This lack of certainty means they cannot make use of social space in the same way'. The consequences for the working-class women in research by the author was that they often spoke of coming away from meetings with school staff feeling that they 'hadn't been listened to'. While the middle-class mothers in the study could be assertive in interaction with teachers, the working-class women's high levels of doubt and anxiety mostly resulted in apologetic, tentative approaches to staff or occasionally escalated into displays of temper (Reay, 2000). Then, as one of them commented forlornly, 'there's no way you're going to get your point of view across'. Furthermore, the middle-class mothers' combination of relative affluence, educational expertise and 'self-certainty' gave them options most of the working-class mothers did not have. While nearly all the working-class mothers talked in terms of 'supporting the school' and 'backing the teacher up' to describe their relationship to schooling, perceiving their role to be a supportive one, many of the middle-class mothers saw their role as a compensatory one. Other mothers, also predominantly middle class, spoke about their efforts to modify the school provision. It was cultural capital, which facilitated this weaving in and out of different roles, and provided the middle-class mothers with options that were not open to their working-class counterparts. This range of options and the ways in which middle-class mothers could draw on them is exemplified in Barbara's account:

> One is the support I give him at home, hearing him read, making him read every night, doing homework with him, trying to get the books he needs for his project. I see that as a support role. The other side, in the particular case of Martin, is where he has had difficulties and finds reading very, very difficult. So a lot of my time has been spent fighting for extra support for him and I mean fighting.

However, later on in the interview she discusses the tuition Martin receives:

> Well he just wasn't making enough progress in school so we decided we'd have to get him a tutor.

Cultural capital is implicated in mothers' ability to draw on a range of strategies in support their children's schooling. As well as financial resources, key aspects of cultural capital such as confidence in relation to the educational system, educational knowledge and information about schooling all had a bearing on the extent to which mothers felt empowered to intervene in their child's educational trajectory and the confidence with which they embarked on such action. For Angie, whose account stresses over and over again the importance of education, her lack of cultural capital, manifested in personal feelings of incompetence, a lack of confidence, and a sense of ignorance in relation to educational matters, mitigated against her embarking on any action with a sense of efficacy:

> I have tried, I really have. I knew I should be playing a role in getting Darren to read but I wasn't qualified. Therefore it put extra pressure on me because I was no good at reading myself, it was too important for me to handle and I'd get very upset and angry at Darren.

In stark contrast to the expectations of contemporary Government policy, working-class mothers who feel ill equipped to engage in educational repair work in the home and lack financial resources are reliant on the school to get the job done. For Josie, in particular, the school had come to be perceived as 'the last and only resort'. Her personal history of immigration, working-class background and academic failure resulted in a sense that there were no other options:

> When I went to see his teacher I was pretty upset about Leigh not reading and it may have come across like 'how come Leigh's not reading. If you aren't hearing him read what are you doing then?' I was maybe coming across like that but what I meant was, can he possibly have some extra time. Can someone hear (sic), for God's sake, give him some extra reading and let him get on because it's making my life harder. I was getting so anxious about him not reading 'cos I couldn't really help him. I'd get upset and frustrated and it wasn't doing Leigh any good because if he can't read what was happening. (Josie)

There is no need to explicate the subtext of inequity lurking beneath Josie's words because Josie goes on to provide her own cogent summation of how increasing reliance on parental involvement within the British educational system is perpetuating educational inequalities:

> You need parental involvement. You need parents to be able to complement what you're doing but that's all it should be. It shouldn't be any more. You see not all

> people speak English, not all parents read and write so how can they help their children at home. They're at a disadvantage anyway so when they come to school they've got to have the help there. You should just be able to say to the teacher "Look, I can't do it. You're qualified, can you do something about it?" without the teacher getting all upset about it. There's a lot of parents who can't, just can't do it.

In Josie's words there is a glimpse at the ways in which ethnicity complicates the workings of cultural capital, at times compounding its impact as in this case, at other times operating in more diffuse ways. Josie's history of immigration makes it difficult for her to comply with teachers' standards of appropriate parent-school relationships. As Lareau and McNamara Horvat (1999) found in relation to African American parents, when minority ethnic parents like Josie display frustration and anger about their inability to meet the school's demands they are dismissed as difficult and unhelpful. Other working-class mothers also resisted a construction of themselves as their children's teachers. This ambivalence about assuming a teaching role was rooted in these mothers' lack of dominant cultural capital and was related to a variety of factors. As well as the complications of ethnicity for mothers like Josie, women's own negative experiences of schooling, feelings that they lacked educational competencies and knowledge, and a related lack of confidence about tackling educational work in the home all played a part. Without these essential ingredients of cultural capital, the time of mothers such as Angie and Josie did not count to anything like the same extent as that of their middle-class counterparts. Yet, it is mothers like Josie and Angie who are being targeted under current educational initiatives despite the fact that they are the mothers with the least resources with which to meet government demands for parental involvement.

Part 3: Ensuring 'You're in Good Company': Mobilizing Cultural and Economic Capital

In the second research project on choice of secondary schooling, Helen Lucey and I have tried to show how choice policies are re-privileging the middle classes after 'the equity blip' caused by the introduction of comprehensives in the 1960s and 1970s (Tomlinson, 2001). Possession of economic, cultural and social capitals, and 'a feel for the game' generated by middle-class habitus, mean their families are engaging in a range of exclusive and exclusionary practices that provide their offspring with real as opposed to the illusory choices of their working-class counterparts. Working-class parents infrequently lived within the catchment areas of the highest achieving schools, but even when they did, powerful barriers grounded in a sense of relative worth often came into play. As can be seen in the quote below, in addition to any other reservations they may have, a lack of entitlement made it difficult for many working-class families to comply with the free market spirit of school choice policies:

> I think it would be nice for her to go to Royden Girls'. I know it's got a very good reputation but then again I thought what if the other girls think she's not good enough to go there. (Mrs Jones)

In contrast, the 'entitled' middle classes are able to use 'choice' to insert their children into 'better schools in better areas' (Brown, 1995; Byrne & Rogers, 1996). The growing policy focus on parents as educational consumers encourages and exacerbates the deployment of middle-class cultural capital in ways which lead to increasing social segregation between schools and pupils. Outlining the choices available to parents under the new UK educational markets, Jordan (1995) describes four main strategies:

- they have powers to influence collective decisions (voice);
- they can choose to live in an area where the local schools provide what they seek for their child (voting with the feet);
- if their child can pass the relevant exams and interviews they can choose a selective school (exit); or finally,
- they can choose to move out of the state system and into private education (self-exclusion).

The disposition to employ one strategy rather than another is influenced by the relative weight of economic to cultural capital in families. Bourdieu uses the analogy of a game of roulette to describe how individuals 'play the educational game':

> Those who have lots of red tokens and few yellow ones, that is, lots of economic capital and little cultural capital, will not play in the same way as those who have many yellow tokens and few red ones. (Bourdieu, 1993, p. 34)

In relation to secondary school transition, self-exclusion nearly always requires high levels of economic capital while exit is often a strategy employed by middle-class families high in cultural capital and relatively low in economic capital. In the study a disproportionate percentage of children applying to selective schools were children of teachers or in lone mother families. There are parallels here with the findings of Edwards and Whitty (1997) that the students who benefited from the Assisted Places scheme came predominantly from families high in educational and cultural capital while low in economic capital. Voting with the feet can be viewed as a disposition of those families in an intermediate position in the educational field. The dearth of middle-class children in a majority of the eight primary schools in the study illustrates how 'voting with the feet' was already an established middle-class practice in both Ashbury and Eastcote. As one middle-class mother commented of her area of Eastcote:

> I know probably 50 people who've moved out. I could think of 50 people who have moved off for better schools. The system's now determined by where you can afford to buy a house to get into a school.

Peter failed three selective school examinations. The only non-selective state school option he and his family were prepared to consider was Westbury, a high performing, non-selective comprehensive, but too far away from their existing home to make admission a possibility. At the last moment the family brought a property in the catchment area of this school and Peter obtained a place there. Robson and Butler (2001), in their study of middle-class communities in London, found secondary schooling was the primary motivation for the out migration of middle-class families from Brixton. In this inner city area in South London, 76 per cent of the families with children were considering relocating for the sake of their education and 8 per cent were in the process of doing so at the time of the research study. Many of the middle-class families in the study were also anxiously considering relocation. As Mrs Tennison commented:

> I actually feel less inclined to send her to a local school. Now it feels less of a good option really . . . I've been thinking about could we move. It would be difficult. I mean so many people have moved from this area.

A significant number of the middle-class families in the study were sufficiently rich in economic capital to contemplate moving in order to ensure that they were in the catchment area of a 'desirable' school. 'Desirable' in this context invariably meant a sizeable cohort of middle-class children. A recent issue of *The Sunday Times* 'Parent Power' (Elkin, 2003) advises its middle-class readers 'Even if your child is still in the early years of primary school start thinking about secondary education now and consider moving house immediately. You'll be in good company'.

Exit is another middle-class strategy at the primary-secondary transition stage. Middle-class parents, especially those rich in cultural capital but not rich enough in economic capital to exercise 'choice by mortgage', seek to bypass what they perceive to be the failings of the state system by entering their child for selective school exams. Only 33 Year 6 children out of the original sample of 454 took entrance exams for one or more selective schools, (although they represented almost a third of the middle-class children in the sample). All but one of the 33 were from professional middle-class families. Mrs Millar's rationalization below is typical of their reasoning for choosing selective schooling:

> I thought, because the exam results at the local school really weren't very good at all, and I didn't want her to be in an atmosphere where only 38 per cent of children got 5 good GCSE passes. And I didn't want her to be in an atmosphere of not being able to achieve the basic minimum, that is way below the national average. Children who want to learn should be surrounded by other children who want to learn as well, that's why we've put her in for selective schools.

Underlying such middle-class narratives on secondary school choice is an implicit, and sometimes explicit, sense of their own child's specialness; of children being too clever and able to go to local state schools. As this mother goes on to assert 'Latymer and Alice Owen (two extremely high achieving selective schools) are the only schools reasonably clever children can go to'. Here we see cultural capital operating again as a sense of entitlement, in this case as a sense of specialness, the barely articulated feelings that you and your family 'are more deserving than most'! We can glimpse below the reproductive aspects of all this, of how a sense of entitlement like many aspects of cultural capital is inherited:

> Mrs Douglas: If he got into either of the selective schools it would be fantastic really because he would be guaranteed a place at university.
> Mr Douglas: And King William's is very much a super traditional grammar school—you couldn't get more—it's just like the one I went to.

Threaded through these examples cultural capital can be seen in operation, not just as a disposition to choose but also as the ability to get the choices one wants. In contrast, the vast majority of working-class families either recognized existing exclusions, as Mrs Jones did, excluding themselves from places where they were already excluded or made risky choices that inevitably failed (see Reay & Lucey, 2003).

Finally, self-exclusion is a possibility only for those families rich in both cultural and economic capital, unless children do well enough in entrance exams to merit a scholarship, an achievement which would suggest particularly high levels of cultural if not economic capital. Only a tiny number, two to three middle-class children in the sample, moved across from the state to the private sector. (This was because most middle-class families living in the two areas who were considering private schooling had already moved their children before the stage of secondary school transfer). Mr Robinson first attempted to get Gregory into a high-achieving school for boys despite living well outside the catchment area. As Mr Robinson insisted 'it's the only school in the area we can see him being happy in'. When Gregory's appeal for a place at Welland Boys' failed, the family decided 'the state system isn't going to work for Gregory' and sent him instead to a progressive, fee-paying boarding school outside London.

Part 4: Gifted and Talented Programmes: A Way of Recognizing Middle-class Cultural Capital in Working-class Schools?

The examples above all suggest a close relationship between cultural and economic capital, but that was not always the case. In the ESRC (Economic and Social Research Council) Teaching and Learning programme the author has been involved in, the focus was on social class in the classroom. It was found that in relation to Gifted and Talented (G&T) programmes even when working-class children were recruited on to the programmes they never stayed, nearly all dropping out within the first term. In interviews with the working-class 'withdrawers' they all talked about feeling awkward and out of place in the G&T groups claiming that: 'it's not my sort of thing' 'Its for really clever children' none of my friends go so I felt all on my own' 'it's really for posh kids'. The only two working-class children who seemed to be thriving in the G&T's and were still in the group two years after the initial start date were Navid and Yussef. It was initially thought that they were working class because that is what their teacher said they were, but when there was a deeper look, their social positioning was far more complex. Navid, Iranian, and Yussef, Nigerian, were both born in their countries of origin but moved to the UK with their families when they were babies. Both families are now poor and subsisting on state benefits. They also live on one of the most demonized council estates in the area. As a consequence Navid and Yussef have learnt to do 'working-class lad' very well. But that is not all they do. They are cultural omnivores (Peterson & Kern, 1996), dipping and mixing the elite cultural tastes of their families with the more univore tastes of the working-class children in their school. All four parents are university educated and are clearly working with very different educational horizons for their children than the working-class parents living in the area. Yussef and Navid may have access to little economic capital but they maintain a strong sense of entitlement and academic confidence, the legacy, it is suggested, of their parents' cultural capital. While none of the working-class boys or girls originally assigned to the group have managed to survive the designation of being a 'G&T', Navid and Yussef are both thriving in the group apparently without having to pay the costs in terms of wider working-class peer group censure. In order to make sense of their success in fitting into both the G&Ts and retaining status among the working-class peer group, there is a need to focus on both their assets of cultural capital and their lack of economic capital. It is a mixture that paradoxically works very well for them in the context of inner city working-class schooling. They combine the cultural resources to cope with both the academic demands and social interaction within the Gifted and Talented group with enough 'rough boy street cred' never to fear being made fun of. The example of Navid and Yussef illustrates how cultural capital can work without the support of economic capital, but it is important to reiterate that Navid and Yussef were the only working-class children who succeeded in Gifted and Talented programmes across the eight primary schools research was carried out in and they were not even working class.

It can be argued that the Gifted and Talented programme is primarily about recognizing and rewarding dominant cultural capital despite Government rhetoric to the contrary. The norm is, as has been shown through data from the other research studies, for cultural capital to be working in conjunction with economic capital, although, as Bourdieu asserts, the disposition to employ one educational strategy rather than another is influenced by the relative weight of economic to cultural capital in families.

Conclusion

The new educational marketplace and the policies underpinning it are allowing the growing middle classes to either re-establish their historic educational advantages or newly achieved status positions. Educational policy in relation to state schooling is accelerating away from the more egalitarian, radical stances of the 1960s and 1970s—child-centred education and comprehensive education (Tomlinson, 2001). There is now a growing synergy between middle-class cultural capital and education policy. This is more than a process of education policy recognizing and responding to middle-class cultural capital. The agentic nature of contemporary middle-class parenting is central to the processes at play (Ball, 2003). As asserted at the beginning of this article, the mobilization of middle-class cultural capital both feeds into and has been fuelled by policy initiatives that prioritize the role of parents in the education of children. In particular, the policy emphasis on parental involvement in schooling, and initiatives such as the Gifted and Talented programme, work to maximize the potential of the already advantaged and are exacerbating class inequalities in education. More generally, the mobilization of cultural capital through educational policies relating to school choice and assessment and testing have generated increasing segregation and polarization both within and between schools (Reay, 2004a).

Therefore, can educational policies counteract the strategies of the middle classes to ensure their continuing advantage? Policies such as Gifted and Talented, in common with policies to increase working-class access to higher education, have a number of contradictory, clashing effects. Whilst nominally directed at 'the bright underachieving' working classes they are highly susceptible to becoming yet another vehicle for middle class 'over-achievement'. Over 30 years ago Bernstein (1970) wrote that education cannot compensate for society and his words still ring true for the 21st century. There needs to be far reaching changes across society and not just within the educational system. The issue is not simply one of the right educational strategies and sufficient cultural and economic resources. While cultural capital brings with it both a propensity and the resources to play the educational game effectively, it does not determine behaviour in the educational field. Elsewhere, the author has begun to focus on middle-class parents who attempt to 'act against self-interest' (Reay, 2004b); those middle classes who, in spite of high levels of both economic and cultural capital, actively invest in inner-city comprehensive schooling. With Sayer (2004), the author would argue very strongly that this is an issue of hearts and minds, a question of ethics and moral principles, just as much as it is an issue of capitals and strategizing. It goes right to the heart of what it means to be 'a middle-class parent'. Currently all the dominant educational discourses celebrate 'the individualized, rational, self interested middle classes'. There is a desperate need to rehabilitate other, more re-distributory ways of mobilizing cultural capital other than 'getting the best for your own child'; to harness both cultural and economic capital to the revitalization of 'the common good'.

Note

[1] Increasingly, the working classes are caught up in dominant discourses of parental responsibility for children's education and there has been a corresponding growth of working-class anxiety and involvement in children's schooling, but it has yet to match the intensity of middle-class anxiety and involvement.

References

Aschaffenburg, K., & Maas, I. (1997). Cultural and educational careers: The dynamics of social reproduction. *American Sociological Review, 62*, 573–587.

Ball, S. (2003). *Class strategies and the education market: The middle classes and social advantage.* London: Routledge Falmer.

Beck, U. (1992). *The risk society.* London: Sage.

Bernstein, B. (1970). Education cannot compensate for society. *New Society*, 26 February.

Bourdieu, P. (1977). Cultural reproduction and social reproduction. In J. Karabel & A. H. Halsey (Eds.), *Power and ideology in education.* New York: Oxford University Press.

Bourdieu, P. (1986a). The forms of capital. In J. G. Robinson (Ed.), *Handbook of theory and research for the sociology of education.* New York: Greenwood Press.

Bourdieu, P. (1986b). *Distinction*. Cambridge: Polity Press.

Bourdieu, P. (1991). *Language and symbolic power*. Cambridge: Polity Press.

Bourdieu, P. (1993). *Sociology in Question*. London: Sage.

Brain, K., & Reid, I. (2003). Constructing parental involvement in an education action zone: Whose need is it meeting? *Educational Studies, 29*(2/3), 291–305.

Brown, P. (1995). Cultural capital and social exclusion: Some observations on recent trends in education, employment and the labour market. *Work, Employment and Society, 9*(1), 25–51.

Byrne, D., & Rogers, T. (1996). Divided spaces: Divided school. *Sociological Research Online, 1*(2). Retrieved from http://www.socreline.org.uk.socreline/1/2/3.html

Department of Education and Science. (DES) (1985). *Better schools: A White Paper*. London: HMSO.

Department of Education and Science (DES) (1986). *Education Act*. London: HMSO.

Department of Education and Science (DES) (1988). *Education Reform Act*. London: HMSO.

Department for Education and Employment. (DfEE) (1997). *Excellence in schools*. London: HMSO.

Dumais, S. A. (2002). Cultural capital, gender, and school success: The role of habitus. *Sociology of Education, 75*, 44–68.

Edwards, A., & Warin, J. (1999). Parental involvement in raising the achievement of primary school pupils: Why bother? *Oxford Review of Education, 25*(3), 325–341.

Edwards, T., & Whitty, G. (1997). Specialisation and selection in secondary education. *Oxford Review of Education, 23*(1), 5–15.

Elkin, S. (2003, November 9). How to get a coverted place for your child. *The Sunday Times* Parent Power Supplement, p. 4.

Ganzeboom, H. B. G., De Graaf, P. M., & Robert, P. (1990). Reproduction theory on socialist ground: intergenerational transmission of inequalities in Hungary. In A. L. Kalleberg (Ed.), *Research in social stratification and mobility, Vol. 8*. (pp. 3–84) Greenwich, CT: JAI Press.

Jordan, B. (1995). *A Theory of Poverty and Social Exclusion*. London: Polity Press.

Lareau, A., & McNamara Horvat, E. (1999). Moments of social inclusion and exclusion: Race, class and cultural capital in family-school relationships. *Sociology of Education, 72*, 37–53.

Lareau, A., & Weininger, E. (2003). Cultural capital in educational research: A critical assessment. *Theory and Society, 32*(5–6), 567–606.

Mahar, C. (1990). Pierre Bourdieu: The intellectual project. In R. Harker, C. Mahar & C. Wilkes (Eds), *An introduction to Pierre Bourdieu*. London: Macmillan.

McNamara, O., Hustler, D., Stronach, I., Rodrigo, M., Beresford, E., & Botcherby, S. (2000). Room to manoeuvre: mobilising the 'active partner' in home–school relations. *British Educational Research Journal, 26*(4), 473–490.

Merttens, R., & Vass, J. (1993). *Partnership in maths: Parents and schools*. London: Falmer Press.

Mohr, J., & DiMaggio, P. (1995). The intergenerational transmission of cultural capital. *Research in Social Stratification and Mobility, 14*, 167–199.

Moore, R. (2004). Cultural capital: Objective probability and the cultural arbitrary [Special Issue on Pierre Bourdieu]. *British Journal of Sociology of Education, 25*, 4.

Office for Standards in Education. (Ofsted) (1994). *Reporting pupils' achievements*. London: HMSO.

Office for Standards in Education. (Ofsted) (1995). *Guidance on the inspection of nursery and primary schools*. London: HMSO.

Peterson, R., & Kern, R. (1996). Changing highbrow taste; from snob to omnivore. *American Sociological Review, 61*, 900–907.

Reay, D. (1998). *Class work: Mothers' involvement in their children's primary schooling*. London: University College Press.

Reay, D. (2000). A useful extension of Bourdieu's conceptual framework? Emotional capital as a way of understanding mothers' involvement in children's schooling. *Sociological Review, 48*(4), 568–585.

Reay, D. (2004a, forthcoming). Mainly roughs and toughs: Class, race and representation in the inner city. *Sociology*.

Reay, D. (2004b, forthcoming). *Middle-class metropolitan habitus and dilemmas of educational choice.* Paper to be presented at The British Educational Research Association Conference UMIST, Manchester September 2004.

Reay, D., & Lucey, H. (2003). The limits of choice: Children and inner city schooling. *Sociology, 37*(1), 121–142.

Reynolds, D., & Cuttance, P. (eds) (1992). *School Effectiveness: Research, Policy, Practice.* London: Cassell.

Robson, G., & Butler, T. (2001). Coming to terms with London: Middle-class communities in a global city. *International Journal of Urban and Regional Research, 25*(1), 70–86.

Sayer, A. (2004, forthcoming). *The moral significance of class.*

Skeggs, B. (1997). *Formations of class and gender.* London: Routledge.

Sullivan, A. (2001). Cultural capital and educational attainment. *Sociology, 35*, 893–912.

Tomlinson, S. (2001). *Education in a post-welfare society.* Buckingham: Open University Press.

Fields and institutional strategy: Bourdieu on the relationship between higher education, inequality and society

Rajani Naidoo

This paper takes as its focus the concept of 'field', which has received relatively less attention than Bourdieu's other concepts such as 'cultural capital' and 'habitus' in the sociology of education. The development of the concept is outlined to present Bourdieu's understanding of higher education as a field consisting of cognitive and structural mechanisms that mediate sociopolitical and economic forces while simultaneously reproducing fundamental principles of social stratification. As an illustration of its widespread application, Bourdieu's framework is applied to develop an analytical understanding of institutional strategies developed by South African universities during a period of political instability. Drawing insights from the South African case study and Bourdieu's empirical research, the article concludes that Bourdieu's theory may be seen to have transcended more simplistic conceptions of universities as closed systems detached from the sociopolitical complex or as mere reflections of external power relations. However, the strict relational nature of Bourdieu's framework and his concept of the 'arbitrary' have placed limits on the extent to which his theory can offer a more in-depth account of the relationship between higher education and society.

Introduction

At the heart of Bourdieu's work on higher education has been his desire to expose higher education as a powerful contributor to the maintenance and reproduction of social inequality. This overarching focus has led to a significant theoretical and empirical contribution to sociological understandings of the relationship between universities and society. Bourdieu has attempted to achieve an 'unveiling' of the functioning of higher education through his development of the core concepts of 'field', 'capital' and 'habitus'. While these constructs function fully only in relation to one another, this paper has, as its focus, a critical exploration of the concept of 'field'.

It begins by presenting Bourdieu's theoretical framework to examine how the concept captures the sense of higher education as a force that mediates, and at the same time reproduces, fundamental principles of social classification. As an illustration of its widespread application, the framework is applied to develop an analytical understanding of divergent admission policies developed by South African universities during a period of political instability. Drawing insights from this study and Bourdieu's empirical research, the strengths of the field concept are outlined. In the final section, limitations as well as directions for further development are presented.

The field of higher education

According to Bourdieu, social formations are structured around a complex ensemble of social fields[1] in which various forms of power circulate. The relative autonomy of fields varies from one period to another, from one field to another and from one national tradition to another (Bourdieu, 1993). In much of Bourdieu's research and the work of others drawing on his framework (see, for example, Grenfell & James, 1988; Robbins, 1993; Delanty, 2001), the intellectual field of university education is conceptualized as a field with a high degree of autonomy in that it generates its own values and behavioural imperatives that are relatively independent from forces emerging from the economic and political fields.

The field is structured in hierarchy in the sense that agents and institutions occupy dominant and subordinate positions. These positions depend on the amount of specific resources that are possessed in relation to other occupants. Bourdieu refers to these field-specific resources as 'capital'. Capital may be viewed as the specific cultural or social (rather than economic) assets that are invested with value in the field which, when possessed, enables membership to the field.[2] The type of capital operating in the field of university education is an institutionalized form of cultural capital that has generally been termed 'academic' capital. In some instances (see *Homo Academicus*; Bourdieu, 1998), Bourdieu distinguishes between two forms of capital: 'academic capital', which is linked to power over the instruments of reproduction of the university body; and 'intellectual' or 'scientific capital', which is linked to scientific authority or intellectual renown. In other instances, however (for example, in *The State Nobility*; Bourdieu, 1996), the two definitions appear to merge and 'academic capital' is defined as an institutionalized form of cultural capital based on properties such as prior educational achievement, a 'disposition' to be academic (seen, for example, in manner of speech and writing), and specially designated competencies. It is in this second sense that 'academic capital' is used in this paper.

Bourdieu develops an understanding of the operation of practices occurring in higher education by the use of the concept 'strategy'. which is understood as a specific orientation of practice. In contrast to the way the term is used in ordinary language, where it is based on conscious calculation, strategy in Bourdieu's theoretical apparatus is dependent on 'habitus', which as a result of socialization engenders in individuals a 'disposition' below the level of consciousness to act or think in certain ways; and on the network of objective relations between positions that agents or institutions occupy in the field. A major insight in Bourdieu's work is that even though the location of agents and institutions within a common field presupposes a minimum level of agreement around basic principles, the field of higher education is in fact not a product of total consensus, but the product of a permanent conflict. The manifestations of these strategies are referred to as 'position takings' (Bourdieu, 1993, p. 35). These position-takings are inseparable from the objective positions occupied by the agent or the institution as a result of their possession of a determinate quantity of specific capital (Bourdieu, 1993). Agents and institutions individually or collectively implement strategies in order to improve or defend their positions in relation to other occupants. The importance of this theoretical framework allows Bourdieu to develop what he calls a 'general science of the economy of practices' within which university practices that purport to be 'disinterested', and hence non-economic, can be analysed as 'economic' practices in the sense that they are directed towards the maximizing of symbolic gain (see, for example, Bourdieu, 1993). Bourdieu is adamant, however, that this does not mean reducing such struggles to the logic of economism.

Bourdieu's central concepts of 'field', 'capital', 'habitus' and 'strategy' are brought together in a relational framework to illustrate how it is precisely through this relative autonomy and through the hierarchical structure of the field that the social reproduction function of higher education is achieved. Higher education is conceptualized as a sorting machine that selects students according to an implicit *social* classification and reproduces the same students according to an explicit *academic* classification, which in reality is very similar to the implicit *social* classification (Bourdieu, 1996). While Bourdieu's use of a machine metaphor at first sight appears to confer a self-sufficient dynamic upon social structures (Bourdieu, 1996, p. 52), it is the internal cognitive workings that are of particular interest to him. Acts of cognition are implemented to select and consecrate what is classified as 'academic' and therefore what counts as valid criteria for entry and success in higher education. He labels these categories of perception 'academic taxonomies' (Bourdieu, 1996, pp. 17–19) and defines them as 'principles of vision and division' that structure academic judgements. Bourdieu's (1988, 1996) empirical studies reveal that this academic taxonomy is in fact organized according to the hierarchy of qualities commonly ascribed to the dominant group. The education system therefore designates those endowed with cultural capital, which is generally inherited as a result of social origin, as 'academically talented.' In this way, higher education establishes a close correspondence between the social classification at entry and the social classification at exit without explicitly recognizing, and in most cases denying, the link between social properties dependent on social origin (such as class) and academic selection and evaluation.

It is through the concept of homology that Bourdieu emphasizes the functioning of higher education as a relatively autonomous field that nevertheless contributes to social inequality. He defines homology as a 'resemblance within a difference' (Bourdieu and Wacquant, 1992, p. 106) and the concept appears to apply to both structural and functional qualities of fields. Each field mirrors the social space in having its own autonomous and heronomous poles, its own dominant and dominated agents and institutions, its mechanisms for reproduction and its struggles for usurpation and exclusion. Thus, many of the strategies function as 'double plays' (Bourdieu, 1996, p. 271) in the sense that although these field-specific strategies are not expressly conceived as such nor the product of conspiracy among the dominants in the various fields, they are objectively organized in such a way that they contribute to both the accumulation of field specific capital and to the reproduction of the structure of 'social space', defined by Bourdieu in an under-theorized way as 'class structure' (Bourdieu & Wacquant, 1992).

The higher education system thus acts as a 'relay' in that it reproduces the principles of social class and other forms of domination under the cloak of academic neutrality. It also acts as a 'screen' (Bourdieu, 1996, p. 36) that permits the realization of social classification in guises that allow it to be accomplished invisibly. In this way, universities contribute to the 'misrecognition' and therefore 'naturalization'[3] of structures of domination.

South African universities in transition

In this section of the paper, Bourdieu's theoretical concepts are applied to the relationship between universities and forces for change in South Africa in the period 1985–1990 in order to illustrate their value (see Naidoo, 1999). The period of the study, which directly preceded the negotiated settlement that the Afrikaner Nationalist Government was compelled to enter into with revolutionary black organizations, has been characterized as a 'pre-revolutionary' one (Price, 1991). The dominance of the Afrikaner Nationalist government, which had segregated and hierarchically stratified South African society in line with the policy of apartheid, was challenged by a powerful mass-based political movement, the Mass Democratic Movement (MDM). The MDM, which had close links to the banned African National Congress, aimed to dismantle and replace the structures of 'racial capitalism' with alternative social, political and economic arrangements (Lodge & Nasson, 1991). In an attempt to stem the tide of revolt, the government initiated a series of minor reforms in 1985, which included the lifting of the 1959 legislation that segregated universities according to race.

In this period of political rupture between 1985 and 1990, alternative belief systems from the MDM drew on nationalist and socialist ideology to question the independence of universities from the political context. In a society that comprised 69% Africans and 17% whites, high status universities remained almost exclusively white. The de-segregation of higher education resulted in unremitting pressures on these universities to suspend highly selective meritocratic arrangements and to develop policies based on notions of disadvantage and redress, particularly in relation to African students, who had suffered extreme forms of discrimination under apartheid. Universities were also expected to transform themselves from elite to mass-based institutions. The aim of the research was to analyse the translation of the sociopolitical forces within universities in the development of new admission policies. While the original study focused on a range of forces emerging from the state and capital, this paper will focus exclusively on the forces arising from the MDM.

The South African field of university education

The first step of the research process was to construct the field of university education in South Africa. An analysis of the specific capital that was valourized in the field, the historical evolution of the relationship between the political context and the different types of universities, and their own position-takings, resulted in the field being hierarchically structured into a dominant, an intermediate and a subordinate tier. The dominant tier consisted of white English-medium universities that were set up in the colonial era for the British community. In 1959, under apartheid laws, these institutions were designated exclusively for white students. These universities were research intensive, internationally recognized and offered high-status postgraduate programmes. In the intermediate tier were the Afrikaans-medium universities, also designated white, which were set up by the Afrikaans community during the Anglo-Boer war. Universities that were set up for the different groups of black South Africans were in the subordinate tier. These institutions were poorly resourced, had almost no research infrastructure and offered low level of study such as diplomas (Hendry & Bunting, 1993). The field of higher education was also structured into autonomous and heteronomous sectors according to the degree of state control and the extent to which institutions were able to reject external political determinants and obey the specific logic of the university field. The white English-medium universities were relatively free of direct state control and were positioned in the autonomous sector. They distanced themselves from the political context and, although they opposed the segregation of universities, for much of their history they did not take a formal stance against other aspects of apartheid. They adhered to the internal laws of the field and developed products destined primarily for the intellectual field. The white Afrikaans-medium universities, located in the heteronomous sector, identified with the apartheid political project and contributed to the reproduction of apartheid culture (Davies, 1996). Black universities were also located in the heteronomous sector and were subject for much of their history to direct and violent state control and repression.

In this section, I will draw on material from two case study institutions located in contrasting positions in the field to illustrate how the particular historical development and the internal structure of the field mediated sociopolitical forces. Dominant representations rather than the micro-politics of each university will be presented. In order to capture the processes of change, Bourdieu's theoretical framework was supplemented with methodological strategies based on materialist approaches to discourse analysis. Interviews and institutional documents were therefore discursively analysed to capture the principles and underlying assumptions structuring accounts of admission policy development. This approach will be outlined in later sections of this paper.

The first case study, which appears under the pseudonym Mount Pleasant

University, was an elite, historically white English-medium university located in the dominant and autonomous sector of the field. The second case study, which appears under the pseudonym Freedom University, was a historically black university that was designated for that sector of the black community designated 'Coloured'. Freedom University was located in the subordinate and heteronomous sector and was subject to direct state control. The two universities developed divergent and controversial admission policies in the 1985–1990 period.

Mount Pleasant University

At one level the political crisis appeared to have had an unprecedented impact on Mount Pleasant University's position of independence from the political field. For the first time since its inception, the university issued a public statement opposing apartheid and the Nationalist Government. However, there was less of a shift in relation to admission policies. In the face of increasing pressure for change, the traditional admission policy (hereafter referred to as the Standard policy) was maintained and strengthened. This policy allocated more than 90% of student places and admitted those who achieved the highest scores in the school leaving examination (the matriculation examination). The vast majority of African students who achieved poor grades from racially segregated and inferior schools therefore continued to be excluded.

Documents and interviews, especially at faculty level, reveal a collective denial of social and political factors that might impact on universities, even in a country that appeared to be on the brink of a revolution. The institutionalized belief that entry to the field should be based purely on academic criteria and should be detached from social categories such as race, class or gender functioned to exclude moral and political pressures to address the issue of disadvantage. In addition, in the face of declining numbers of white applicants, a surge in black applications and an improvement in black matriculation results, the university implemented a number of additional policies. The argument was that these policies were necessary because the pool of talent in the country had decreased. A policy to limit undergraduate growth was instituted and the places available in a number of first-year undergraduate courses were reduced. Finally, students for whom English was a second language (which included the majority of black students) were required to take an English-language proficiency test. These policies acted as a further barrier to the admission of black students.

Forces for redress were instead deflected to an adjunct admission route, the Selective policy, which admitted a small number of African students. In the period of study, no more than 1% of places was allocated by the Selective policy and these student were generally admitted to subdegree courses, thereby insulating mainstream programmes from students from non-traditional backgrounds. In one sense, the admission of students on the grounds of ethnicity eroded the strict operation of academic principles. However, the concept of 'academic potential' became part of the institutional discourse and students were admitted depending on their results in a test designed to measure academic potential. The implementation of 'latent' academic ability as a criteria for selection thus displaced the social criteria and re-inscribed academic principles, and indeed academic merit.

The judgements implemented by powerful agents at Mount Pleasant University did not appear to be conscious and direct responses to external forces or, as some commentators have implied, inherent racism on the part of deans who attempted to exclude black students from an institution that was predominantly white. My analysis of interviews indicated that the systems of classification that were implemented appeared to be part of an orientation to conserve institutional arrangements that a new system of admissions could potentially threaten. New criteria were resisted because academics were concerned that an influx of students from poorer educational backgrounds would threaten institutional arrangements such as the proportion of time allocated to research and would endanger the high progression rate of the university. It was feared that these changes would endanger the status of the university in the intellectual field. Although informants vehemently denied any association, analysis of the legitimate academic capital (or what informants understood to be 'typical' students) were found to coincide closely with qualities possessed by students from the white schooling system. Thus, although powerful agents such as deans did not appear to be excluding students in any direct sense on the grounds of ethnicity, their strategic interventions to conserve the traditional properties constituting admissions and to protect traditional academic practices functioned to exclude the majority of African applicants.

Freedom University

The second case study university, which appears under the pseudonym Freedom University, was located in the subordinate sector. Freedom University took the opportunity offered by the political crisis to challenge its status as an ethnic state-controlled university. The university forged an alliance with the MDM that resulted in the university remaining locked in the heteronomous sector. However, the political stance against apartheid and its aim of developing an alternative model of university education attracted a significant number of radical academics with high levels of academic capital. The university's position-taking and the influx of academic capital resulted in the university ascending to a dominant position relative to other black universities in the subordinate sector of the field.

Freedom University challenged the academic principles on which entry to the field was granted. The principle of academic merit, which was represented by dominant universities as fundamental in determining who would gain admission, was systematically eroded. Matriculation results as an indicator of academic merit were regarded as inappropriate in a society in which black students were forced into a poorly resourced inferior school system. A direct relationship between the operation of academic merit, the exclusion of black students and the system of apartheid was construed, and informants implied a collusion between the elite white universities and the government in maintaining a racial hierarchy in South African society.

Admissions strategies drew on discourses embodying the notion of 'redress' and 'rights' from the political field to construct new categories of admission and to argue that admission policies should compensate those who had been denied university access through apartheid policies. The university developed a non-selective and open admissions policy termed the 'Peoples Admission Policy', through which all students who met the statutory conditions for entry to higher education were accepted. In addition, in contrast to policy trends at other universities, Freedom University increased student growth.

In 1989 the university acknowledged that the rapid growth rate had placed unbearable pressures on university staff and facilities. A new admission policy was developed that incorporated two mechanisms. The first mechanism, which was presented as a continuation of the open admission policy, consisted of computerized random selection through which 80% of student places were allocated. The second consisted of the application of various criteria through which the remaining 20% of student places were filled. Social criteria such as race, class and gender were applied. In addition, all students who showed 'academic achievement' were automatically admitted as part of the 20% of accepted students.

At one level, the policy developed in 1989 drew directly on political discourses to replace the academic criteria that were dominant in the field with criteria based on principles of random and social selection. At the same time, however, academic principles were re-introduced by automatically selecting students who had achieved high matriculation grades. My analysis of the representations of the divergent classificatory principles underlying selection criteria revealed an almost complete absence of any recognized relationship of contradiction between the two policy discourses. For example, when discussing student selection through social criteria, the matriculation score was presented as an inappropriate measure. When discussing criteria based on academic skills, the matriculation score was presented as an appropriate indicator of success at university. This perhaps emphasizes the fact that individuals are structured by the field while continuing to structure it. However, one consequence of the ambiguity of the admission policy was that it led to different groups of students claiming the 'right' to be prioritized for admission on the basis of either possessing good academic grades or possessing attributes of greater social disadvantage relative to other students. These challenges to admission policy that led to student strikes and other political action contributed to the crisis that engulfed the university in the 1990s.

A mediating field

The strategies developed by these two universities must be situated in the specific context of the 'pre-revolutionary' political situation, during which mechanisms maintaining the relative autonomy of the field of university education from the sociopolitical context appeared to be partially and temporarily suspended. Alternative belief systems drawing on socialist principles became embedded in popular consciousness and the principles structuring the field of university education were challenged. In this context, Mount Pleasant's position of dominance was threatened by the actions of a subordinate institution. The threat posed by Freedom University may be illustrated by the fact that each Dean at Mount Pleasant, and the majority of senior managers, with no prompting from the interviewer, launched an attack on the admission policies developed by Freedom University.

The findings also point to the importance of the historical evolution of relationships between institutions and the sociopolitical complex. Such relations influenced the extent to which specialized structural and discursive mechanisms were developed. The relative independence of Mount Pleasant led to the development of complex discursive mechanisms that were independent from the political and economic context. These mechanisms were deployed to reposition, exclude and restructure political forces in the development of a differentiated but relatively coherent admission policy.

In contrast, Freedom University's close relationship to the sociopolitical complex led to an institutional context that was not conducive to the development of discursive mechanisms that were independent from external social and political discourses. The university did not appear to have recourse to specialized mechanisms that it could deploy in response to the contesting sociopolitical forces impacting on the institution. It appeared to respond to the political crisis by simply excluding or appropriating, rather than restructuring sociopolitical forces that emerged from the political field.

These presented findings also point to the significance of the location of institutions in the internal power relations of the field. The admission policy, which served to publicly codify the appropriate capital required to enter the university field, became a crucial locus of struggle because it served to legitimize or delegitimize the principles underlying the recognition of existing capital in the field. Mount Pleasant's position of structural dominance oriented powerful agents in the institution to relate to external forces in such a way that the institution's position of dominance was protected. Sociopolitical forces were excluded from the standard admission policy, and deflected to an adjunct policy. Further restructuring occurred in relation to the Selective policy to ensure that traditional academic principles underlying admissions were, in the final analysis, conserved. In this way, Mount Pleasant University sought to ensure that the academic principles underlying the recognition of legitimate capital in the field was maintained and that its position of structural dominance was protected.

The development of the admission policy at Freedom University can be seen as a strategic action taken by an institution located in the dominant fraction of the subordinate sector of the field of higher education during a time of social upheaval. External political principles were imported to erode the academic principles upon which power relationships in the field were based and which placed the university in a subordinate position. However, the growing dissonance between an admissions policy based on social criteria and the internal logic of the field, as well as the university's own ascendance in the field, also resulted in the appropriation of discourses around academic merit that were valourized by dominant institutions. The absence of an overarching institutional discourse that could restructure such discourses in a coherent manner was unavailable, resulting in an ambiguous and contradictory admissions strategy.

The extent to which the two case study universities contributed indirectly to the reproduction of the racial hierarchy in South Africa is a complex one. At one level, a simple indicator of the extent to which such policies reproduced racial stratification may be measured by the proportion of students classified African, originating from the most dominated sectors of society, that were admitted to each university. In this sense, the admission policies of Mount Pleasant University, which admitted mainly white students from dominant positions in society, while largely excluding African students, can be seen to have contributed to reproducing fundamental racial divisions. The policies developed by Freedom University, on the other hand, which resulted in the largest enrolment of African students relative to all other non-African universities in the country, can be seen to have challenged racial divisions.

What is unclear, however, is the extent to which each university contributed to placing students in more privileged positions in society at the point of graduation. The admission strategies developed by Mount Pleasant University could have enabled an elite minority of African students to access more privileged positions in society. On the other hand, while Freedom University provided access to large numbers of African students, what is debatable is whether such students were placed in a more privileged position in the social structure of South African society. Researchers have indicated, for example, that alternative educational strategies may inadvertently entrench the hierarchy between privileged and disadvantaged students in capitalist society by conferring on students a qualification that is not recognized as sufficiently 'academic' by other universities or by employers (see, for example, King, 1993). In this sense, the admissions strategies developed by Freedom University, which were constructed by the direct appropriation of political principles, may not have resulted in a redistribution of academic capital to Black students; nor did such strategies lead to the development of an alternative type of capital that could erode the dominant principles of academic capital to function in a relatively autonomous field.

The contributions of field theory

The South African case study, Boudieu's research and research located in other national contexts (see, for example, Tomusk, 2000; Deer, 2003) indicate the significant contribution of the concept of 'field' to sociological understandings of the relationship between higher education and society. Research has tended to conceptualize universities as closed systems that are detached from the sociopolitical complex or as reflections of external power relations within a determinant social structure. More recently, a number of sociologists have placed the relationship between sociopolitical forces and universities firmly on the agenda. However, a conceptual apparatus through which the macro forces and institutional practices could be analytically related has not been adequately developed. Researchers have in general theorized two conceptual levels: the one level that sees policy as being determined at the level of macro-social relations, and a second level that allows considerable explanatory autonomy to human agency within institutions. The relationship between the two often appears to be either largely arbitrary or, alternatively, the macro forces appear to provide the theoretical backdrop while the analysis at the level of the institution provides descriptive evidence for the grand theoretical framework. The incorporation of Bourdieu's framework, by conceptualizing universities as existing in specialized fields, alerts researchers to the interaction of external forces with the logic and structure of the field of university education and illustrates how external determinants may be restructured, repelled or even reversed. Theoretical representations of universities as existing independently of one another are also replaced with an understanding of universities as imbedded in complex relations of power with other universities. University responses can therefore be conceptualized as a type of 'position-taking', which is dependent on the institutions structural position in the field and which is oriented to safeguarding or improving this position. Bourdieu's theoretical constructs therefore make a significant contribution to understanding, first, the relationship between macro sociopolitical forces and universities and, second, why institutions within the same system develop divergent strategic responses to external pressures.

Bourdieu's 'field' concept also has particular ramifications for the relationship between the massification and democratization of higher education. Bourdieu's work illustrates that it is precisely because the field of higher education consists of institutions that are classified in hierarchy that it can fulfil this classificatory function. Through acts of subjective and objective selection, a high proportion of students originating from different regions in social space are selected by institutions that traditionally supply the very same regions of social space. The structuring of the field of higher education, while establishing internal homogeneity in terms of social origin and disposition within each institution, establishes stark differences in social origin and therefore disposition between the student and staff populations in institutions positioned at different levels of relative hierarchy. It is therefore not individual universities, but higher education as a system that contributes to reproducing and legitimating the 'ensemble of distances' that constitute social structure (Bourdieu, 1996).

Limitations and further developments in the work of Bourdieu

In this section, I will outline two important limitations related to Bourdieu's focus on social reproduction that are of relevance to the concept of 'field'. First, Bourdieu's methodological strategies cannot be easily applied to contexts characterized by social conflict and change. In his empirical work, Bourdieu analyses the relationship between educational institutions and political forces by identifying the underlying principles structuring activities in universities and illustrating how these principles are related (and, in fact, reproduce) the dominant principles (mainly based on class) structuring society. This analytical strategy results in two limitations. First, the exclusive focus on the dominant principles structuring society excludes an analysis of social forces that are strong enough to challenge dominant forces but too weak to entirely displace such forces. Second, Bourdieu's mapping of the underlying principles structuring the activities in the field of university education exclusively onto the dominant principles structuring society may be seen to be analogous to viewing cinematic stills exclusively at the beginning and at the end of a sequence of actions—we are not able to view the series of steps by which the initial action relates to the final action. This methodological strategy renders the process by which educational or social principles are produced and reproduced invisible to analysis. By excluding the *process* by which such principles are produced, Bourdieu excludes the key mechanisms by which universities appropriate social forces to reproduce selected principles while excluding and displacing other social forces. His approach therefore leads to less illumination of university practices.

On the other hand, however, Bourdieu's thinking tools do not prevent the incorporation of other perspectives to complement the limitations. One way to ensure that process, contradiction and change are included in Bourdieu's framework is to incorporate materialist approaches to discourse analysis. Such language-based analyses have been adopted by a wide range of sociologists including Rizvi and Kemmis (1987) and Ball (1994). In the aforementioned accounts, policy is conceptualized as emerging from contested relations of power within institutional and social settings, and is therefore the product of negotiation, struggle and compromise. In this sense, policy texts and statements may be conceptualized as ideologically constructed products. Representations of policy will therefore embody, in implicit and explicit form, many of the contradictory and contesting social and political forces that were part of its production. The application of methods of discourse analysis to documents and interview transcripts is therefore likely to reveal the constitutive discourses that structure such texts and is therefore likely to render the processes of policy development more visible to analysis. The incorporation of methods of discourse analysis within the meta-theoretical framework of Pierre Bourdieu (see Naidoo, 1999) therefore makes it possible to analyse two sets of relations: the principles and underlying assumptions structuring various discourses in relation to other discourses and the relationship between the different discourses and the structural positions held in the institutional field within which such discourses are produced.

The second limitation in Bourdieu's general theory of fields is that there is little focus on the internal content of a given field. Li Puma (1993) has stated that Bourdieu holds an 'absolute substantive theory of arbitrariness' to the extent that the content of a cultural product such as a text, a painting or a theoretical development is arbitrary and could just as well have been replaced by an alternative product to serve the same function. All that is necessary in Bourdieu's model is for the cultural product to produce distinction as a means of expressing and reproducing relations of class inequality. In relation to his work on higher education, Bourdieu focuses on structural positions and position takings in the struggle to impose and monopolize academic authority. The content and internal structuring of knowledge is therefore excluded from analysis, and academic products are perceived as mere emanations of the respective positions occupied in the field that relate in a homologous pattern to social structure. This is a key gap in Bourdieu's work. The work of Basil Bernstein (1996) on the intrinsic structuring of knowledge indicates that differential knowledge structures have a decisive impact on the social relations and academic products in any given field. Moore and Maton (2001), for example, drawing on Bernsteins' framework, illustrate how developments in mathematics can be traced to the impact of the discipline of mathematics as a specific knowledge formation, rather than as a mere reflection of field relations. Bernstein's proposition that sociological accounts of the relationship between education and society need to incorporate both symbolic structures and social relations as part of one system for the purposes of analysis is therefore crucial to the further development of Boudieu's framework.

In conclusion, a question that needs to be posed is the extent to which Bourdieu's field concept remains relevant in the context of current developments in higher education. Bourdieu's theoretical and empirical work was developed in the context of a 'social compact' that evolved between higher education, the state and society over the last century and that led to the insulation of universities from direct market pressures (Slaughter & Leslie, 1997; Marginson & Considine, 2000). However, Government perceptions of higher education as a lucrative service that can be sold in the global marketplace has begun to eclipse the social and cultural underpinnings of the social compact. Relatedly, the belief that universities require a relative independence from political and corporate influence to function optimally, which was in turn linked to the need for guaranteed state funding, academic tenure and professional autonomy, has been eroded. These changes have resulted in the implementation of funding and regulatory frameworks that revolve around neo-liberal market mechanisms and new managerialist principles (Avis, 1996; Williams, 1997; Deem, 2001). Such developments have led to a growing and relatively unmediated influence of economic forces on the field of university education, which has in turn resulted in the undermining of cultural capital and the valourization of economic capital.

While Bourdieu has not focused on the growing commodification of university practices and products, his theoretical concepts remain valid in the present context. First, Bourdieu's framework is predicated on the knowledge that the relative autonomy of fields vary from one period to another and from one national tradition to another. The conditions for the relative autonomization or de-autonomization of fields has also been developed and clarified (see Bourdieu, 1992; Vandenberghe, 1999). Second, his insight that the field of higher education is not a product of consensus but the product of a permanent conflict is also important. In an era where both academic and economic forces exert powerful structuring effects on universities, the field of higher education is likely to become the locus of power struggles over the legitimate capital required to attain dominance. Preliminary work on the effects of forces for commodification (see, for example, Naidoo & Jamieson, 2002) indicates that elite universities are more likely to possess the financial and cultural resources to restructure or redeploy forces for commodification in order to re-legitimize academic capital, and so protect their position of dominance in the field. Subordinate universities, on the other hand, which admit students from disadvantaged backgrounds, are more likely to be buffeted by market forces. Bourdieu's framework is therefore likely to continue to play an important role in contributing to sociological understandings of the extent to which commodification is likely to erode or exacerbate social equity.

Acknowledgements

The author would like to thank Madeleine Arnot and Joe Muller for their support and guidance in the development of the empirical work on which this paper is based. The author would also like to thank Hugh Lauder, Ian Jamieson, Graham Thom and the two anonymous referees for their helpful comments on earlier versions of this paper.

Notes

1. The differentiation of the social world from a state of non-division, regarded as characterizing primitive society, to the separation of diverse social functions in more complex society (e.g. scientific thought from religious thought, and art from worship) has previously been analysed by Durkheim. For an illustration of how Bourdieu draws upon and extends the Durkheim's thesis, see Bourdieu and Wacquant (1992, pp. 12–14).
2. Bourdieu defines capital in a formal sense as accumulated labour in its 'materialised' or 'embodied' form, which when 'appropriated' by agents 'enables them to appropriate social energy in the form of reified or living labour' (Bourdieu, 1986, p. 241).
3. Bourdieu explains this effect of 'naturalisation' by proposing that existing relations of domination are maintained because individuals' minds are structured according to cognitive structures that are issued out of the very structures of the world, and thus perceive the organization and distribution of power in society as 'natural' (Bourdieu & Wacquant, 1992, p. 168). Education plays a key role in this process by converting and consecrating, and thus naturalizing, social divisions in terms of both cognitive classifications and material privilege.

References

Avis, J. (1996) The enemy within: quality and managerialism in education, in: J. Avis, M. Bloomer, G. Esland, D. Gleeson & P. Hodkinson (Eds) *Knowledge and nationhood: education, politics and work* (London and New York, Cassell).

Ball, S. J. (1994) *Education reform: a critical and post-structural approach* (Buckingham, Open University Press).

Bernstein, B. (1996) *Pedagogy, symbolic control and identity: theory, research, critique* (London, Taylor and Francis).

Bourdieu, P. (1986) The forms of capital, in: G. R. Richardson (Ed.) *Handbook of theory and research for the sociology of education* (New York, Greenwood Press).

Bourdieu, P. (1988) *Homo Aademicus* (Cambridge, Polity Press).

Bourdieu, P. (1992) *The rules of art: genesis and structure of the literary field* (Cambridge, Polity Press).

Bourdieu, P. (1993) *The field of cultural production* (Cambridge, Polity Press).

Bourdieu, P. (1996) *The state nobility* (Cambridge, Polity Press).

Bourdieu, P. & Wacquant, L. J. D. (1992) *An invitation to reflexive sociology* (Cambridge, Polity Press).

Davies, J. (1996) The state and the South African university system under apartheid, *Comparitive Education,* 32(3), 319–332.

Deem, R. (2001) Globalisation, new managerialism, academic capitalism and entrepreneuralism in universities: is the local dimension still important?, *Comparative Education,* 37(1), 7–20.

Deer, C. (2003) Bourdieu on higher education: the meaning of the growing integration of educational systems and self reflective practice, *British Journal of Sociology of Education,* 24(2), 195–207.

Delanty, G. (2001) Challenging Knowledge: The University in the Knowledge Society Buckingham (Open University Press).

Grenfell, M. & James, D. (Eds) (1988) *Bourdieu and education: acts of practical theory* (London, Falmer).

Hendry, J. & Bunting, I. A. (1993) *Universities in South Africa* (Cape Town, University of Cape Town).

King, K. (1993) *Education policy in a climate of entitlement: the South African Case.* Unpublished discussion paper, (Centre for African Studies, University of Edinburgh, Edinburgh, UK).

Li Puma, E. (1993) Culture and the concept of culture in a theory of practice, in: C. Calhoun, E. Li Puma & M. Postone (Eds) *Bourdieu: critical perspectives* (Cambridge, Polity Press).

Lodge, T. & Nasson, B. (Eds) (1991) *All, here, and now: black politics in South Africa in the 1980s* (London, Hurst and Co. & Ford Foundation).

Marginson, S. & Considine, M. (2000) *The enterprise university: power, governance and reinvention in Australia* (Cambridge, Cambridge University Press).

Moore, R. & Maton, K. (2001) Founding the sociology of knowledge: Basil Bernstein, intellectual fields and the epistemic device, in: A. Morain, I. Neves, B. Davies & H. Daniels (Eds) *Towards a sociology of pedagogy: the contribution of Basil Bernstein to research* (New York, Peter Lang).

Naidoo, R. (1999) *Admission policies and the politics of access: a case study of two South African universities (1985–1990)*, Ph.D. dissertation, University of Cambridge.

Naidoo, R. & Jamieson, I. (2002) Consumerism in higher education and its implications for a high skills society. Paper presented at the *European Conference for Educational Research,* Lisbon.

Price, R. M. (1991) *The apartheid state in crisis: political transformation in South Africa 1975–1990* (Oxford, Oxford University Press).

Rizvi, F. & Kemmis, S. (1987) *Dilemmas of reform: the participation and equity program in Victorian schools* (Geelong, Deakin Institute for Studies in Education).

Robbins, D. (1993) The practical importance of Bourdieu's analyses of higher education, *Studies in Higher Education,* 18(2), 151–163.

Slaughter, S. & Leslie, L. (1997) *Academic capitalism: politics, policies, and the entrepreneurial university* (Baltimore and London, Johns Hopkins University Press).

Tomusk, V. (2000) Reproduction of the 'State Nobility' in Eastern Europe: past patterns and new practices, *British Journal of Sociology of Education,* 21(2), 269–282.

Vandenberghe, F. (1999) 'The real is relational': an epistemological analysis of Pierre Bourdieu's Generative Structuralism, *Sociological Theory,* 17(1), 32–67.

Williams, G. (1997) The market route to mass higher education: British experience 1979–1996, *Higher Education Policy,* 10, 275–289.

Violent youth or violent schools? A critical incident analysis of symbolic violence

KATHRYN HERR and GARY L. ANDERSON

Utilizing critical incidents primarily from a year-long ethnographic study of a single gender middle school, the authors attempt to capture the mechanisms of symbolic violence as described by Bourdieu and Passeron in *Reproduction in Education, Society and Culture* and by Bourdieu in latter publications. Our analysis suggests that problems of persistent social inequality, crime, and incarceration are linked to symbolic forms of violence that occur in schools and that current policies attempting to address these issues are flawed, based on a limited theorization of violence.

> You cannot cheat with the *law of the conservation of violence*: all violence is paid for, and for example, the structural violence exerted by the financial markets, in the form of layoffs, loss of security, etc. is matched sooner or later in the form of suicides, crime and delinquency, drug addiction, alcoholism, a whole host of minor and major everyday acts of violence. (Bourdieu 1998: 40)

Bourdieu's 'law of conservation of violence' is a powerful explanatory tool for understanding the continuum – from symbolic to physical forms – of violence that exists in schools. While violence and school safety are near obsessions in today's schools, the origins of violence are undertheorized. This article will use the law of conservation of violence and the theory of symbolic violence to help explain how violence is generated symbolically within schools, reproducing larger systems of structural violence and spawning local instances of emotional and physical violence (Herr 1999). Our analysis will suggest that problems of persistent social inequality and school violence are linked, and that current policies attempting to address these issues are flawed, based on a limited theorization of violence.

Headlines warn us of the current climate of danger in the culture in which we live. Schools rehearse student lockdowns in anticipation of Columbine-style shootings. Students are scrutinized for weapons and gang colours. State funds for additional counsellors are diverted for the purchase of metal detectors. Additional monies for more youth detention centres and prisons have been allocated should other interventions fail. Courses on violence prevention have sprung up in the curriculums of colleges of education. Professional development workshops for teachers offer instruction on recognizing gang signs and preventing the growth of gangs in schools. School districts debate arming the guards in local public schools so they are evenly matched with the dangers they face.

Males (1998) points out that these fears do not match statistical realities and that the crime rates on the rise are not among minority youth; rather, rising crime rates fall more within white collar crime categories, such as the Enron, Worldcom and other Wall Street fiascos. Yet the lens on youth, particularly minority youth, constitutes what Cohen (1972, cited in Welch *et al.* 2002) terms a 'moral panic', where a 'person or group of persons emerges to become defined as a threat to societal values and interest . . .' (p. 3). Exaggerated claims as to the dangers posed by groups of youth establish this climate of 'moral panic'.

Ironically, some argue, violence may be partly a result of the social policies we have devised to contain it. More than two million Americans are in prisons, which are among the most violent social institutions in the world. Nearly two-thirds of these prisoners are in prison for non-violent (usually drug-related) crimes, but are often schooled in violence on the inside (Parenti 1999). As these prisoners' terms end they return to their economically devastated communities with few social or vocational skills. We will suggest that schools, like prisons, may actually generate violence (although through very different mechanisms) rather than contain it. Although schools are often characterized as a safe oasis in the violence of inner-city neighbourhoods, we suggest that this view is due to an undertheorization of violence and a misperception of apparently orderly schools and classrooms as violence-free.

Thus, while there are exaggerated claims surrounding some forms of violence, other manifestations remain virtually invisible. Bourdieu and Passeron (1990) describe two ways 'of getting and keeping a lasting hold over someone': overt (physical or economic) violence or symbolic violence – censored, euphemized, unrecognized violence. This latter form often occurs, for example, when children are labelled in schools, when women are marginalized through various forms of sexism, or when unequal power relations are hidden through attempts to characterize them as natural. Drawing on critical incidents taken from a year-long ethnographic study of a public middle school experimenting with school-wide, single sex classes (Herr and Arms 2002), we explore how symbolic violence in schools and classrooms is related to physical and structural forms of out-of-school violence.

Pierre Bourdieu and symbolic violence

Bourdieu elaborated his theory of symbolic violence, with Jean-Claude Passeron, in sometimes excruciating detail, in *Reproduction in Education, Society and Culture*, a book that appeared in French in 1970 and in English in 1977.[1] In his preface to the 1990 second edition of the book, Bourdieu discusses the ways his theory of symbolic violence was misunderstood and conflated with more reductionist Althusserian theories of 'state ideological apparatuses' that were popular when the English translation of his book came out. In American educational scholarship, the book has frequently been cited as a negative example of Marxist overdeterminism; it was often lumped together with another book popular at the time, Bowles and Gintis' (1976) *Schooling in Capitalist America*, also a widely misunderstood and little read, but much cited, book about social reproduction. These analyses were used as a foil for theories of resistance which argue that previous Marxist work failed to understand the role of human agency in social reproduction.

Without entering into a lengthy debate about the relationship between the social scientist's identification of social regularities, on the one hand, and the phenomenological experiences of social subjects, on the other, suffice it to say that Bourdieu's theory of symbolic violence is more theoretically rich and generative than has been portrayed by its detractors. For this reason, we will cite at some length excerpts from his theory, so that the reader can appreciate the complexity of a theoretical perspective too often reduced to an explication of merely one of its concepts ('cultural capital' or 'habitus'), stripped from the theoretical richness of his exposition on symbolic violence in this early work.

A major tenet of the *Reproduction in Education, Society and Culture* was the idea that the social reproduction of privilege from generation to generation could partly be understood in economic terms (tax codes, inheritance laws, the appropriation by capitalists of the surplus value of workers' and women's labour, etc.), but that the rarity of social class upward mobility during most historical periods had to be partly understood also in cultural terms. The book lays out the subtle and usually unconscious mechanisms through which dominant groups in society make their own particular form of cultural capital appear to be the natural way of being in the world. Thus, taking arbitrary cultural capital (e.g. white skin, a particular way of pronouncing words, a manner of dress) which has no inherent superiority and succeeding in imposing it as a dominant social norm through social institutions, particularly through formal schooling (and more recently the mass media), represents, according to Bourdieu, a form of 'symbolic violence'.

Bourdieu and Passeron (1990) describe how symbolic violence is accomplished through ongoing *pedagogical work*. This pedagogical work is done through childrearing, which he calls *primary pedagogical work* or through other social institutions outside the family, such as formal schooling, mass media, etc., which he describes in the following passage:

> Insofar as it is a prolonged process of inculcation producing internalization of the principles of a cultural arbitrary in the form of a durable, transposable habitus, capable of generating practices conforming with those principles outside of and beyond any express regulation or any explicit reminding of the rule, pedagogical work enables the group or class which delegates its authority to pedagogical action to produce and reproduce its intellectual and moral integration without resorting to external repression or, in particular, physical coercion. (p. 36)

Key to Bourdieu's theory of *social/economic* reproduction is how *cultural* reproduction occurs and, for subordinate groups, the disconnect between the cultural capital they obtain through child-rearing (*primary pedagaogical work*) and cultural capital implicitly valued in formal schooling and the mass media. Thus, in Bourdieu's terms, the 'legitimate addressees' of pedagogical work (primarily in schools) are those groups who already have acquired the dominant habitus through childrearing and other early cultural experiences.

Some scholars use the term 'culturally relevant pedagogy' or 'culturally responsive pedagogy' to describe a pedagogy that is effective with children from low-income and culturally diverse families (Ladson Billing 1995, Gay 2000). However, implicit in their work is a recognition that most dominant teaching and schooling practices have traditionally been culturally-relevant in the sense that they have tended to be congruent with the primary habitus of white, middle-class families.

This primary habitus is inculcated through the 'primary pedagogical work' of early upbringing and is ultimately characteristic of a group or class, becoming the basis for the subsequent formation of any other habitus:

> Because in any given social formation, the dominant mode of inculcation tends to correspond to the interests of the dominant classes, i.e. the legitimate addressees, the differential productivity of the dominant pedagogical work according to the groups or classes on whom it is exerted tends to be a function of the distance between the primary habitus inculcated by primary pedagogical work within the different groups or classes and the habitus inculcated by the dominant pedagogical work (i.e. the extent to which education or acculturation is re-education or deculturation, depending on the group or class). (Bourdieu and Passeron 1990: 46)

Meier (2002) explains how this symbolic violence occurs in schools,

> . . . what the most successful students had going for them was that even in kindergarten, with their hands eagerly raised, they were ready to show off their school smarts. Starting on day one, certain forms of knowledge and skill – the stuff they've eagerly brought with them from home – was confirmed and honoured, thus increasing their self-confidence to take still more risks . . . But many other students never found a replacement for a school and teacher who didn't recognize their genius, who responded with a shrug or a look of incomprehension as they offered their equally eager home truths. They too soon learned that in school all they could show off was their ignorance. Better to be bad, or uninterested, or to just silently withdraw. (p. 15)

Two important Bourdieuan concepts are alluded to in this passage. First, Meier's allusion to the reaction of students who are victims of symbolic violence represent strategies that run the gamut from the relatively passive internalization of their lack of worth to 'being bad', or engaging in forms of resistance discussed at length by Willis (1977) and others.

Second, the shrug or the 'look of incomprehension' captures the spirit of symbolic violence, which is inflicted on students most often by well-meaning, capable, caring teachers. These teachers are often simply incapable of recognizing, much less valuing, the cultural capital the student brings to the classroom. This child's cultural capital, which has high exchange value at home, since it is a product of primary pedagogical work, has little exchange value in a classroom led by a teacher unfamiliar or unappreciative of the child's cultural capital. This is more than a problem of cross-cultural misunderstanding or ignorance, since one's cultural capital is part of one's habitus and is viewed as simply the natural order of things. This is closely related to Bourdieu's notion of 'misrecognition'. Teachers take their habitus for granted 'precisely because [they are] caught up in it, bound up with it; [they] inhabit it like a garment. [They] feel at home in the world because the world is also in [them], in the form of the habitus'(Bourdieu 2000).

In fact, according to Bourdieu and Passeron (1990), it is the very invisibility of the operation of symbolic power that makes it so effective:

> Every power to exert symbolic violence, i.e. every power which manages to impose meanings and to impose them as legitimate by concealing the power relations which are the basis of its force, adds its own specifically symbolic force to those power relations. (p. 4)

In this way, inequitable social relations are maintained not simply through bad teaching, as current school reform efforts assume, but through the everyday 'pedagogic actions' of 'world class', dedicated and caring teachers. This is one reason that much feminist scholarship that promotes an ethic of caring in schools often fails to understand how a caring attitude can function as a velvet glove that serves to obscure the exercise of symbolic violence or even collude in making the dominant habitus seem more universal and natural.

While Bourdieu describes his theory of symbolic violence as it operates at the level of pedagogical action, he also discusses implications for the institutional and systems level. He continuously reminds us that these micro (home, classroom) and meso-level (school) practices of symbolic violence (cultural reproduction) produce macro-level outcomes as they 'contribute to the reproduction of the relations between the groups or classes (social reproduction)' (p. 54). The following example illustrates how symbolic violence operates at the classroom and school levels and suggests why the theory of symbolic violence is a necessary compliment for empirical research into such issues.

Exposing symbolic violence at the institutional level

One of the authors was involved in an evaluation study that served as a cautionary tale about doing empirical work without an understanding of how symbolic violence works to reproduce inequities. Johnson Elementary School was an inner-city magnet school in a large Southwestern US city. Students were drawn from both its low-income, largely Chicano, neighbourhood and from middle-class, mostly white, neighbourhoods from 'the heights'. The school was considered exemplary and magnet school parents stood in long lines to get their children enrolled. The curriculum was arts-centred and classical music was piped into the halls during the school day.

After a few years, some parents from the school's low-income neighbourhood who felt their children were not thriving, approached the district's Director of Research and Evaluation for information on their children's progress. The director initiated an evaluation study of the school, disaggregating achievement outcomes according to whether students were magnet or local students. The achievement outcomes of the neighbourhood students were, as everyone suspected, far below the middle-class, magnet students; however, to their surprise the researchers also discovered that their outcomes were significantly below those of two nearby non-magnet elementary schools serving a demographically similar population. Apparently this highly regarded magnet school was educating half of the student population well and neglecting the other half.

One of the authors was brought in, along with doctoral students from a qualitative research class, to observe classrooms to see if any teachers favoured one group over another. We fully expected to observe patterns that would help us understand how and why the neighbourhood students were marginalized. Elaborate observation protocols were used to identify friendship patterns among students, which students were called on in class, which students were 'engaged' in learning, student seating arrangements, etc. Teachers were interviewed about their knowledge of students, teaching techniques, attitudes, etc. The research team turned up no obvious differences in how students from the two groups were treated. Researchers and community members were at a loss to explain why magnet students were thriving, while neighbourhood children were falling further behind both the magnet students and their demographic counterparts in nearby schools.

While the discrepancy in academic outcomes was widely reported and spurred a change in school administration and the conversion of the school to a dual language school, the reason of why one group of students flourished while another group languished was never fully understood. While no empirical data were produced that directly linked the students' low achievement to symbolic violence, had we entered the field using a framework based on Bourdieu's theory of symbolic violence, we might have designed the study differently. Rather than seek visible signs of differential treatment of children that could be documented through observations and interviews, we might have documented differences in the primary and secondary habitus of teachers, students, and administrators, and instances of well-meaning incomprehension across habituses. Closer attention to the congruence of practices at the classroom and institutional level (such as the choice of classical music in the halls) with the primary habitus of the children might have led us to a better understanding of how symbolic violence operated at this particular school.[2] Such methods would still perhaps be inadequate since, as Bourdieu points out, it is the very invisibility of symbolic violence that makes it so powerful, an invisibility sustained through the misrecognition of the dominant habitus as natural, and therefore legitimate, rather than as a cultural arbitrary.

Bourdieu and the analysis of critical incidents

While empirical studies informed by a theory of symbolic violence represent one way to go about attempting to make symbolic violence visible, another approach is suggested by Bourdieu himself. While the analysis of critical incidents is seldom associated with the work of Bourdieu, his theory of symbolic violence suggests that this approach is a fruitful way into studying the invisibility of symbolic violence.

In his discussion of institutionalized educational systems Bourdieu describes how idiosyncratic forms of pedagogic action are discouraged through institutionalizing and standardizing the inculcation of the dominant habitus, which is not seen as arbitrary, but rather is invested with institutional authority and legitimacy. Given the extent to which the dominant habitus is standardized, institutionalized, and tightly legitimated throughout the educational system, how would one study these invisible forms of legitimation, these non-events (Anderson 1990)?

Bourdieu marshals empirical data that documents the reality of social reproduction in France, and similar data are widespread throughout the US. However, the processes he describes that make the social reproduction of unequal outcomes appear to be a natural outcome of merit, charisma, diligence, etc., are harder to pin down. He suggests a possible method, although this method has been elaborated in more detail by others.

Bourdieu and Passeron (1990) suggest that educational systems, in inculcating students with a cultural arbitrary that is vested with pedagogic and institutional authority, avoid the need to justify or assert in any explicit way their right to do so through processes of institutionalization and legitimation: 'In short the persistence of an educational system proves that it resolves by its very existence the question raised by its existence' (p. 62). The day-to-day, institutionalized practices of schooling appear natural, and this grammar of schooling has persisted for decades, if not centuries. But, according to Bourdieu, cracks appear in its legitimacy, 'when one examines moments in the institutionalizing process when the questioning of the legitimacy of the pedagogical action and the masking of this question are not simultaneous' (Bourdieu and Passeron 1990: 62). Bourdieu uses the examples of the ancient Sophist teachers who,

> proclaimed their educative practice as such without being able to invoke the authority of an institution . . . Similarly, at moments of crises when the tacit contract of delegation legitimating the educational system is threatened, the teachers, placed in a situation not unlike that of the Sophists, are called upon to resolve, each on his own behalf, the questions which the institution tended to exclude by its very functioning. (. . . One teacher finds he is called a Communist for having explained Marxism to the sixth form; another learns he is suspected of religious propaganda for having thought it necessary to explain what the Bible is . . .). (pp. 62–63)

Other authors have expressed a similar understanding of the potential of critical incident analysis to illuminate those institutional moments in which forms of symbolic violence are made a bit more visible as tiny cracks appear in the legitimacy of institutional authority. Institutional cultures carry a 'reality-defining function' (Hargreave 1995, cited in Angelides 2001), with administrators in a legitimating role, where they mediate the social construction of organizational reality (Anderson 1990). Analysis of critical incidents invites a probing into workplace norms that help construct institutional realities and can stimulate reflection on institutional practices, exposing underlying motives and structures. It can be a way of studying the 'invisibility of the phenomenon' and interrupting 'its redefinition as a non-issue' (Anderson 1990: 39).

For example, in the context described above, the discrepancy between the academic outcomes of the children from the low-income neighbourhood and their counterparts in nearby schools, threatened the legitimacy of an 'exemplary' magnet school and opened up the possibility of further unravelling of the operation of symbolic violence at the school.

Definitions of critical incidents vary from those who see them as 'surprises' or 'problematic situations' (Schon 1983), to 'highly charged moments and episodes that have enormous consequences for personal change and development' (Sikes *et al.* 1985, cited in Angelides 2001: 432), to 'mostly straightforward accounts of very commonplace events that occur in routine professional practice' (Tripp 1993: 25). The naming of an event as a critical incident can come from any individual in an institution and signals that an event has occurred that potentially becomes the stimulus for reflection (Schon 1983); it signals a turning point of sorts, provoking a change in the life of an institution or a person working in it (Tripp 1993).

The naming of an event as critical potentially interrupts institutional meaning management and invites reflection on business as usual; for the administrator charged with the role of legitimating institutional practices, the analysis of a critical incident can pose a threat and, ironically, needs to be carefully managed. In this sense then, critical incidents are not 'things' that happen independently of the norms of the institution but rather are a manifestation of the institutional culture; their analysis potentially unearths assumptions that remain largely unexamined or outside the realm of public awareness.

In a further attempt to illustrate how symbolic violence plays out in schools, we produce two critical incidents in the following section, drawn from a year-long study of a public middle school experimenting with single-sex classes. As noted above, critical incidents can document the common-place workings of a school as well as more highly-charged incidents. In the following cases we present two very different classrooms and discuss how two teachers either reinforce or attempt to interrupt symbolic violence in their classrooms.

The incidents are drawn from two different classrooms of eighth grade boys. The school in which they are located primarily draws students from its surrounding low-income neighbourhood and the population of the school is overwhelmingly students of colour (African American, Latino, and Cambodian). The single sex classrooms afforded an opportunity to focus on the school experience of boys of colour. Classes were observed on an ongoing basis and teachers and students interviewed throughout the school year. The following accounts are drawn from these observations and interviews.

Critical incident 1: 'They've been terrible'

Many teachers in the school struggled with their all-male classes and Ms R. was no exception. The classes throughout the school are large, with 35 students jammed into classrooms intended for smaller numbers. Ms R. was initially squeamish about giving permission for observations in the boys' class, explaining 'they've been terrible'. Nonetheless, she did grant permission and as our relationship developed, she often asked for feedback or suggestions. Although departments had instructional coaches who were to be resources for the teachers, they also evaluated the teachers, something both coaches and teachers saw as being at cross purposes. As one coach put it, when he came into the classrooms he felt as welcome as Typhoid Mary.

Ms R. was an experienced teacher, but at the elementary, rather than middle school level; in the suburbs, rather than in an urban setting. A white woman, Ms R. had little experience with students of colour and confessed to being a bit intimidated by the boys in her class, many of whom were larger than her. In fact, there had been a fight in her girls' class the week before and Ms R had cried; one of the girls told her that it was 'almost worth the fight for them to see how much she cares about them'. Ms R. said she 'really, really wants her students to learn' but she has been struggling to create a learning environment in her classroom; it has, in fact, been near pandemonium. Ms P., an African American educational assistant, has been assigned to the room to help out.

The following incident is drawn from field notes of Ms R's class, a 2½-hour math/science block. It is mid-November of the school year. The first 15 minutes are homeroom time and, on this day, all the homerooms are to discuss the school's 'word of the week': respect. Teachers have a lot of latitude regarding how they conduct the homeroom time.

Description of critical incident 1

Boys come spilling into the room, some leaping over desks on their way in. Ms R. insists they go back out and enter the room all over again. Once they are in the room she tells them that today there will be no warnings, that the first infraction will earn them a call home. She switches on the overhead where the word respect is written; the rest of the page is covered up. 'Respect', she announces, 'copy this definition in your notebooks'. She uncovers the rest of the overhead and reads aloud, 'Respect is doing what the person in charge of you tells you to do'. Boys are opening notebooks and looking for writing utensils. Ms R. continues, 'The first thing you've got to learn here is to respect the teaching going on and the learning of fellow students'. She tells them they are not to question assignments and suggests that outside of class they confront those who are 'pulling the class down – talk to them outside of class, tell them what they're doing'. The room is now somewhat quiet and the boys are writing.

Ms R. has written their assignment on the board – to copy pages of the science text into their notebooks. 'The first thing I've asked you to do is a no brainer. Hopefully something will stick in your head'. Ms R. went on to say that the second assignment will be a 'bit more'; it involves looking up a word. Boys are grumbling and one asks Ms P. why they need to copy pages from the book. 'Cause these are her instructions and you can't question what she tells you'. Marvin, one of the students, replies, 'I'm not doing this; it's too much'. Ms P. tells him 'You've got to face reality; you come to school to work. We're not going to discuss this; you're too argumentative'.

The room is quiet. Some boys are not writing at all; they have their heads down on their desks, eyes closed. There's an occasional noise in the classroom but overall it is 'peaceful'. The boy beside me has been diligently copying pages of the science book; he looks to see how much more there is, sighs, puts down his pencil for a little while and stretches his hand. Fifty minutes pass and the boys are writing or dozing. Some are being pulled out of class by Ms R., for some infraction I deduce, since phone calls are being placed to these boys' homes. The phone is near the classroom door and the cord stretches to the outside; the calls home can be overheard in a sort of stage whisper and are a backdrop to the continued copying of the science book.

I notice that a group of boys in the back of the room are stretching to see something outside the window; the window looks out over an entrance to the school and the school's parking lot. I must have looked curious because one of them mouths to me, 'There's cops out there'. The room starts to stir as boys notice the scene outside the window. Finally, Ms P. says 'it's probably the DARE officers; the sixth and seventh graders have DARE'.

Soft murmuring begins in the room; Ms R. reminds them she'll call home. The boys are getting their names on a list on the board to go to the bathroom. It seems like most of the boys want to go to the bathroom and the list grows. More boys stop writing and talk to those around them. Ms R. says, 'Okay, no bathroom!' The boys groan.

There's excitement in the back of the room as the boys watch the unfolding scene outside the window. Sergio, a fellow 8th grader at the school, is being led away by two policemen. The whole room is trying to see what's happening. Sergio gets in the police car and it pulls away. Ms R. calls the room to order, 'Sit up straight! Feet on the floor! Let me see everyone's feet flat on the floor. Everyone put your pencil in the tray . . .'

She begins a math lesson, passing out a math work sheet, but the boys are not paying attention. Ms R. tells the boys 'I can't go any lower in math; make an honest effort to solve them'. But by now the boys are talking among themselves, speculating on why Sergio has been taken away by the police and no one appears to be paying attention to Ms R. who is trying to get them to work on the math work sheets. A boy calls out, 'Hey quiet! Administrators are here!' An assistant principal pops her head in the door; the room is quiet and she moves on.

Epilogue to critical incident 1

Ms R. never returned after the school's winter break in December. An African-American male teacher was hired to take her place; he had previously worked at the youth detention centre and it was commonly thought that he was brought in to restore some order to the classroom. After a few weeks he was fired because he threw one of the boys up against a wall and had his hands around the boy's neck. A third teacher was hired, a young African-American male teacher, who remained with the class for the rest of the school year. Two of the boys transferred out of this class and moved into Mr Y's classroom (described below); in looking back at their classroom experience these boys observed: 'They had three different teachers already because the way the students act . . . they just act up how-they-want-to-act-wise. It's like they don't have no self-esteem for themselves . . . The teachers, they didn't really care. They the one that was getting paid. It wasn't their education that was lost'.

Discussion of critical incident 1

This classroom will sound familiar to those who have spent time in low-income schools. Of all the classrooms observed in this school, this one was only slightly worse than many. Symbolic violence is perhaps exacerbated in this case by differences of race, class, and gender. A white, female, middle-class teacher attempts to teach a group of low-income, male students of colour. However, while these differences undoubtedly contribute to the incomprehension between teacher and students, symbolic violence is embedded in the 'explicit pedagogy' of the educational system. In this sense, teachers are largely interchangeable. According to Bourdieu, an 'implicit pedagogy' consists of those practices that teachers have acquired informally as well as the particular habitus they, largely unconsciously, model for students. In this latter sense, race, class and gender are implicated, but as we saw above, two middle class, African-American men followed the same explicit pedagogy (Character Counts: 'respect', etc.) and one appeared to have the same general view of the students that the white, female teacher had.

Here the symbolic violence is seen in the failure on the part of the teacher to recognize the students' abilities. Through her behaviours and statements, she makes it clear that she does not believe that these students have a primary habitus that provides them with the tools to be high-achieving students. Images are of students with heads on their desks, getting their names on the board for bathroom breaks – anything to get out of the classroom – taking themselves out, in effect; and why not, since the day-to-day dynamic is one that violences and denigrates their sense of selves?

As Ferguson (2001) points out, Bourdieu's concept of symbolic violence

> is particularly useful for an examination of punishment practices as symbolic enforcers of a cultural hegemony in the hidden curriculum. He directs our attention to the manner in which this type of violence operates through taken-for-granted notions of the form and content of 'proper' behaviour overlooked by liberal notions of schooling. For example, 'politeness', in his view, 'contains a politics, a practical immediate recognition of social classifications and of hierarchies between the sexes, the generations, the classes, etc'. (p. 51)

The very means by which the boys take themselves out of the violence – heads down, long lists to get out of the room by going to the bathroom – become incorporated into the punishments of the classroom: 'Heads up! Feet on the floor!' No bathroom privileges. Definitions of respect reinforce dominant rules and privileges without being open for questioning or alternative constructions. All of these are instruments of symbolic violence in this particular class, while serving as a means to create a 'respectful' classroom environment. The police car pulling up outside the classroom window seems an all-too-ready metaphor for the end results of this kind of education; as pointed out at the beginning of this article, all violence is ultimately paid for, 'matched sooner or later in the form of . . . a whole host of minor and major everyday acts of violence' (Bourdieu, 1998: 40).

Critical incident 2: 'Just a regular day'

When an observation I had set up for the day fell through, I spontaneously stopped into Mr Y's classroom before school; Mr Y. readily agreed to let me observe but warned that I would see 'just a regular day'. Mr Y. taught a 2½-hour Humanities block. It was purely chance that I landed in Mr Y.'s classroom but after the first time observing it, I came back again and again, enthralled by the rich learning environment I found.

Mr Y. is a white man in his mid-50s. He is an experienced middle school teacher and when the opportunity came up to work at the school he requested a transfer as he was interested in teaching single-sex classes, particularly the boys. He had read much of the current literature on boys and schooling and, during interviews with me, he often peppered his comments with references to this body of work. Mr Y. said that there was just one rule in his classroom: no one was allowed to interrupt the learning process. In fact, on the first day of school, he convened his class in the auditorium, explained this rule to them, and indicated that should they choose to follow it, they then were free to follow him into their regular classroom.

Description of critical incident 2

Boys were lined up in the hallway outside the room and when the morning bell rang they quickly went in and took their seats. Mr Y. announced that homeroom this morning was SSR (sustained silent reading) and he and the boys commenced to read. There was virtually no interaction during this 15-minute period, with everyone in the room reading.

At 8:15, when SSR was over, Mr Y. offered, 'This is the advantage of getting to be a good reader, of not just little books' and started to tell the boys about the book he was reading: 'It's a book by Frank McCourt, a book about an Irish immigrant' and noted that some of their parents or the boys themselves are immigrants. He explained that, 'in the racial politics of NYC in the late 40s and 50s, the Irish', and he reads from the book, 'were not as low as a PR or a Negro'. He asked the boys what a PR was and one of them supplied 'Puerto Rican'. They discussed racial politics a bit and then Mr Y. read them a brief excerpt from the book, explaining that McCourt was 'just thinking about all these things'. He told the boys that these 'are the kinds of things you can do. McCourt is an excellent writer and was also a teacher for 30 years'.

It was the end of homeroom and time for history. Mr Y. said, 'Paper and pencil out; history books open to page 90'. There was bustling in the room as the boys reached into their desks to get their books. 'Waiting. Still waiting', Mr Y. said. The boys instantly settled down. Mr Y. was poised beside the overhead projector. 'Okay, I have two things, one for the real world, one for decoration'. He turns on the overhead and 'Double Bubble Thinking Map' appeared on the screen. Mr Y. told the boys that the school had determined that notes will now be graphed like this, that each classroom had been asked to use this format. The map consisted of several interlocking circles, with areas to be filled in; it appeared to be a visual means of organizing note taking on a given topic. 'You have to have a sense of humour to go along with this', he remarked to the boys. They briefly went over the format of the double bubble thinking maps and then moved on to 'the real world', a discussion regarding the American Revolution and the creation of the balance of powers in the Federal government and with the power of the states.

Mr Y. began with a review of why the revolution occurred. The boys quickly offered information related to this and there was a sense that they'd gotten it down, that they are remembering this information from another day's work. Mr Y. moved to the overhead and graphed the information they were offering, saying, 'This is one of the ways you'd write it down' to conform to the mapping being asked for by the administration.

They continued the review. William got called on and volunteered, 'I wasn't listening' but Mr Y. stuck with him and William came up with the answer. Mr Y. commented to the class in general, 'Don't sell yourselves short when you know the answer. Just pause . . . and think!' The class continued with this kind of ready give-and-take. It was a lot of information peppered with comments by Mr Y. such as 'it's just a few short years until you're voting', stressing to them why they needed to know how the government works. One student supplied the end of a phrase for Mr Y. who replied, 'Thank you, Chris; it would have taken me an hour to get that out'. Later, when Chris offered another answer, Mr Y. observed, 'Glad you're sitting there today Chris; you keep my brain working'. As the class rolled on, he responds to virtually each boy in this manner, calling them by name, sometimes doing a check-in ('Steve, did you understand what I was saying?'), sometimes underlining a point ('Make sure you get the information down or you're going to be stuck'), and sometimes graphing the material into the double bubble map framework on the overhead, 'translating' the classroom talk into this format.

At one point Mr Y. paused and told the boys that, 'this could be on your writing prompt in January', on the statewide writing assessment in January, that the state has outlined broad areas which may be in the eighth grade writing section. For emphasis, he reread part of the paragraph they'd just finished.

They briefly discussed the writing assessment and the Stat 9s that the class would be taking later in the school year; the whole school was under an injunction to raise test scores and the whole topic had provided a bit of a pressure cooker. Mr Y. pointed out that a lot of white students pick up much of this information 'on their Grandmother's knee', but that, unfortunately, the knowledge the boys brought from their own families didn't appear as part of the testing process. Mr Y. made clear that the testing regime was not an even playing field, in terms of the test questions reflecting the mainstream culture of whites, but concluded with his confidence that they'd do well, that they'd work on these 'valued' areas in the classroom 'so you'll be ready'.

They continued reading and discussing the history text until Mr Y. told them they had about 10 minutes to construct their double bubble maps. As the boys worked, Mr Y. made his way around the room, quietly chatting with a number of the boys. I heard him ask a very thin boy if he had had breakfast today. 'No'? 'Why'? 'There wasn't any cereal in the house'. My Y. asked him if his father would give him money to go to the grocery store. 'Yes'. 'That's good', Mr Y said. He later told me the boy is the only son of a very elderly father; the younger mother died earlier this year. The time for working on the double bubble maps is nearly up; Mr Y. mused aloud that he thought they'd 'post these outside in the hall since the administration likes this kind of thing. This is not for us; it's for the management'.

Epilogue to critical incident 2

'You should have seen us on the playground last year', two of the boys in Mr Y's class commented; 'we were always in trouble, fighting and stuff'. I expressed surprise, since I had often watched them out playing basketball during the lunch recess this year, laughing and playing ball. When I asked them what made the difference, one of the boys observed, '. . . like sometimes if I don't get my feelings out, I start getting mad at everybody and stuff', but that in Mr Y.'s room this year they talk among themselves and he had come to realize that other boys had thoughts, feelings and experiences similar to his own. 'I just talk and tell them my stuff, my business and stuff, and then I just go outside and I'm all happy, all nice. So it's better for me because you never know, it might lead up to a fight or something and I'd end up getting kicked out'.

In addition to this kind of open and expressive atmosphere, the boys felt Mr Y. helped hone their analytic skills to 'read the world'. 'Mr Y. tells us the real deal. He doesn't give us no crap; he just tells us the real stuff, what's really going on in the world'. They have come to believe they have futures, through his constant references to 'when you're in high school . . .' or 'when you're old enough to vote . . .' Because they had futures to protect, it became important to be able to remain in school and do well; in their current experience of school, they felt this was more of a possibility for them.

Discussion of critical incident 2

The boys themselves were linking the open expression on multiple levels that they experienced in this classroom and the diffusion of pent up anger and frustration. Having experienced the spill of their frustration into the playground the previous year – resulting in fights – they were in a good position to contrast that with the learning situation this year. This year, they could actually play on the playground, enjoy a game of basketball. The outlet for expression could come in the classroom, as they found their primary habitus valued, while getting explicit instruction on the knowledge those privileged by the curriculum and educational systems take for granted. They were being let in on the 'real deal' of how the dominant culture works. While this knowledge is not to be confused with being allowed access to privilege or the fruits of a meritocracy, it is a far cry from the symbolic violence they had experienced in school in the past, and, for this year at least, it is a reprieve from the business-as-usual experiences of school.

It is important to note that this instruction took place in a supportive community of learners, where the boys found commonality in their struggles. They had the opportunity to find commonality with each other, to learn that their frustrations and issues were not theirs alone, but also part of the experience of others. At the end of the school year, they organized for collective action when the school perpetrated, from their vantage point, an injustice. They could work toward their own school success while working to interrupt and question business-as-usual school practices. They were able to bring the collectivity they experienced in the classroom to tasks beyond it, acting in concert for change on their behalf and for others beyond their classroom. Just as Bourdieu made the case that 'all violence is paid for' (Bourdieu 1998: 40) and erupts on societal as well as personal levels, we posit that interrupting symbolic violence at one level can potentially ripple through and initiate interruptions across micro, meso and macro levels, displacing business as usual, or at least shedding light on it.

Cultural analysis and social reproduction

Bourdieu's work on symbolic violence is infrequently cited in recent US work on teaching, and learning, and multicultural education that examines culture and student achievement, perhaps because to many he seems frozen in the 1970s, the decade in which his work on education appeared. Bourdieu may also be ignored by many multiculturalists because he is associated with neo-Marxist writers of the same period, like Basil Bernstein, Louis Althusser, Bowles and Gintis and others, who worked to understand how unequal social relations were reproduced through social institutions. Not only did many of these white male writers focus more on social class than on gender and race, they were also often characterized as overly deterministic and structural in their analyses, leaving little room for what came to be known as 'a language of possibility'. While there is not room here to defend these authors, suffice it to say that the focus on a language of possibility has too often resulted in more optimistic, but narrower, analyses and an avoidance of linking micro-processes in schools and classrooms to broader mechanisms of social reproduction.

Moreover, much of the work focused on issues of violence and alienation in schools is framed through traditional psychological constructs, like motivation or needs, such as belongingness and caring (Osterman 2000). These studies focus on behaviour as if it were independent of its socio-historical context. While critique of the ways schools fail to meet the socio-emotional needs of children and adolescents is important, such studies remain embedded in a narrow psychological paradigm that limits solutions to classroom or organizational interventions.

What is lost, then, in even the most sophisticated writing on diversity and school achievement, is the multilevel analysis provided by Bourdieu. Most analyses of race, class, and gender diversity in education leave undertheorized the link to larger macro forces, leaving the reader to infer that if low-income students and students of colour have higher levels of motivation and achievement then they will be more competitive in the, presumably legitimate, meritocratic system, through which good jobs and other resources are allocated. By leaving these assumptions unexamined, much social and cultural analysis in education can become itself a form of symbolic violence. This is even true of much multicultural work that focuses on issues of gender and race.

In laying out his materialist theory of the economy of symbolic goods, Bourdieu is clear that cultural capital is just one in a series of forms of capital that dominant groups and classes use to maintain dominance.[3] Bourdieu's wholistic theory of symbolic violence carefully lays out the mechanisms through which cultural reproduction helps to sustain social reproduction. For all of its indignation, introspection and, often, confrontational style of writing, contemporary cultural analysis in education is often timid about pointing a finger at dominant groups and their mechanisms of control. Without a wholistic analysis of how cultural reproduction links to social reproduction and the needs of a neo-liberal, globalized economy, such work can be easily absorbed into the current 'Leave no Child Behind' legislation and discourse which substitutes rhetoric for resources for poor and minority communities.

Implications for leadership

Mr Y.'s strategies helped students deconstruct the mechanisms of symbolic violence in the classroom. In addition, he helped them access the dominant discourse, demystifying how they are often 'set up' by school experiences that pretend to foster the meritocracy. While this is an empowering practice for students, it can leave them vulnerable to potentially being 'picked off' as individual actors when they begin to critique or express themselves in broader arenas beyond the classroom. When this deconstruction and explicit instruction is combined with the sense of community that the students experienced, it seeds the ground for collective action and political citizenship. Students with this kind of knowledge are rightly viewed as a threat to the legitimacy of the schooling enterprise and this is even more the case when they are a collective force. The question becomes one of how their critique and collective action is received by educational leaders who are charged with the caretaking of the boys and their educational experiences. Is there an equivalent stance that school leaders can take? As credentialed agents of the state, are they even less likely to open up spaces in which the mechanisms of symbolic violence can be deconstructed?

Deborah Meier (1995), the former principal of Central Park East Secondary School in New York, talks about her commitment to produce students who are experienced in the skills of political citizenship. She talks about how the school reacted when students decided to stage a demonstration at City Hall after the Rodney King verdict in Los Angeles. The event was seen as an opportunity for the school to create 'teach-ins' and help students experience this form of civic participation, while making sure they were safe by sending along teachers and giving parents the option of keeping them home the day of the demonstration. Mr Y. was not part of a school culture that encouraged examination of symbolic violence nor the skills of political participation and he was seen more as a threat than as an exemplary teacher.

In the 1970s, theories like Bourdieu's led to critiques of public schooling as agents of social reproduction. More recently, with the threat of privatization, many critical educators are defending public schools and trying to find ways to open up spaces to work critically within them. Meier (1995) defends public schools, but has chosen to work only in small charter schools, where such cultures have a better chance of developing.

More recently Bourdieu suggested that altering symbolic forms of violence will require more than its deconstruction within the scenarios in which it is played out. In regard to masculine domination, he suggested that the perpetuation of domination does not principally reside in the site in which it is most immediately played out – the domestic sphere, but rather in surrounding institutions where it is developed and imposed, opening up a vast field of action for feminist struggles (Bourdieu 2001). Likewise, the classroom and school, while important in a cultural sense, are not the principal sites in which social reproduction is played out, nor are they likely sites for ameliorating all social ills, as current reform efforts in schools unwittingly promise. Just as Bourdieu's theory of symbolic violence involves many forms of capital and many sites of oppression that occur on multiple levels, altering relations of domination will require struggle on many fronts, including, both the critical pedagogical action of committed teachers who understand how symbolic violence operates, and large-scale political struggles, such as the recent global confrontations against the World Trade Organization.

However, programmes that credential teachers and administrators need to prepare committed and critical teachers and administrators who understand the mechanisms of symbolic violence. Interestingly, the two teachers who were observed in the single-sex school and who were the most adept at helping students demystify symbolic violence evoked the names of local university professors they had had in their credential program who inspired them to be critically reflective about their teaching and their understanding of why low-income and minority students fail academically. There is an equal need for supportive principals who are also trained to encourage rather than stifle student critique. Too often the most perceptive and critical students and teachers are framed by administrators as problems, instead of allies, in their efforts to combat symbolic violence.

Fine (1991) using the notion of 'institutional silencing' described what happens to students who are victims of symbolic violence, but who have critical insights into its operation:

> Those students, particularly low-income students, whose lives, self-conscious critique, or even naïve questions pierce the fragile veneer of equal opportunity, typically pay a price . . . They may be sent off to a psychologist for assistance, classified as insubordinate, seen as a cause for a suspension, or labelled – usually for life – as a student with 'special needs'. Some students, especially those who are academically successful, learn to mute their own critique. (pp. 61–62)

Those students who can no longer tolerate the daily forms that symbolic violence takes, flee schools and are channelled into, at best, low-wage work or, at worst, the juvenile justice system and, ultimately, incarceration. Many deal with the hurt of symbolic violence by self-medicating with drugs and alcohol. Fine (1991) provides evidence that school dropouts are generally psychologically healthier, less willing to continue to allow the daily battering of what's left of their identities and sense of self worth.

The consequences, however, are clear. These include the continued social reproduction of the savage inequalities that characterize the US as we move into 21st century, inequalities of income and financial assets that rival the Guilded Age of the 1920s. For poor and minority youth – particularly males, two violent options are the most viable, incarceration or the military. What we have attempted to illustrate is that those two violent options are only one end of a continuum of violence that starts in the schools and in many homes. It is important to keep children safe in schools from daily forms of physical violence; however, addressing symbolic violence in schools will not only provide opportunities for individual and collective empowerment, but will also help to reduce instances of physical violence, in and out of schools. If, as a society, we pay for all forms of violence, as Bourdieu (1998) suggested, then the continued symbolic and structural violence of the schools, the media, systemic corporate greed and corruption – which bolsters dominant group and class interests – assure that the violence, the social and racial inequities associated with crime, gangs, prisons, and the military will likely continue. But there are other alternatives.

Notes

1. Although the book was co-authored, Bourdieu has gone on to further develop and integrate the theory of symbolic violence into his subsequent work. In this article we will refer to the theory of symbolic violence as associated with Bourdieu, while recognizing Passeron's early contribution.
2. Of course, the solution here would not be to eliminate all remnants of the dominant culture. Such a strategy tends to 'ghettoize' the curriculum and leaves the disconnect between primary and secondary habitus intact. A pedagogy is needed that helps student demystify how symbolic violence works, freeing them to embrace their primary habitus while appropriating the dominant one (i.e. to achieve dual identities).
3. Others are economic capital, social capital, linguistic capital, and educational capital.

References

Anderson, G. L. (1990) Toward a critical constructivist approach to school administration: Invisibility, legitimation, and the study of non-events. *Educational Administration Quarterly*, **26**(1), 38–59.

Angelides, P. (2001) The development of an efficient technique for collecting and analyzing qualitative data and the analysis of critical incidents. *International Journal of Qualitative Studies in Education*, **14**(3), 429–442.

Bourdieu, P. (1998) *Acts of resistance: Against the tyranny of the market* (New York: The New Press).
Bourdieu, P. (2000) *Pascalian meditations* (Stanford, CA: Stanford University Press).
Bourdieu, P. (2001) *Masculine domination* (Stanford, CA: Stanford University Press).
Bourdieu, P. and Passeron, J. (1990) *Reproduction in education, society and culture*, 2nd edn (London: Sage Publications).
Bowles, S. and Gintis, H. (1976) *Schooling in Capitalist America: Educational reform and the contradictions of economic life* (New York: Basic Books).
Ferguson, A. A. (2001) *Bad boys: Public schools in the making of Black masculinity* (Ann Arbor, MI: The University of Michigan).
Fine, M. (1991) *Framing dropouts: Notes on the politics of an urban public high school* (Albany: SUNY Press).
Gary, G. (2000) *Culturally responsive teaching: Theory, research, and practice* (New York: Teachers College Press).
Herr, K. (1999) Institutional violence in the everyday practices of school: The narrative of a young lesbian. *Journal for a Just and Caring Education*, **5**(3), 242–255.
Herr, K. and Arms, E. (2002) The intersection of educational reforms: A study of single gender academies in a public middle school. In A. Datnow and L. Hubbard (eds), *Doing gender in policy and practices: Perspectives on single sex and coeducational schooling* (New York: Routledge Press).
Ladson-Billings, G. (1995) Toward a theory of culturally relevant pedagogy. *AERJ*, **32**, 465–492.
Males, M. (1998) *FramingYouth: 10 Myths about the Next Generation* (Monroe, Maine: Common Courage Press).
Meier, D. (2002) *In schools we trust: Creating communities of learning in an era of testing and standardization* (Boston: Beacon Press).
Meier, D. (1995) *The power of their ideas: Lessons from a small school in Harlem* (Boston: Beacon Press).
Osterman, K. (2000) Students' need for belonging in the school community. *Review of Educational Research*, **70**(3), 323–367.
Parenti, C. (1999) *Lockdown America: Police and prisons in the age of crisis* (New York: Verso).
Schon, D. A. (1983) *The Reflective Practitioner: How Professionals Think in Action* (New York: Basic Books).
Tripp, D. (1993) *Critical Incidents in Teaching* (London: Routledge).
Urso Spina, S. (2000) The psychology of violence and the violence of psychology. In S. Urso Spina (ed.), *Smoke and mirrors: The hidden context of violence in schools and society* (Lanham, MD: Rowman & Littlefield), pp. 177–209.
Welch, M., Price, E. A. and Yankey, N. (2002) Moral panic over youth violence: Wilding and the manufacture of menace in the media. *Youth and Society*, **34**(1), 3–30.
Willis, P. (1977) *Learning to labor: How working class kids get working class jobs* (New York: Columbia University Press).

Bourdieu and the Social Space of the PE Class: Reproduction of Doxa through Practice

LISAHUNTER

ABSTRACT *This paper considers the social space of one physical education (PE) class in the middle years of schooling. I endeavour to tease out the dialectic between the discursive spaces available to the students positioned within this space and the construction and negotiation of student subjectivities. Using the conceptual tools of field, habitus, practice, capital, illusio, and doxa provided by Pierre Bourdieu and of embodied subjectivities from post-structural feminism, three particular spaces are explored, namely: 'the good student', 'hetero/sexism' and 'the body'. I argue for a (re)turn to conversations around* PE as a learning area *and* learning as embodied *as a way to meet the needs of* more *young people through PE. Like others, I also question PE's existence as it is currently configured in the school curriculum.*

Introduction

Young people's subjectivities and their construction within the practices of physical culture have received some attention previously (see e.g. Broekhoff, 1972; Kirk & Tinning, 1994). More recent attention has included work by Leahy and Harrison (2001, 2004), Light (2001), Satina (2001), Sykes (2001), and Wright (1998). However, a number of silences, gaps or largely undisturbed spaces still exist in the literature pertaining to young people in the health and physical education (HPE) field. One such gap includes the *social space* of the HPE class, a space where subjectivities are constructed and negotiated in particular ways in dialogue with the available discursive spaces.[1] Applying the conceptual tools of Pierre Bourdieu, in particular field, habitus, practice, capital, illusio, doxa and symbolic violence, I will describe one such social space of a physical education (PE)[2] class consisting of 24 students and their teacher in their middle years of schooling. The discursive spaces around 'the good student', 'hetero/sexism' and 'the body' within a sport-dominant PE field show how only some subjectivities could be legitimate and in turn complicit in reproducing much of the doxa, or taken-for-granted assumptions and beliefs, associated with PE. This paper concludes by adding to an already existing, but largely unheard, call to practitioners in the field, in schools and in teacher education. This call is to challenge particular discourses and their categories maintained through PE, current configurations that make impossible other ways of being and arguably result in oppressing, marginalizing or alienating young people from positive orientations to themselves and physical culture. I conclude by arguing for a (re)turn to conversations around *PE as a learning area* and *learning as embodied* as a way to meet the needs of more young people through PE in schools and justify/question PE's existence in the school curriculum.

Theoretical Framework: The Field and Players in the Game

Researchers have explored the significance of student corporeality within the discourse of schooling (Gore, 1998; Kirk, 1998a; Reid, 1998) focusing on the disciplining or control of students' bodies. Findings from this work strongly suggests that the surveillance and control of students' bodies has been a dominant discourse in schooling, manifested through formal schooling practices such as lining up, raising one's hand to speak or asking permission to urinate, and informal playground practices, such as boys playing out physical violence within a frame of acceptance not available to girls. These practices become more obvious, although no less insidious, within aspects of the curriculum that apply directly to the body. PE is one formal space in the school curriculum where the body becomes the focus of/ for observation. Kirk and Tinning (1994), Vertinsky (1992) and Wright (1998) suggest that the history of PE has been discursively driven by controlling, disciplining, gendering, and shaping an objectified body. These discourses become apparent in the way sport, health and gender, for example, are understood.

A more dynamic understanding of teaching and learning as contextualized, contested, and embodied necessitates a theoretical framework that illuminates multiple, interrelated dimensions. I draw heavily upon the work of Bourdieu to explore the way in which discourses associated with the body, both within the classroom context and through the *field* of physical education, create discursive spaces for constituting the *embodied subjectivities* of those within the social space. Bourdieu refers to field as:

> a network, or a configuration, of objective relations between positions objectively defined, in their existence and in the determinations they impose upon their occupants, agents of institutions, by their present and potential situation (situs) in the structure of the distribution of species of power (or capital) whose possession commands access to the specific profits that are at stake in the field, as well as by their objective relation to other positions (domination, subordination, homology, etc.). (Bourdieu & Wacquant, 1992, p. 97)

The field of PE, then, is made up of a structured system of social relations between the educational authority, PE teacher educators, PE curriculum writers, health and sport professionals who have influence over curriculum and practices, individual school administrators, PE teachers, and PE students. Any analysis of discourses and the individual devoid of a social context is flawed and limited because it denies the *relational positioning of the individual* within social fields. The body highlighted by Bourdieu's concept of habitus is paramount in *reading* an individual, *categorizing* and *positioning* them within a field.

Interconnected to the concept of field is *habitus,* the corporeal dispositions that interact with the social relations. Habitus works similarly to subjectivity, but *emphasizes embodiment* and the role of the body in constituting habitus, as well as being constituted by habitus (Bourdieu & Wacquant, 1992). This dialectic becomes important in understanding the intertwining of material and symbolic practices in the construction of the subject, such as linguistic conceptions of the construction of corporeality. Bourdieu's emphasis on social structures is balanced by his conceptualization of agency. However, acting as an agent may be mediated by influences that are beyond conscious realization. Therefore, agents may actually reproduce the very structures that limit them. These become important points to discuss when arguing for people's ability to reflect and be reflexive, to act as an agent. Agency can be contextualized in the positioning of young people as *not-adults,* as students, and within the discourses of particular subject areas such as PE. It is through the tension between being subjected to meaning inherent in the discourses of

PE and becoming an embodied agentic subject that PE may constitute and construct the habitus of young people. At the same time, the habitus of young people also has the *potential* to constitute and construct the PE field. This dual process, being constituted and constituting, is central to understanding *habitus as being constantly negotiated—that is constructed/ing, reconstructed/ing and maintained/ing.*

Lois McNay (2000) suggests the internal diversity of habitus is under theorized by Bourdieu, and others claim that habitus is too deterministic and inadequately precise (Giroux, 1983; Nash, 1990; Jenkins, 1992; May, 1994). Unlike these critics I read Bourdieu's concept of habitus to be useful in that it pays attention to the intersection of symbolic and material dimensions of power on, through, and by the body as well as highlighting the mutually constituting and therefore relational importance between the concepts of field and habitus, structure and agency. For me, habitus is compatible with Davies' (2000) articulation of subjectivity which includes the potential for 'constitutive agency of *authority*' (p. 15). Although *subjectivities* could theoretically suffice there is a danger of linguistically slipping the body away with the everpresent influence of Cartesian dualism. As such a (politically feminist) preferable concept for my work is *embodied subjectivity/subjectivities,* a conceptual tool that, like Kristie Fleckenstein's (2003) *somatic mind,* is a generative structure rather than a determining principle—an orientation that suggests potentialities (Grosz, 1994; Wright, 1996; Davies, 2000). A person can be conceptualized as a multifaceted intersection of various subject signifiers or markers including, but not limited to, gender, class, race, sexuality, and corporeality. Within categories such as *adolescent* or *boy* or *Aboriginal* there are more differences than similarities. Local and contextual factors are important, and are variable across contexts for any one individual (Brooks, 1997). Because of this variability, the post-structuralist notion of subjectivities is more helpful than that of identity to encapsulate multiple, unpredictable, contradictory and complex contextual inter-relationships of selves that make up a person in any one timespace (Lovell, 2000). It allows for conceptualizations of difference within and between individuals—as internal and external diversity (Hird, 1998).

In drawing our attention to habitus, bodies, and subjectivities, we must also attend to *practice* (Bourdieu, 1998). Culture is embodied and reproduced through participation in social practices in day-to-day activities produced by the interaction of fields and habitus, through social structures and agents. Through practice, social structures become embedded in the habitus, mediating discourses between habitus and social fields. As with the concept of agency, actions occur through processes that may be beyond conscious control or awareness of the individual. 'Habitus reveals itself... only in reference to a definite situation. It is only in the relation to certain structures that habitus produces given discourses or practices' (Bourdieu & Wacquant, 1992, p. 135). Practice is therefore 'the product of a habitus that is itself the product of the embodiment of the immanent regularities and tendencies of the world' (p. 138). This is illustrated by the student reproducing oppressive practices of sexism, sometimes unconsciously taken up in the habitus as a result of normalizing practices of the society into which s/he was born and learned to re-enact.

In this paper, the analysis of practice is done within the social space of the PE class. This space is held together through the concept of *capital,* where capital acknowledges the value of something by members of a particular field and, in turn, the distribution of that value yields two principles of differentiation: economic capital and cultural capital (Bourdieu, 1998). The more people have in common in a given social space, the closer they are. They are distributed according to the volume of the different kinds of capital they possess, and according to the relative weight of the different forms of capital

(Bourdieu, 1998). The forces active in the field define specific capitals, in relation to a field, and conferring power over the field (Bourdieu in Wacquant, 1989). Bourdieu's concept of capital therefore goes beyond an economic form, to include social, symbolic and cultural forms, differentiating between the source and nature of the operating power. These will be explained further.

While economic capital still refers to wealth, the other forms of capital ultimately translate into economic capital, providing there is a means for exchange. A network of lasting relations, a belongingness or connectedness with others in the field, defines social capital. Cultural capital marks the product of education or the academic market as connected to individuals in the form of accent, disposition or learning, as connected to objects such as books, qualifications or possessions, and connected to institutions such as having a secondary school education in a state school as opposed to a private school or university. Symbolic capital (Bourdieu, 1998) draws from any of the abovementioned capitals and is given value by a particular groups' perception of what is legitimate and/or valued; for example, some young people may be perceived as good students and therefore afforded more symbolic capital than those not perceived as such. The accumulation of symbolic and material forms of capital influences one's location in social space, in turn determining the kinds of possibilities for accumulating different forms of capital and the abilities to redefine or legitimate the forms of those capitals. Bourdieu (1986) also referred to physical capital as a form of cultural capital, although Shilling (1993) argues that 'the corporeal is too important to be seen merely as a subdivision of another form of capital' (p. 58). Shilling develops the concept more broadly through his contribution to the sociology of the body, arguing that physical capital encompasses the symbolic value of the exterior surface of the body in the form of shape, physique and appearance. The physical body is the external manifestation of the habitus as well as constituting the habitus warranting inclusion in understanding the definitions and practices where the body is central. This is particularly pertinent to schooling and PE.

To compliment this theoretical framework several other concepts require mention. *Illusio* is an investment that one has in maintaining *the game* or the social space and its outcomes. One does not necessarily play the game consciously but 'one is born into the game, with the game; and the relation of investment, *illusio*, investment, is made more total and unconditional by the fact that it is unaware of what it is' (Bourdieu, 1990b, p. 67). Those who have a *feel for the game* are complicit in reproducing the *doxa,* the presuppositions of the game, through illusio, so as to maintain their positioning, the allocation of capital, and the legitimation of the forms of capital to be allocated. *Symbolic violence* then is 'the violence which is exercised upon a social agent with his or her complicity' (Bourdieu & Wacquant, 1992, p. 167). Symbolic violence may occur through *misrecognition* where the violence is not even recognized as such by the individual, 'the fact of recognising a violence which is wielded precisely inasmuch as one does not perceive it as such' (p. 168). Distinction between people is necessary for some to accrue capital and be positioned in a way to maintain the game. As such, those not able to access capital must give consensual validation to those who can. As I hope to demonstrate, in attending to the body formally the field of PE produces physical capital through gaze, performance, measurement and categorization. Such attention often means that the symbolic violence operating through unofficial discourses that maintain and reproduce the mind/body dualism and essentializing categories are not problematized. So too a particular doxa is maintained rather than critiqued and reconstructed to be more inclusive and engaging for young people.

The Game in Practice: Who Is On the Team, Sidelined, a 'No Show', Banned?

Twenty-four students participated in an 18-month study that formed the data source for this paper. The students were from one Year 7 class, during their final year of primary school, who then spread to nine Year 8 classes in their first year of secondary school or middle school. A classroom generalist teacher and PE specialist teacher worked with the students in Year 7, and five specialist health and physical education (HPE) teachers were primarily involved with the classes in Year 8. The primary school was situated within a working class/lower middle class suburb of an Australian metropolitan city. Although several students transferred to middle class schools in other suburbs, most moved to the corresponding government co-educational high school in the same suburb.

I used a multi-method approach for data generation in an attempt to include as many students' perspectives as possible over the 18 months of fieldwork. The methods included interviews, field observations, questionnaires, journals, videoing, photography, and Qsorts. The data were analysed using the tools of both qualitative and quantitative methods, critical discourse analysis, descriptive statistics and Qmethodology. The study drew from a number of theoretical perspectives including critical pedagogy, post-structural feminism, cultural studies, and youth studies. Through the use of these perspectives, the study attempted to analyse the relational positioning of 24 students within their physical education class using Bourdieu's conceptual tools of habitus, field, capital, and practice. This paper draws on that study.

The Field: Physical Education or PE-as-Sport?

Many students regarded PE to be synonymous with sport: '[PE is] running and swimming and playing like soccer or something' (Bradley, I1, 78[3]). The nature of the field of PE, how it impacted on the embodied subjectivities of the young people in it, and how it was experienced as a social space acted as a *structure.* The structure was constitut *ing*, and constitut *ed* by, practices of agents located at the macro (HPE community) and micro (classroom) levels of PE. At the macro level these include the practices of curriculum and policy document writers, researchers and teacher educators, those working in sport, health and related government agencies, and teachers, the teacher acting as a mediator of discourses between the macro and micro levels of the field (Hunter, 2002a,b). Particular discourses such as sport, health, fitness, age, body, gender, sexuality, social class, and ethnicity interacted through agents to shape the field, circulating between the macro and micro levels.

Included in the micro level were the lived experiences of the teacher and students within the class. As the student above noted, discourses associated with PE have strong roots within sport and health, and vice versa, to the point where they are understood to be synonymous. Programs such as *Aussie Sport* (Australian Sports Commission, 1990) and *Health Promoting Schools* (National Health Promoting Schools Association, 1997) supported by government and practised in schools are underpinned by dominant discourses of sport and health. So too does sport, health and fitness dominate the *official* discursive practices of PE (Tinning *et al.,* 1994). *PE-as-sport* has constructed: a narrow conceptualization of movement as technical and utilitarian; an imbalance in the experiences provided for students, emphasizing for example regimented and controlled sport based movements, rather than exploratory experiences such as in creative dance; and the replication of oppressive practices, such as found in competition, and misrecognized as *normal.* In a

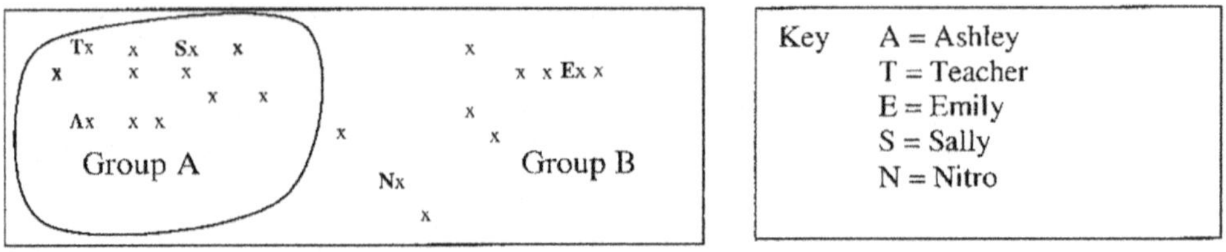

FIG. 1. Representational value positions toward physical education.

subtler and perhaps more elusive way, the *unofficial* discourses associated with sport, including gender-ing, sex-ing, and body-ing, also operated to constitute the field of PE.

Many students spoke of PE by *naming* it as sport: 'Yeah, coz like if you like didn't do sport or anything you like wouldn't be fit and healthy' (Emily, I1, 145). Emily also illustrates the assumption of the positive relationship between PE participation and health, an illusion about her lived experiences and one upheld by the field of PE. The doxa of sport/health/fitness was based upon presuppositions that worked as unofficial discourses including healthism, blaming the individual for their health rather than considering social situations, individualism, competition and comparison, and positivist scientism, in particular sports sciences. The subject positions that were therefore rewarded in PE were legitimated as competent display of skill performance, appearance of health and *ideal* body type (not being fat), knowledge about the objectified biomedical body, displays of competitive fitness indicators, and being a *good student.* Those students able to take these positions accrued capital and therefore had an investment in reproducing the *game,* arguably unaware of their complicity in maintaining these legitimated subject positions. Misrecognizing that *sport is good* for one's health and therefore worthy of participation justified PE in the curriculum, under a restricted conflation of sport with PE. As such, those students who could not take up legitimated subject positions, for example, someone who was labelled *unfit* or *fat,* but continued to participate, were also complicit in reproducing the social space, albeit as targets of symbolic violence.

Players Take Up Their Positions on the Field: The Good Student, Hetero/ Sexism and the Body

The construction of positions in the field of PE was partially realized through the teacher's role. The teacher was central, but not exclusive, in the legitimation and assigning of capital valued by the field. Many of the students referred to the teacher's centrality in the form of knowledge and codes of behaviour: 'He might show you the stroke or he might demonstrate it and he'd just tell us what to do' (Ashley, I1, 408). 'The teacher says you've done it very well that's when you know you've done it correctly' (Nitro, I1, 322). A form of symbolic violence common in schooling kept many of the students *in their place* as they mis/recognized their role as unquestioning of authority. Others created pockets of resistance which in turn labelled them as *bad students* by *both* the teacher and *good students.* Although various forms of capital were being legitimated and afforded within the PE class, here I focus on physical capital to illustrate how students' positioning may be conceptualized.

The value positions towards PE taken up by the teacher and students in the class are represented in Fig. 1.[4] Those in Group A, including the teacher and students such as Ashley and Sally, valued working hard through skill acquisition, good grades and working on social skills such as cooperation and tolerance. These were the more *serious students* or those who wanted to *phase the teacher.* The students in Group B, including Nitro and Emily, identified strongly with *different* values, including a chance to talk with friends, have fun, and get good grades without too much effort or having to think about others. The students in this group were marginalized and labelled as resistant, disruptive, or *not keen workers* by the teachers and other students.

> Mr Spears: Mmm, in relation to other Year 7s we've had [here] the last few years they were quite a difficult class to take... I find them particularly in phys ed unmotivated, not overly keen, um been a difficult class since they've been in Grade 1... Nitro I think is uncooperative unless he's doing something he really likes and if he doesn't really like it he spits the dummy,[5] and the girls like Emily, constantly, doesn't matter what you say, it always has to end up with laughs, it annoys me. (I1, 7–22)

Those who did not value PE for the reasons the teacher did arguably had less access to capital and less influence on the construction of the field.

Importantly, resistance had different origins or reasons and took different forms such as opting out or disrupting. As such, those resisting did not have an affinity with each other, reducing any agency to change the field had they operated together, hence these students were positionally marginalized and strategically isolated. Particular students positioned closely to the teacher in values, the *serious students* and *pleasers,* had bought in to the *game* and were therefore *on the team* and a part of maintaining the game. They had accumulated the necessary capitals through legitimation by the teacher and many of the students, through the taken-for-granteds and symbolic violence, to be important ways of being. In particular capital was defined in relation to sport/health/fitness, being a good student, their gender and their bodies. Those marginalized were either *sidelined* (e.g. note from parents to sit out of PE), *no shows* (had excuses not to attend class), or *banned* (removed from class by the teacher), reducing their ability to recreate the field and increasing the maintenance of dominant discourses complicit in the practices of the teacher and affiliate students.

The Good Student

The discursive space of the *good student* in the PE class highlights how symbolic capital operates to endorse particular subjectivities and not others. Specific ways of looking and behaving increased one's capital accrual and legitimation as a good student, such as hegemonic masculinity within the context of *PE-as-sport.* The discursive space of the good student in PE is shaped by characteristics of competence, competition, comparison, display, skill, and fitness, through a sport discourse. To accrue physical capital in PE, a student must be able to recognize the discourses of sport and operate successfully within them. Not to engage with these discourses means a label of 'not good' which is reinforced publicly every time the students participate, or avoid participation. The good student was 'Someone... that's really good at sport coz he wins almost every event' (Emily, I3, 341–342). The concept of the good student, similar to Clarke's (1992) concept of the *competent student,* was powerful in that it constituted particular students as successful through the embodiment of a particular construction of the field. The students who were able to recognize and effectively work within the discursive spaces available to them became more closely aligned to the discourses operating through the teacher, particularly when this included discourses from the school field, emphasizing behaviour and effort. This *classification* or category is explained by Bourdieu (1998):

> Habitus are generative principles of distinct and distinctive practices (what [one] eats, how she eats)... But habitus are also classificatory schemes, principles of classification, principles of vision and division, different tastes. They make distinctions between what is good and what is bad. (p. 8)

Good students' embodied subjectivities were displayed as good at sport, compliant in behaviour, and demonstrative of effort. They had physical capital in the form of skill, fitness and or corporeal appearance, legitimated through teacher approval, support and attention. By the teachers' continual reinforcement of these capitals for those with the *right* attitude, the students learned what a good student was. The discourses of sport and school positioned the good students closer to the teacher. The discourses and physical proximities worked together to maintain and reproduce the dominant aspects of the field.

This was evident, for example, in the teacher's praise of those who finished pool laps quickly and returned to their blocks to wait for the next instruction, as opposed to those who struggled to complete or resisted the activity and were either ignored or reprimanded. Through this pedagogical relationship those already positioned with power held together the legitimated practices in PE-as-sport and students learned who was either *not good* or *bad*. Ashley, a good student, explained, 'There's some people who are bad at PE but they don't listen much and that's why they're bad at it... Here, here [pointing] there's the badder ones having a good old chat' (I1, 559 & 721). Students like Ashley maintained this position while others, like Nitro, slipped between good and bad depending on their engagement with the various discursive spaces. Nitro was afforded leniency in expectations of effort because others took it for granted that he was a 'good' PE student given his physical capital, his corporeality and ability to perform skilfully and with speed:

> Most of them are [good]... That'd be me, Ashley, Nelson... Bernie, Emily... Sally, umm Toni. Toni gets into trouble sometimes, Tammy, I think that's all... I'm pretty good at it, I think I'm pretty good I can beat some of my friends when I'm competing with them, that's if I do... And the teacher tells you you're good at it. (I1, 424–37)

Some students, who recognized they were not good PE students, rejected the version of PE expected by the teacher. When given the choice students took the opportunity to leave PE altogether, focusing instead on their club sports activities or recreation, or moved into a life of sedentary practices. Some students used their own positions of power or agency to redirect the path of the class's activities to suit their own purposes. For example, Emily told a supply teacher that they were to do netball rather than soccer and Nitro wrestled with another student at the shallow end of the pool instead of continuing with laps. A significant number of students also resisted participation in the dominant space. Strategies included wearing a knee guard in case the teacher announced that running would be part of the activity or leaving the required sun hat behind to disqualify one's self from participation, an option taken by some when they wanted to avoid the *boring stuff.*

As with entry into many social fields, a novice's entry shows naiveté to the potentialities of the field. Within PE, the students were not aware of learning and movement possibilities outside those narrowly defined through sport. They were defining themselves as good or bad in terms of this specific field, which in turn opened or closed spaces for engagement. Bourdieu (1990b) explains this perpetuation as follows:

> The earlier a player enters the game and the less he (sic) is aware of the associated learning ... the greater is his ignorance of all that is tacitly granted through his investment in the field and his interest in its very existence and perpetuation and in everything that is played for in it, and his unawareness of the unthought presuppositions that the game produces and endlessly reproduces, thereby reproducing the conditions of its own perpetuation, (p. 67)

The field of PE reproduces the conditions of its own perpetuation through teacher and student subjectivities, and the strong links to sport, and the associated practices and discourses. Marginalization in and dissatisfaction with PE—along with its devaluation by many of the disengaged students—came from practices within the field. Although the good students, like Ashley and Sally, were well positioned to seek continuance when the choice became available, others, like Emily and Nitro, decided not to.

Hetero/Sexism[6]

After age, gender was perhaps the most dominant categorical space in which students were discursively constituted at school. Teacher/student language and practices referenced individuals as to whether they were *boys* or *girls*. This discourse, construed as *natural*, gendered many of the practices within the social space. Students articulated the significance of their bodies in gendered practices that also related to sexuality and sexual orientation practices in less visible ways. Gendered discourses worked through language, corporeality, physical proximity, and relationships to establish a dominant order of heterosexual masculinity over heterosexual femininity (Wright, 1996), other ways of being silenced.

The PE teacher, like many other teachers, constantly referred to students as boys and girls and always in a particular order, 'OK, let's make a start. Boys and girls walk up to the other end behind a block' (Fg1: 52). The gendered language became constituted in the students' subjectivities, and they reconstituted the dominant discourse through their practices. Gender separation in some activities also reified heteronormative dualism by reinstantiating as *natural*, assumed biological differences attributed to boys and girls. When testing for fitness, the teacher separated the students according to their test results and gender saying 'girls over here and boys over there. Line up with the highest scores to lowest scores. Stand in order' (Fb3: 8, 15–20). This was common practice, regardless of whether they were measuring sprint speed, height, anaerobic power or coordination. Performance was constantly on display as physical capital, and it was always differentiated and ordered by gender.

As in primary school, separation according to gender also continued as *normal* practice in secondary school, played out spatially in terms of where students waited for teachers at the beginning of class and in different activities. Another example of the separation of the genders through the daily practice of the PE class again comes from a teacher:

> Today we're going to measure. Ok boys, you have to pick the 600 [gram javelin]. You can pick any of these [and he shows them the green javelin]. The orange is the heaviest—you can usually tell be the thickness. The girls have to have the smaller ones. (Fb3: 6, 29–33)

Unpacking the doxa of ordering gender through sport, the taken-for-granted assumptions about gender also point to the level of symbolic violence through this hegemonic ordering.

Gender was also played out through students' spatial relationships to each other such as sitting as two gendered groups at the beginning of class. When the students viewed this practice (via video playback during their interview) very few could articulate the reason for gender separation: 'Oh, because, I don't know, we just sit like that' (Sally, I1, 881–2). After further questioning, Sally attempted an explanation also used by other students, 'Because we don't like boys, they're horrible, I don't know, we just sit like that [there's a reason] ... I don't know, I think so but I don't know it (laughs)' (I1, 915–18). Through her words, Sally references gender as a *natural* and dichotomized difference, based upon only two opposing ways of being;—heteronormative masculine and feminine. Those students who attempted to explain the practice could not go beyond the misrecognitions associated with the gender discourses, continuing to use totalizing and polarizing explanations such as 'like the boys are just mucking around and the girls are usually trying' (I1, 681).

Through corporeal practices, PE provided a space where structures of sexuality were reinscribed and reconstituted as gendered practices based on complementarity and heteronormativity. The sexual gaze of the *opposite sex* was noted by some: 'Andrew's an idiot... Coz he's so small, he's so annoying... He just sits there and looks at me. Like yuk, piss off' (Emily, I2. 142–6). Being under the *evaluative gaze* (Bartky, 1988) of boys was reported as a reason for girls not wanting to engage in PE. Postures that covered the body, such as standing with their arms across their torso or across their waist and chest with hand across their face were common amongst the girls during the swimming lessons: 'It's close to swimming and I get nervous coz I hate going in togs with all these boys around. Yaaaah. I hate swimming with all these boys around coz they look at you like that, especially if you've got a big body. Like me' (Sally, I1, 1002). In turn, however, some girls used their physicality to gain capital. The legitimized appearance was a *hyperfeminine* ectomorph—*not fat,* with developing breasts and a fine-featured face clear of blemishes. Two students referred to as *attractive* by students of both genders often moved around the pool in minimal swimming garb to remain close to several of the boys and to avoid engagement with the physical activity. Some boys had noted the girls' appearance as *physically attractive* while describing other girls as *fat* or *smelly* and indicating a dislike in interacting with them. The tension for some girls was between being physically active, therefore not appearing feminine, or trying to display a feminized sporty appearance while avoiding being labelled *butch* or *lemon.*[7]

Within the dominating discourse of sport, hypermasculinity was valued by many of the boys who wanted to appear more muscular. Those who were small, not sporty, and not yet showing physical signs of puberty were not able to obtain physical capital through appearance or performance. In Nitro's case, his practices seemed to be a display of heterosexuality as well as same-sex social dominance. During swimming classes, he gained the attention of other students, by a clowning display of his well-developed biceps and abdominals. While doing athletics in PE, specifically the shot put, he continued this display, as noted in my field notes:

> As soon as the teacher left, Nitro again performed the incorrect technique that looked like a caber toss. On retrieving the shot he held it up under his shirt-sleeve imitating a body builder showing off his biceps. He then relocated the shot to his pectorals to display to his two friends either large pectorals, or, given the way he was holding the shot and an imaginary one in his other hand, his large breasts... He commented that the school tracksuit was *gay* and returned to the circle for another *toss.* This time, he picked up a second shot

> dangling both between his knees like a pair of swollen testicles, laughing as he showed his friends. (Fb4: 9, 38–49)

Particular discourses of body, gender and sexuality made possible the access to physical capital through performed heteronormativity within the field of PE-as-sport. Simultaneously, this reified capital served to reproduce each of these dominant discourses.

The visibility of physical characteristics and the hormonal changes occurring for some of the students provided a biological reading of the body (Bourdieu, 1990a,b) through the discourses of gender and sexuality. However, many of these perceived displays (e.g. hair cut, clothes worn, ways of walking, ways of talking) had been socially constructed from the gendered positions, understood as biological. All students were *obviously* male or female despite the *lack* of visibility of primary or secondary sex characteristics[8] among many of the students. Routines around public clothes changing and the wearing of 'togs'[9] made some physical characteristics more visible. For several of the girls, exposure of the body, as an object of others' gaze, led to an *awareness* that others were looking at them and in *covering up* practices using their arms or towels. Swimming sharpened the merger between bodily and gender discourses.

Normative structures of gender and sex function to promote particular sexual relationships underpinned by biological discourses. Like sex and gender, sexuality was also ascribed to bodies. Sexuality was often performed through heteronormative speech acts, such as calling someone or something gay to indicate illegitimacy, abnormality, or unacceptability. Choice of clothing, a lack of physical prowess, or a lack of friends meant some students were ostracized, and therefore referred to as *gay* and constructed as *other,* thus linking this discourse with non-sexualized performances rather than upon sex/uality.

In the only other reference to sexualities outside heteronormativity, Emily identified lesbianism and pregnancy as negative states of being that were located on herself and her friend, states with which neither wanted to be associated:

> I like Anthony (laughs) ... he's the only partially good-looking one (laughs). Tim's an idiot coz in Drama, um, we did this thing, it was like make up and Mia told me that she was a lesbian and I told her I was pregnant and then he went and spread it that I'm a piece of shit. (Emily, I2. 136–8)

For Emily out of her drama role, to be incorrectly constructed as either lesbian or pregnant was a technique employed by students to reduce her capitals and positioning within the class. Through the language and practices like those experienced by Emily, the dominant state of being heterosexual and a virgin had more legitimacy than other ways of being. The dominant discourses had been reproduced rather than challenged.

In practices outside the class, that is, in lunch-time free play, it was interesting to note both the resistance to the dominant discourses of heteronormative masculinity and femininity but also the way in which dominant practices reinscribing and reinscribed by gender were reasserted with a reference back to PE. As one female student noted:

> Since girls never bring a ball, we play with the boys ... football and soccer as well ... girls are on one team and the boys are on the other. Sometimes if the girls are doing really badly one good person on the boys team will come over and help us and it's mainly just like PE when we do it. (I1, 203–11)

In statements like this made outside of PE and referencing non-PE activities, the dominance of boys over girls in sport is again reified. This student, like many others, took for granted that if the girls were not succeeding *against* the boys, it was because they were girls. Having a boy on the team was expected to rectify the *problem.* Through practices in PE, under the guise of equity or equal teams, the dominant discourse of a hierarchical gendering dualism was reinforced and embedded in the student subjectivities. The belief that males are better and can therefore help females becomes reinforced in practice.

These few examples of gender and sexuality operating in the field of PE demonstrate how heteronormativity is reproduced and how the field closes spaces for alternatives to dualistic, normative and gendered heterosexual orientations. Connell (1998) notes:

> Issues of gender are, at one level, issues about how personal lives are arranged and conducted. It is through critical reflection on personal experience, often, that people come to realize the significance of what has been taken-for-granted—such as the [hegemonic] masculinity of sport, and the use of sport to make and confirm masculinities, (p. iii)

Connell describes the critical reflection that is absent from the PE field manifested in all of the PE sites in the study. Instead, the field of PE reproduces dominant forms of gender and sexuality discourses, despite some resistances, and beyond much of student and teacher consciousness, but constituted through both discourse and corporeality.

The Body

'[I'm concerned] if I get like really, really, really, really, really fat coz I'm already fat. I'll probably get anorexic or something' (Emily, I1, 39–40). Emily highlights the reification of the surveilled body in PE (Broekhoff, 1972). A particular bodily appearance, or *'the look'* (Featherstone, 1982), is legitimated through PE, resulting in those close to the ideal accruing capital and those further from the ideal not. Prior examples have demonstrated that the body is paramount in the constitution of one's subjectivity when engaging with the field of PE specifically and in schooling more broadly. The mind/body dualism promoted in schools, in conjunction with emphases in PE on objectification and performance, appearance and gaze, operated to construct particular discursive spaces in which students' subjectivities are differently legitimated and alienated.

Students come to know the body through the physical sciences and objectify the body through gaze, measurement, and comparison (Pronger, 1995). Bodily discourses also operate sensually and emotionally (Lyon, 1997), yet there is a gap in this research and little space within the field of PE to know the body in this way. Ultimately, students become disembodied in classes, such as maths and English where a disembodied mind and cognitive processes become the focus (Davis, 1997). At the same time, discourses operate to present the student's body as an object to be controlled (Kirk, 1998b). The separation of body from mind is legitimated through the often-disparate association of each with particular school subjects, rather than understanding the student as embodied, where subjectivities are manifested through movement and corporeality. An epistemology based upon Cartesian dualism is reproduced within education placing the mind as dominant and separate to the body. This is illustrated in many students' comments, like Nitro's differentiation between PE and maths:

> Maths? It's more tougher ... Like in swimming it's like you have to do something but in maths you have to concentrate and you have to write things and all that. So it's more really tough than doing PE. In PE it's just relaxed, you can talk whenever you want. If you're talking in maths you just get a detention straight away. (Nitro, I1, 816–18)

Nitro differentiates between *doing* in PE, that is, using the body, and *concentrating* in maths, that is, using the mind. This separation values particular knowledges, or ways of knowing (cognitive, 'theory') over ways of doing (activity, 'practice'), reinforcing the mind/body hierarchy.

As described in the previous section, physical capital and social positions were influenced by comparisons of performance, such as placement in races and comparisons of throwing distances, and one's physical dimensions, including height, weight, and arm span. As Sally noted: 'you have to weigh yourself... it's just horrible. Look at how skinny and tall I am' (I1, 335 & 910). Emily learned about her heart as a pump and her lungs as billows, 'stuff like, the pumps in your heart or something like that' (I3. 66). The students' bodies acted as a reference point from which they constituted their subjectivities, through a very deterministic relationship between field and subjectivity, and through the accrual of physical capital.

Consequently, some students were very conscious of the *look* and how closely their reality came to the ideal, shaped by discourses of sport, health and fitness, admittedly not necessarily exclusive to the PE class. Nitro knew the capital to be gained through a muscular physique: 'I think [PE's] for your health and um for your fitness, to get you fit ... It helps me get more fit, helps me get ah ... huge I guess, very big' (I1, 104–110). By 'big', Nitro was referring to physique and muscle definition. Nitro's physique was rewarded with physical capital in the form of positive comments from others, whereas other students' capital (e.g. Emily's) was diminished, especially through the increased opportunities of gaze provided by PE: 'But I hate [PE] because you have to wear the togs because it makes me look fat and everyone teases me because I'm fat' (I1, 759).

The body was a *thing* to be *looked after* and worked on in PE in order to access physical capital: 'Because, like you learn how to look after your body and (pause) stuff, and swimming, like you can learn how to rescue people and you could run fast and get a career in sports and stuff' (Sally, I1, 302). This *shape* or *look* about the somatic surface of the body carried with it physical capital. However, Bourdieu (1990b, 1999) also conceptualizes the body as a visual manifestation of the habitus. The students used this visuality in a number of ways. Through misrecognition, the performance-competence discourse was played out against those with particular body types. If one was competent, displayed through their performance, as Emily did in swimming, their *fatness* was sometimes overlooked by others, although they themselves made reference to *being fat*. However, in the case of others, visual markers of a body that was not legitimate within the discourses of either PE or youth culture was associated with incompetence. Several students legitimated their lack of competence through visual markers of fatness. They continued to be seen, or see themselves, as fat, and concurrently, they had no expectation of being competent. The body discourse available through PE arguably gave these students the tools to misrecognize the relationship between appearance and competence—a possible explanation for their lack of engagement with the activities and reproduction of low physical capital. The public exposure of bodies, experienced in PE change rooms and with showering, has been identified as a negative experience of PE for some students (Flintoff & Scraton, 2001). To avoid any gaze upon the body, whether of contours or competence, students resorted to strategies such as moving to the back of lines when expected to demonstrate a skill or sitting out of PE altogether.

Time Out: Moving Beyond Categorization

The discourses associated with the body, through PE, are important spaces for constituting embodied subjectivities and therefore necessitate explicit critique both within the field and by the students. Bourdieu (1990b) suggests that this critique cannot be reduced to the familiar concept of 'body image', which he explains as being 'a subjective representation largely based on the representation of one's own body produced and returned by others' (p. 72). Rather, the body is understood through 'classificatory schemes', such as gender, ethnicity, and class. These categories pose oppositional values, such as male or female, and are 'one of the fundamental principles of the perception that agents have of their body and also of their whole relation to the body' (p. 72). The bodies required from the PE field and the spaces for compromise between the actual and the *ideal* offer opportunity for engagement with PE or a realization that one does not belong. In effect, while some students learn what they *can* do and who they are, many learn what they *can't* do, who they are not or cannot be.

Numerous possibilities for students' subjectivities are conceivable, but are not part of students' formal conversations in understanding how physical capital may be afforded to some and not to others. Instead, these bodily inscriptions are played out implicitly through discourses associated with gender and sport, for example. When these discourses are incurred implicitly, certain students *naturally* acquire physical capital, and others do not. Those with a physicality that approximates the *ideal* body and sportsperson are rewarded through the legitimation applied by both those with the capital, and withheld from those without. Bourdieu (Bourdieu & Passerson, 1977) suggests that this is what schooling is all about—that inequality is necessary and that it comes about because everyone is playing a particular game that reproduces that inequality. Despite resistances the body is heavily legitimated implicitly by compliance, whether in a person's favour or not, with the dominant discourse of body.

Physical Education as a Learning Area

Learning to *be* is an important if not pre-eminent purpose of schooling and is predicated on ways of understanding/enacting one's subjectivities. More importantly, discursive spaces created from conceptualizations of young people as adolescents, and therefore still *becoming*, are problematic. PE is *potentially* a very powerful catalyst for learning, through, and as a result of, the somatic surface of the body, manifested in movement, and contextualized in social relationships (e.g. Martinek, 1997). Whether this potential is used in socially just and empowering ways is the issue. Given its history and its appropriation of sweeping association with sport, PE has demonstrated its powerful use of these discourses in enculturing bodies, embodied subjectivities, young people's bodies, students' bodies, to be understood and reproduced in particular ways. I argue that these ways marginalize many young people from PE, physical activity, health and their bodies, and reduce positive spaces for different subjectivities to exist. It could be argued that PE does more harm than good, its practices demonstrating a failed health intervention at best and a damaging learning space at worst. Through the assimilation of legitimized practices, such as those encouraged in sport, some people have been able to access cultural and social capital through their physical capital. However, others have been resoundingly reminded of what they lack, closing spaces for opportunities involving movement or an understanding of one's subjectivities, and closing spaces for difference. By redefining what a good student in PE could *be* like or *look* like, within and outside sport discourses, there may be spaces for more students to successfully position themselves (and be positioned by others) as good, that is, of *value* and to participate.

PE as a field could potentially model what being an embodied learner would be like. The first step would be for teachers and students to challenge the doxa of PE, as part of PE. Two learning experiences then need to be worked through with students. The first is learning associated with one's subjectivities, one's embodiment as a participant in the field of PE, that is, how we are constituted within the field of PE and how we participate as agents in the reproduction or re-creation of those fields. The second is learning associated with one's positioning within society based upon signifiers—such as age, gender, sexuality, ethnicity, and bodily appearance—and the legitimization process that affords some people social, physical, cultural, and symbolic capital not possible for others.

Learning as Embodied

Learning, as embodied, needs to be a part of PE if the field is to break from its oppressive reproduction of essentialized bodies through narrow categories. Expanding possible bodily discourses to disrupt the mind/body dualism, objectification and performance, appearance and gaze within the field of PE may offer spaces for students to understand and explore their bodies beyond those currently constraining the field. Learning particular ways of *becoming* an *adult* body, ways of moving, controlling and surveilling the body, seems to be part of the project of schooling upheld through the doxa of adolescence. Through PE *and* schooling, the knowledge about bodies, and therefore embodied subjectivities, needs to be challenged as constructed, essentialized and limited, and as manifestations of selves. This knowledge must make, or include, an epistemological and ontological shift about learners and knowledge. Through understanding the construction of knowledge that frames the field, more students might become more aware of the discourses operating as well as the need to critically act towards these discourses. Synchronously, an awareness of the complicit or agentic participation of teachers and students in reproducing discourses and circles of influence, needs to be raised. Only when these become explicit though may students begin to move beyond the superficial and constraining ways of relating to themselves through the field. Becoming aware of these superficial relations, people, students and teachers may come to understand learning as embodied and may be able to critique their own social construction and positioning within the social processes imposed in institutions such as schooling. I reserve my hope that those currently privileged by contemporary discourses might participate in a reconstruction of a more inclusive and socially just space.

Knowledge as cognitive, learning as an individual process, adolescence as a biologically-driven stage, and intelligence as only working with knowledges from particular fields are discourses we need to critique to understand the role of school in the creation of particular types of citizens, to understand the part young people, individually and collectively, can play. New ways of knowing as well as new knowledge that incorporates selves as embodied may open up the way for a respect for difference and as political spaces to disrupt oppressive practices already inherent in PE, schooling and the positioning of young people within our society. As Bourdieu (1990b) proposes, the body operates 'below the level of consciousness ... it does not represent what it performs, it does not memorize the past, it enacts the past, bringing it back to life' (p. 73). This suggests that the body, as the visible manifestation of embodied subjectivities, also needs to become explicit, operating at the level of consciousness if we are to move beyond the reproduction of past oppressions.

To constantly ignore embodied subjectivities in education, whether through the field of PE or the field of schooling is itself oppressive, in the spaces created for young people, for their opportunity for agency and for the construction of their subjectivities during, and beyond, their middle years of schooling. Further exploration of the nature of young people's subjectivities is necessary to understand how they might be situated in the multiple discourses that constitute the fields of PE, schooling and broader society, and how these discourses allow for engagement or disengagement by different ways of being. We need these to be considered if we are to shift our practices towards *better* forms of schooling, reconfigure the field of sport = PE, and create a more diverse, inclusive, just and generative society.

Acknowledgements

Thanks to Doune Macdonald and Richard Tinning for their guidance with the research on which this chapter was based, Delia Hart and the reviewers for their comments on drafts of this paper, and particularly those individuals who participated in the research. Thanks also to Lisa Patel Stevens and Jen Vadeboncoeur for their suggestions and patience in teasing out and communicating the important issues. Portions of this paper are taken from Hunter (in press) Who gets to play? Kids, bodies, and schooled subjectivities, in: J. Vadeboncoeur & L. Patel Stevens (Eds) *Re/Constructing 'the Adolescent': Sign, Symbol and Body* (New York, Peter Lang Publishing).

Notes

[1] A discursive space is one where particular meanings are made according to the discourses shaping that space. For example, an economic discourse might operate in business, whereas a medical discourse might operate in the emergency section of a hospital. The discursive space of an HPE class might include discourses around sport, health, fitness and gender.

[2] Although the classes referred to in this paper were actually health and physical education classes, they were often named as and operated as physical education classes.

[3] Indicates data source reference of speaker or field notes.

[4] A Qsort test was employed (ordering 40 value orientations towards physical education). Figure 1 illustrates the results of the test that shows the value orientations of the teachers and students to physical education. By focusing on Function 1 (Eigenvalue of 73.2%) it is possible to recognize two groups of people within the class (Group A and B). Function 1 separated the class on their values towards physical education as a chance to talk with friends, have fun, and get good grades without too much effort or having to think about, or take into account, others. A further separation using Function 2 was valid between clusters 2 and 3 within Group A (although with a much lower Eigenvalue of 26.8%). This discriminated between those who highly valued being with friends, agreeableness towards the teacher, and not having to work too hard (the pleasers) and those who were very motivated towards working hard through skill acquisition, for good skill outcomes and therefore grades (the serious students).

[5] 'Spits the dummy' is a colloquialism for having a temper tantrum.

[6] Gender is used to denote the socially constructed dichotomized categories of masculinity and femininity into which boys and girls are contained. Although these categories are assumed by the naturalizing discourse of biology to be based upon sex, there is argument to suggest that sex is also a socially constructed category taken for granted within the doxa of biological determinism.

[7] A lemon is a disparaging term used to describe as a lesbian.

[8] Primary sex characteristics are the actual reproductive systems such as ovaries and testes whereas the secondary sex characteristics are bodily characteristics of adult males and females produces from hormones. These would include pubic hair, change of voice, breast development and sexual desires.

[9] Togs are bathing costumes or swimwear.

References

AUSTRALIAN SPORTS COMMISSION (1990) *Aussie Sports Activities Manual for Children with Disabilities* (Belconnen, ACT, Australian Sports Commission).

BARTKY, S. (1988) Foucault, femininity and the modernization of patriarchal power, in: I. DIAMOND & L. QUINBY (Eds) *Feminism and Foucault: Reflections on Resistance*, pp. 61–86 (Boston, North Eastern University Press).

BOURDIEU, P. (1986) The forms of capital, in: J.G. RICHARDSON (Ed.) *Handbook of Theory and Research for the Sociology of Education*, pp. 241–258 (New York, Greenwood Press).

BOURDIEU, P. (1990a) *In Other Words: Essays towards a Reflexive Sociology* (Stanford, CA, Stanford University Press).

BOURDIEU, P. (1990b) *The Logic of Practice* (Cambridge, Polity Press).

BOURDIEU, P. (1998) *Practical Reason: On the Theory of Action)* Cambridge, Polity Press).

BOURDIEU, P. (1999) Language and symbolic power, in: A. JAWORSKI & N. COUPLAND (Eds) *The Discourse Reader*, pp. 502–513 (London, Routledge).

BOURDIEU, P. & PASSERON, J. (1977) *Reproduction: In Education, Society and Culture*) London & Beverly Hills, Sage).

BOURDIEU, P. & WACQUANT, L. (1992) *An Invitation to Reflexive Sociology*) Cambridge, Polity Press).

BROEKHOFF, J. (1972) Physical education and the reification of the human body, *Gymnasion*, 9, pp. 4–11.

BROOKS, A. (1997) *Postfeminisms: Feminism, Cultural Theory, and Cultural Forms*) New York, Routledge).

CLARKE, G. (1992) Learning the language: discourse analysis in physical education, in: A. SPARKES (Ed.) *Research in Physical Education and Sport: Exploring Alternative Visions*, pp. 146–166 (London, Falmer Press).

CONNELL, RW. (1998) Forward. Where the boys are, in: C. HICKEY, L. FITZCLARENCE & R. MATTHEWS (Eds) *Where the Boys Are: Masculinity, Sport and Education*, pp. i–vi (Geelong, VIC, Deakin University).

DAVIS, K. (1997) *Embodied Practices: Feminist Perspectives on the Body*) London, Sage).

DAVIES, B. (2000) *A Body of Writing, 1990–1999* (Walnut Creek, AltaMira Press).

FEATHERSTONE, M. (1982) The body in consumer culture, *Theory, Culture and Society*, 1(2), pp. 18–33.

FLECKENSTEIN, K. (2003) Writing bodies: somatic mind in composition studies, *College English*, 61(3), pp. 281–306.

FLINTOFF, A. & SCRATON, S. (2001) Stepping into active leisure? Young women's perceptions of active lifestyles and their experiences of school physical education, *Sport, Education and Society*, 6(1), pp. 5–22.

GIROUX, H. (1983) Theories of reproduction and resistance in the new sociology of education: a critical analysis, *Harvard Educational Review*, 53, pp. 257–293.

GORE, J. (1998) Disciplining bodies: on the continuity of power relations in pedagogy, in: T. POPKEWITZ & M. BRENNAN (Eds) *Foucault's Challenge: Discourse, Knowledge, and Power in Education*, pp. 231–251 (New York, Teachers College Press).

GROSZ, E. (1994) *Volatile Bodies: Toward a Corporeal Feminism* St. Leonards, Allen & Unwin). HIRD, M. (1998) Theorising student identity as fragmented: some implications for feminist critical pedagogy, *British Journal of Sociology of Education*, 19(4), pp. 517–527.

HUNTER, L. (2002a) Teachers as gatekeepers to physical and social capital. Paper presented at the Australian Council for Health, Physical Education and Recreation National Conference, Launceston, Tasmania, Australia, July.

HUNTER, L. (2002b) Young people, physical education, and transition: understanding practices in the middle years of schooling. Unpublished doctoral dissertation, University of Queensland, Brisbane, Australia.

JENKINS, R. (1992) *Pierre Bourdieu*) London, Routledge).

KIRK, D. (1998a) *Schooling Bodies: School Practice and Public Discourse, 1880–1950*) London, Leicester University Press).

KIRK, D. (1998b) Educational reform, physical culture and the crisis of legitimation in physical education, *Discourse: Studies in the Cultural Politics of Education*, 19(1), pp. 101–112.

KIRK, D. & TINNING, R. (1994) Embodied self-identity, healthy lifestyles and school physical education, *Sociology of Health and Illness*, 16(5), pp. 600–625.

LEAHY, D. & HARRISON, L. (2001) Mind your own body: regulating gendered and sexual subjectivities within the secondary health and physical education curriculum. Paper presented at the annual meeting of the Australian Association for Educational Research, Fremantle.

LEAHY, D. & HARRISON, L. (2004) Health and physical education and the production of the 'at risk self', in: J. EVANS, B. DAVIES & J. WRIGHT (Eds) *Body Knowledge and Control Studies in the Sociology of Physical Education and Health,* pp. 130–139 (London, Routledge).

LIGHT, R. (2001) Practice, the body and research on school-based physical education and sport: the analytic tools of Pierre Bourdieu. Paper presented at the annual meeting of the Australian Association for Research in Education, Fremantle, Perth.

LOVELL, T. (2000) Thinking feminism with and against Bourdieu, *Feminist Theory,* 1(1), pp. 11–32.

LYON, M. (1997) The material body, social processes and emotion: 'techniques of the body' revisited, *Body and Society,* 3(1), pp. 83–101.

MARTTNEK, T. (1997) Serving underserved youth through physical activity, *Quest* 49, pp. 3–7.

MAY, S. (1994) *Making Multicultural Education Work*) Clevedon, Multilingual Matters).

MCNAY, L. (2000) *Gender and Agency: Reconfiguring the Subject in Feminist and Social Theory*) Cambridge, Polity Press).

NASH, R. (1990) Bourdieu on education and social and cultural reproduction, *British Journal of Sociology of Education,* 11, pp. 431–447.

NATIONAL HEALTH PROMOTING SCHOOLS ASSOCIATION (1997) *National Health Promoting School Initiative,* Final Report (Brisbane, National Health Promoting Schools Association).

PRONGER, B. (1995) Rendering the body: the implicit lessons of gross anatomy, *Quest,* 47, pp. 427–446.

REID, J-A. (1998) New times, new ways: methodological problems in researching the Nintendo generation, *Australian Educational Researcher,* 25(3), pp. 37–60.

SATINA, B. (2001) 'Girls don't get muscles!': overcoming gender equity while developing bodily competence during girlhood. Paper presented at the annual meeting of the American Educational Research Association, Seattle, WA.

SHILLING, C. (1993) The body, class and social inequalities, in: J. EVANS (Ed.) *Equality, Education, and Physical Education,* pp. 55–73 (London, Falmer Press).

SYKES, H. (2001) Teaching bodies, learning desires. Paper presented at the annual meeting of the American Educational Research Association, Seattle, WA.

TINNING, R, KIRK, D., EVANS, J. & GLOVER, S. (1994) School physical education: a crisis of meaning, *Changing Education: A Journal for Teachers and Administrators,* 1(2), 13–15.

VERTTNSKY, P. (1992) Reclaiming space, revisioning the body: the quest for gender-sensitive physical education, *Quest,* 44, pp. 373–396.

WACQUANT, L. (1989) Towards a reflexive sociology: a workshop with Pierre Bourdieu, *Sociological Theory,* 7(1), pp. 26–63.

WRIGHT, J. (1996) The construction of complementarity in physical education, *Gender and Education,* 8(1), pp. 61–79.

WRIGHT, J. (1998) Reconstructing gender in sport and physical education, in: C. HICKEY, L. FITZCLARENCE & R. MATTHEWS (Eds) *Where the Boys Are: Masculinity, Sport and Education,* pp. 13–26 (Geelong, VIC, Deakin University).

Mainland Chinese students at an elite Hong Kong university: habitus–field disjuncture in a transborder context

Cora Lingling Xu

ABSTRACT
Drawing on in-depth interview data from 31 mainland Chinese (MLC) students in a Hong Kong university, this article conceptualises MLC and Hong Kong higher education as two dissonant but interrelated subfields of the Chinese higher education field. The article argues that these MLC students' habitus, one that possesses rich economic, social and cultural capital, prompts a strong sense of entitlement to anticipated privileges. However, this sense of entitlement is disrupted by the differential capital valuations across these fields. There is thus notable habitus–field disjuncture, which, exacerbated by the hysteresis effect, gives rise to a sense of disappointment and ambivalence. This article demonstrates how the Hong Kong education credential, which these students initially set out to pursue as a form of capital, can become a disadvantage at multiple levels; the article illustrates that capital valuation and conversion in a transborder context is not a straightforward, but rather a complicated and sometimes contradictory, process.

Introduction

With the People's Republic of China's economic development and growing political influence on the international stage, there has been a steady increase in Chinese students stepping outside China's borders to pursue higher education (HE). In 2014, of the 4.5 million international students worldwide (OECD 2014), more than 690,000 tertiary-level students were from the People's Republic of China. In Hong Kong, the past decade has witnessed a 10-fold increase in the number of mainland Chinese (MLC) students pursuing undergraduate studies at Hong Kong's higher education institutions (HEIs) (University Grants Committee 2015).

Examining student flows from mainland China to Hong Kong, an intra-state yet border-crossing case, would appear to be an intriguing and important addition to the existing literature on international student experience (Brooks, Waters, and Pimlott-Wilson 2012; Fong 2011). In recent years, more research attention has been paid to intra-state student mobility, with the excellent example of Tindal et al.'s (2015) study on student flows between Scotland and England. Such intra-nation student mobility, as Tindal et al. pinpoint, is in effect tightly enmeshed with globalisation forces, given that domestic students are increasingly competing with mobile international students in a globally differentiated HE system.

It is perhaps axiomatic that student mobility provides the mobile student with 'distinction' (Bourdieu 1984), as much research into the geographies and sociology of international student migration has confirmed. Such 'distinction', or symbolic capital, consequent on acquiring international (usually western) credentials, is usually rewarded in the mobile student's domestic labour market upon their 'return trip' (Waters 2012, 130). Nevertheless, as Waters cautions, 'the "value" attached to mobility is not always transparent or easily "read off" an individual's international experiences' (2012, 128). Indeed, it remains unclear whether this necessarily applies in contexts where destinations are not in the Global West (Brooks, Waters, and Pimlott-Wilson 2012), but rather at the periphery of the system (Altbach 1989), such as Hong Kong, an emergent HE destination. In this article, I expound the nuances which demonstrate that not only is such 'value' attached to mobility itself not straightforward and transparent, but also that mobility can sometimes 'backfire', upsetting and disrupting the perceived advantages usually associated with, or assumed to be part and parcel of, cross-border student mobility.

Furthermore, in intra-state border-crossing situations, such as moving from mainland China to Hong Kong, the unique relationship between the two sides of the border constitute a special transborder context, which may give rise to distinctive social conditions that mediate student experiences (Tindal et al. 2015). Research has shown that, depending on the relative positioning of destination countries in relation to countries of origin, this assumed distinction can be problematic. Brooks, Waters, and Pimlott-Wilson (2012, 289) demonstrate that British students may sometimes find that their HE degrees obtained overseas 'impede job prospects' back in the United Kingdom. Li (2013) and Xiang and Shen (2009) also note that certain overseas qualifications may no longer serve MLC students well in the Chinese labour market.

However, this seems paradoxical in the case of Hong Kong. Hong Kong's HEIs have successfully branded themselves as 'best picks for smart, ambitious, internationally-minded higher performers in the mainland school system' (Shive 2010, 5). Opting for Hong Kong as a HE destination was considered a strategic move only accessible to a small fraction of top-scoring students in *Gaokao.*[1] Indeed, as student participants in this study revealed:

> When I was applying for universities, Hong Kong HEIs were the most popular among applicants; you could constantly read in the newspapers about how many *Gaokao* top scorers accepted scholarship offers from Hong Kong. (Yuhan, male second-year, business)

> The heated social discourse ... promoted Hong Kong HEIs as THE best choice for top students like us (Miusi, female graduate, social sciences)

In 2011, for instance, around two-thirds of top-scoring applicants (i.e. *Zhuangyuan*) were declined by the University of Hong Kong because they were not considered to possess the desired potential and overall ability (Wu 2011). Such a high positioning of Hong Kong HEIs may easily engender the assumption that academic credentials obtained in Hong Kong can reap high rewards in the MLC labour market. In view of the cautions about the problematic nature of such assumptions, a question thus arises: how far can the assumed distinction obtained through a Hong Kong degree be portable across the border?

Existing literature on MLC students in Hong Kong HEIs has highlighted the phenomenon of privileged classes deploying different forms of capital to maintain intergenerational advantages, while peasants are largely marginalised in such cross-border HE pursuits (Li and Bray 2006). Lam's (2006) study explicates differing orientations of MLC students, who identify more closely with the national identity, and their Hong Kong counterparts, who exhibit a more salient regional Hongkonger identity. Gao's (2010) data foreground students who are subject to constant 'active' and 'forced' exclusions, and who are caught between the local Hong Kong student community and the dominant MLC student community. Gu (2011) and Gu and Tong (2012) reveal how speakers of Putonghua, Cantonese and English are accorded different symbolic power and how they utilise their multiple linguistic repertoires to project multi-layered identities.

One issue, however, has been neglected in the afore-mentioned body of literature. That is, how do border-crossing students' understandings of these two social contexts that border one another inform/misinform practices? Inversely, how do cross-border HE pursuits shape the cultural and social identities of these students? Indeed, the interrelations between practices and identities have seldom been theorised in the existing literature. Therefore a second purpose of this article is to propose a conceptual vocabulary to provide a means of explanation. In what follows, I firstly introduce my research methods and then explicate the field characteristics and specify the habitus of MLC students in this study.

The study

To adequately address the questions of 'how a transborder context in itself informs/misinforms the practices of border-crossing students' and 'how these students' border-crossings shape their social and cultural identities', I selected the University of Oceania (UO),[2] a top English-medium research-intensive university in Hong Kong, as the site of investigation. Fieldwork took place between September 2013 and May 2014. Posters advertising details of this study were put up around the UO campus to recruit MLC student participants. Attracting more interested participants than originally intended, an online questionnaire was used to collect demographic information that informed a screening process. Because it was anticipated that factors such as students' length of stay in Hong Kong (as directly reflected in their year of study), gender, place of origin and subject may have influenced how they perceived their experiences in Hong Kong, efforts were made to ensure a relatively balanced representation of participants in the screening process. At a later stage, as initial analysis pointed to potential distinctions between current students and recent graduates (i.e. those who pursued undergraduate studies in the UO and were working in Hong Kong at the time of investigation), the snowball sampling strategy was utilised to recruit such recent graduates.

In total 31 participants, comprising 25 current undergraduates and six recent graduates, were recruited. All except for seven, who could not make the second round of interviews, participated in two rounds of individual interviews. To triangulate their interview accounts, participants' written accounts, such as blog entries were collected. Because some of these blog entries were not originally intended for this investigation, consent was obtained from the participants prior to access. Additionally, seven focus groups involving nine MLC participants and 18 of their friends (including both MLC and local Hong Kong students) were conducted.

Subfield characteristics – two dissonant fields

In Hong Kong, 95–98% of the population are ethnic Chinese. Many of them were previously refugees fleeing from natural and political disasters in mainland China. Memories of such disasters coupled with Hong Kong's colonial past and no clear promise of real independence shape a 'transit' mentality (Ong 1999, 2) among the Hong Kong people. Mathews (1997, 3), for instance, posits that on the eve of the return of Hong Kong's sovereignty to China, the Hong Kong people began to 'define themselves as having autonomous cultural identity'. This identity as 'Hongkongers', Mathews contends, involves 'Chineseness plus English / colonial education / colonialism' and 'Chineseness plus democracy / human rights / the rule of law' (1997, 3).

Since its reversion in 1997, following the 'One Country, Two Systems' principle, Hong Kong has been a Special Administrative Region, being guaranteed a high degree of autonomy in running its internal affairs (Chan and Clark 1991). However, there has been a discrepancy in the understanding of 'One Country, Two Systems'. Whereas the people of Hong Kong tend to emphasise the practice of 'two systems' – that is, maintenance of a high degree of autonomy and upholding distinct cultural, political and civil liberties – the Beijing government and the pro-Beijing camp in Hong Kong place more weight on 'one country', emphasising the country's interests and unity (Flowerdew and Leong 2010). Such a discrepancy is widely observed in Hong Kong's public discourse and is constitutive of what I argue later to be the 'anti-mainlandisation discourse' prevalent in Hong Kong (see Xu 2015).

Specifically, Hong Kong's deeper and more frequent interactions with mainland China have triggered sentiments that Hong Kong is becoming 'politically more dependent on Beijing, economically more reliant on the Mainland's support, socially more patriotic toward the [mainland], and legally more reliant on the interpretation of the Basic Law by the National People's Congress' (Hui and Lo 2014, 1106). Socially, closer economic ties between the two entities have engendered a series of controversies, including notable cases such as the 'locust' dispute and the 'maternity ward' controversy[3] (Ma 2012).

Culturally, Hong Kong's official languages include English and Cantonese, a dialect drastically different from Putonghua, the official language of mainland China. Since Cantonese is widely used in everyday life both on and off campus, it understandably becomes a point of tension, especially when juxtaposed with English as a global language and Putonghua as a national language. Research has shown that MLC students' movement across mainland China and Hong Kong has indexed the varying values attached to these three languages, which become 'emblematic of individual and group identities' (Gu and Tong 2012, 502); that is, the mainland China identity and a Hong Kong identity.

In the HE sphere, from its colonial days through to its current Special Administrative Region status, Hong Kong HE has been different, separate and independent from that of mainland China. Hong Kong's HEIs in particular have unique characteristics that distinguish them from HEIs in mainland China (Postiglione 1998). In recent years, in view of the increasing number of MLC students enrolled in Hong Kong HEIs, Hong Kong taxpayers have questioned whether they should sponsor non-local students in government-funded universities when only 18% of local high school graduates get funded places (Gao 2014). As a response to such concerns, Hong Kong's Education Bureau has proposed the withdrawal of the 600 annual subsidised places for non-local students in 2016/17, a significant proportion being MLC students (Yip 2015).

As will be demonstrated in the following, crossing the border between mainland China and Hong Kong immediately subjects the MLC students to a position of having to struggle for legitimacy. This is a clear instance where the 'effects of the field cease' and another field – that is, a 'relatively autonomous social microcosm' – takes over (Bourdieu 1993, 72).

While these students were highly sought-after elite students on the mainland, their presence in Hong Kong became mediated by the host of social, cultural and political dissonances already outlined. Such contrasting situations invoke Bourdieu's depiction of a field: 'a locus of a struggle to determine the conditions and the criteria of legitimate membership and legitimate hierarchy' (1988, 11).

In this sense, I conceptualise HE in China as a field with 'a high degree of autonomy in that it generates its own values and behavioural imperatives' (Naidoo 2004, 458); the MLC and the Hong Kong HE fields are its two major subfields embedded in a complex political, social, economic and cultural entanglement. The UO, the case-study site, can therefore be understood to represent a microcosm of the Hong Kong HE subfield. The types of capital recognised in this micro-field are influenced by the 'specific stakes and interests' (Bourdieu 1993, 72) of the fields within which it is embedded and those which surround it (the political and economic fields). The UO's reputation, stemming from its international ranking and locally perceived prestige, demand of its prospective students a high level of scholastic capital (e.g. top *Gaokao* marks) and cultural capital. This presupposes that MLC students recruited in this study belong to a very selective subgroup of students from mainland China, possessing particular habitus and capital profiles, which I now discuss.

MLC students' habitus

Academically speaking, all 31 MLC students were among the highest echelon of *Gaokao*-takers in mainland China. While two of them were *Zhuangyuan* (top-scoring students in *Gaokao*), 17 received offers from elite universities, including Peking University (PKU), Tsinghua University (THU) and Fudan University. For the remaining 14, half did not apply to any MLC university but reported that their *Gaokao* marks qualified them for top-tiered universities nonetheless. Their *Gaokao* marks served as the most widely recognised form of academic capital transferable across the two subfields of HE. However, as Ruhua (female second-year, business) suggested, apart from academic capital the UO also demands cultural capital (especially 'embodied') (Bourdieu 1986), such as 'English proficiency, but also the way you think and the way you talk' (Ruhua's words). In fact, these MLC students generally possessed rich resources of cultural capital. For instance, most had extensive travel experience within China and five had travelled abroad before coming to the UO. Some of these students had strong training in aspects of classical (high) Chinese culture, such as Chinese painting and calligraphy, and some had been exposed at an early age to western literature, such as Shakespearean works.

Regarding socio-economic status, 11 had been granted full or partial scholarships, among whom only two indicated that they could not afford the cost of living in Hong Kong. The remaining 20 self-financed students had to pay an annual tuition fee of HK$146,000 (£12,304) plus around HK$30,000 (£2528) maintenance expenditure. Two-thirds had parents occupying typical 'middle-class' jobs, such as doctors, accountants and teachers, while the other third had parents from business backgrounds. In terms of self-reported household income, the annual household income was above RMB 360,000 (£37,431) for six of them, between RMB 60,000 and 360,000 (£6325–37,431) for 24 students and below 60,000 RMB (£6325) for only one student. Therefore a majority of these students were from families with middle-class or upper-middle-class income levels.[4]

Since most of these students came from prestigious national or provincial high schools, they constantly talked of high school seniors or classmates in elite universities abroad or in mainland China. Some mentioned powerful family connections in government departments who 'made life easier' or rich family friends sponsoring trips abroad for them. Such social capital has the potential to engender a sense of entitlement, invoking the 'multiplier effect' that Bourdieu (1986, 249) talks of.

Generally these students possessed considerable economic, cultural and social capital, resonating with the image of 'mobile students' that Waters identifies:

> ... generally ... internationally mobile students [...] are financially secure; have the support (emotional and material) of family and friends (i.e. 'social capital'); have been raised in an environment that places great value on formal education and credentials; have highly educated parents; and have experienced overseas travel as a child. (Waters 2012, 128)

However, this begs the question of why these students chose to come to Hong Kong, rather than mainland China or other popular HE destinations, such as the United States, the United Kingdom or Australia. When asked this question, all 31 MLC participants consistently articulated what I argue to be their 'Hong Kong Dream'. Specifically, this 'Dream' bears three characteristics. The first is a desire to change, as manifested on two different levels: to break free from the familiar and mundane life on the mainland, what Longnu (female third-year, sciences) described as a 'stable path, the end of which [she] can anticipate'. The second level was evidenced in their desire to steer clear of the alleged corruption in society and unethical academic practice on university campuses in mainland China (Qiu 2010). The second characteristic rested in their yearning to capitalise on Hong Kong's close alignment with international practices and standards, its English-rich environment, abundant opportunities for exposure to cosmopolitan lifestyles and the chances to gain overseas experiences. The last characteristic was reflected in their rich imaginations of Hong Kong as a sophisticated and inclusive society, which mirrors what Fong (2011) describes as a yearning for the 'developed' world (Xu 2015). Importantly, this Hong Kong Dream was enmeshed with these students' positioning of Hong Kong as a flexible space that would enable them to move with ease post graduation, whether relocating abroad, remaining in Hong Kong or returning to mainland China.

To a great extent, this Hong Kong Dream illuminated the 'scheme of perceptions' rooted in these students' past experiences (i.e. habitus), 'mak[ing] some possibilities inconceivable, others improbable and a limited range acceptable' (Reay 2004, 435). It underpinned these students' expectations and anticipated their likely strategising upon border-crossing. Put differently, these students needed to understand the internal workings, especially the conversion rates of forms of capitals between the two subfields. In view of the field dissonances discussed previously, it is likely that the habitus of the MLC students would encounter disjuncture. Therefore, in what follows, I present evidence to illustrate how these MLC students successfully or unsuccessfully converted/exchanged capitals in the transborder context.

Border-crossing advantages

Some students referred to how their education experience in Hong Kong contributed to positional advantages. For instance, as students in the UO, all MLC students in this study had been issued with Hong Kong identity cards that marked their distinction in comparison with ordinary mainland visitors. Such a distinction was accentuated upon crossing the border between Hong Kong and mainland China. Lingshan (female first-year, social sciences) described this experience vividly:

> ... it felt quite convenient to take the Hong Kong resident channel because mainland visitors had to queue in long, long queues. When I walked past them as a Hong Kong resident, I felt like this ID card ... had given me lots of convenience, and it made me feel like a Hongkonger.

While MLC tourists are regulated, and (in a sense) disadvantaged by rules jointly set out between mainland China and Hong Kong, MLC students like Lingshan can bypass such regulations because their academic (cultural) capital had been converted into an institutionalised form of cultural capital; that is, the rights to residency in Hong Kong. At the border, this new form of cultural capital is ritualised and accentuated overtly, to such an extent that it is turned into a form of symbolic capital (Bourdieu 1986, 245). To some, such recognition of the accordance of an elevated sense of symbolic capital appears to be an instantaneous sign of capital conversion; nonetheless, given the notable field dissonances already discussed, acquiring such symbolic capital can entail a degree of convenience and social recognition. Zhang's (2013, 99) study on Chinese and Taiwanese tourists similarly posits that travel documents as such can enable the traveller to 'negotiate macro-political structures to her/his own advantage'. In some cases, such symbolic capital can enable the MLC students to evade public scrutiny in daily life. Lingshan recalled another incident, this time on her trip back home during the Chinese New Year holiday:

> When we were passing through the border we all had to place our luggage on the bus. There was this [possibly] mainlander whose luggage blocked the way of the next passenger, a female Hongkonger. This woman complained, 'How come you mainlanders' *suzhi* [quality] is so poor?' That male mainlander started to defend himself, in Cantonese, 'I am not a mainlander; I am a Hongkonger'. The woman replied disdainfully, 'Then show me your ID card'. She repeatedly demanded this but the man did not show any such evidence in the end. Seeing this, I was really sad.

This incident further testifies to the degree of symbolic violence this Hong Kong ID card can produce; the perceived and imagined hierarchy of ID cards (i.e. Hong Kong and MLC ID cards) translates directly into a perception of the 'quality' of their respective possessors. Elsewhere, I have discussed in greater detail how deeply such anti-mainlandisation sentiments in Hong Kong impacted on the daily life and concomitantly the self-perceptions of the MLC students in my study (Xu 2015). While Lingshan was made more aware of the strong currency of her Hong Kong residency capital in this liminal space, her short-lived happiness about feeling like a 'Hongkonger' was imbued with a deep level of uncertainty and unease, showing a conflicted habitus, one that was in transition.

Lack of assuredness

Thus far, the MLC students' habitus has been shown to be characterised by a cognisance of the intricate rules of two bordering fields. However, as Bourdieu cautions (Reay 2004), habitus is formed on the basis of understandings and experiences that were available prior to border-crossing. This means the habitus cannot anticipate situations that have not occurred before. For the MLC students, their habitus assumed privileges and generated actions that would maximise capital conversion in the new field of Hong Kong HE. However, in what follows I show that when encountering the new field, these MLC students also confronted situations novel to their habitus, leading to a habitus–field disjuncture and resulted in the need to address difficult emotions.

Xue, for instance, complained about perceiving in herself less of a sense of assuredness compared with peers attending PKU and THU, who considered themselves to be 'God's favoured ones' (*tianzhijiaozi*). Having studied at THU for one preparatory year,[5] Xue recalled that the Deans or the President of THU frequently inculcated in the students such notions as 'you represent the highest standard of the country'. Such inculcation, as Hansen (2013) astutely observes, reflects the Chinese Communist Party's strategy of portraying elite university students for whom there is a high demand in terms of leading the nation.

In comparison, Xue lamented the lack of such a sense of assuredness at the UO. When questioned why, given that the UO has consistently fared better than top MLC universities in international university rankings, Xue suggested 'Hong Kong after all is a smaller place; even if you are the top among seven million people[6] you still don't seem to have so many halos around you'. The drastic difference in scale – that is, being top of 1.3 billion people in comparison with seven million – engendered a sense of loss in Xue. Notably, Xue declined PKU's offer in pursuit of her Hong Kong Dream. However, her habitus established on the mainland predisposed her to be more ready to perceive the social recognition accorded to students in elite MLC universities; in contrast, she was less able to recognise the level of symbolic capital accorded by the UO. As Bourdieu writes:

> … capital exists and acts as symbolic capital … in its relationship with a habitus predisposed to perceive it as a sign, and as a sign of importance, that is, to know and recognise it on the basis of cognitive structures able and inclined to grant it recognition because they are attuned to what it is. (2000, 242)

In fact, there was a tacitly shared sense of loss over abandoning offers from prestigious MLC universities in favour of those from Hong Kong among MLC students on the UO campus.

> In the first semester, I think everybody felt similarly … many people were really low, not knowing why they came here. (Qingwen, female second-year, sciences)

Compared with other international students who usually look up to the host university and culture (Montgomery 2010), 15 out of 31 of the MLC students spoke about this sense of loss resulting from having chosen Hong Kong. This may be related to the sceptical views prevalent in MLC media discourse, which casts doubt on top-scoring MLC students' decisions to come to Hong Kong while rejecting offers from top MLC universities (Dong and Wei 2015). More crucially, we can discern a mismatch between their habitus and the new field: it is clear that the MLC students still operated their durable dispositions (habitus) acquired in mainland China when they encountered the unfamiliar characteristics of the Hong Kong HE field; there is therefore a notable time lag between encountering the new field and the establishment of a transformed habitus. This delay is what Bourdieu and Passeron (1977, 78) term the hysteresis effect:

> …as a result of the *hysteresis effect*…practices are always liable to incur negative sanctions when the environment with which they are actually confronted is too distant from that to which they are objectively fitted. (Bourdieu and Passeron 1977, 78; original emphasis)

Xue's comment thus depicted a troubled transformation, in which her links with the original field had been disrupted and her identity as an elite student at an elite institution was being challenged.

'Double-betrayal'

Internships and jobs applications

Apart from perceiving a lack of social recognition, some MLC students also reported the diminishing value of their education credentials acquired in Hong Kong when applying for internships and jobs both in Hong Kong and mainland China. This sentiment was conveyed by a majority of senior students, especially those in their third year of study or those who were recent graduates. Miusi, a social sciences graduate, spoke about feeling 'doubly betrayed':

> When we turned down offers from PKU or THU, we actually had faith in the credentials of the UO. However, we realise upon graduation that Hong Kong employers have this mindset that 'a monk from outside chants scriptures better' (*wailaide heshang huinianjing*) – in this sense we are betrayed by the Hong Kong employers. Meanwhile, for those of us who return to seek employment on the mainland, we find that compared with peers from top MLC universities who have already established extensive alumni and social networks, we are severely disadvantaged. I feel I am doubly betrayed.

When MLC students chose the UO over top MLC universities, their durable dispositions anticipated that the institutionalised cultural capital acquired in Hong Kong would be highly prized in both the MLC and Hong Kong labour markets. This strong sense of entitlement, however, was frustrated when expectations were not met.

Firstly, as Waters's (2007, 493) study reveals, many Hong Kong employers have themselves been educated in the West so they prefer to recruit those similarly in possession of western degrees. This has led to a devaluation of education capital acquired in local Hong Kong universities, whose graduates are unfavourably viewed as 'less competent'. Although Miusi managed to obtain a job in Hong Kong, the degree of competition she experienced when applying for jobs led her to perceive that her Hong Kong credential was negatively valued.

Xue similarly pointed out that her 'locally educated' identity had reduced her competitiveness in the internship market too, this time when compared with peers from top MLC universities:

> I realised that peers from PKU and THU got more internship positions and better welfare packages in investment banks in Hong Kong than us, that is, those 'educated locally'.

Xue perceived her position to be unfavourable when competing against peers whose universities' offers she had rejected previously. She added that these peers were favoured possibly because of their familiarity with the MLC culture and business environment, which is considered as an important form of cultural capital given that finance companies in Hong Kong nowadays have significantly more business interaction with MLC partners (Shen 2008). Xue's absence from her field of origin had unwittingly deprived her of a legitimate claim to familiarity with MLC business culture. As a result, Xue encountered both a devaluation of her Hong Kong education credential and a lack of legitimate claim to her MLC cultural capital.

Moreover, when competing against other Hong Kong students who were likewise 'educated locally' in Hong Kong universities, more than two-thirds of these MLC students felt they were lacking a competitive edge, mainly due to insufficient linguistic capital or a lack of understanding of the local context. For instance, Min, a final-year psychology student, suggested:

> When I attended internship and job interviews in Hong Kong, the interviewers usually enjoyed talking to me, but in the end they usually had concerns over my Cantonese and whether I could integrate well in their team. Once, I was one of the final two candidate[s] but they eventually picked the local candidate because of my Cantonese.

Not only did Min lack the prized currency in Hong Kong's linguistic market (Bourdieu 1991), Cantonese, the hiring managers' concern about whether she could fit into the team also reflected their reservations about Min's understanding of Hong Kong's local business culture. Min's perception is echoed in Gao's (2014) study, which paints a revealing picture of how Hong Kong employers marginalised non-local applicants for similar reasons. Taken together, this lack of the locally prized linguistic capital and local level of contextual understanding can be considered as a lack of 'local cultural capital'.

Besides these, when returning to the MLC labour market, these students found that they lacked the social capitals accumulated through institutional affiliations that their peers in prestigious MLC universities possessed. These students frequently talked of 'missing out' on chances to establish social networks that were deemed crucial to obtaining a job. For instance, Min said in a focus group:

> In undergraduate years they had loads of internship experience and accumulated substantial connections in the mainland that make job searches easier. For us, being in Hong Kong means it is not practical to get internships or part-time jobs back there. When we return we have no connection whatsoever and have to start all over from scratch.

Additionally, some students complained that the education credentials from Hong Kong were not as well recognised because employers in the MLC labour market were not experienced in assessing comparable qualifications from Hong Kong HEIs: this could be considered a hysteresis effect that MLC employers experience because it will take time for them to become familiar with the Hong Kong HE qualifications.

Applications for postgraduate studies overseas

Opting out of the MLC HE field meant that students' habitus was often in misalignment with the new field. This was evident in their complaints about feeling isolated when applying for postgraduate studies abroad, as Liwan suggested:

> ... it is easier for [peers in MLC universities] to find companions taking the same path. I have a childhood friend in Beijing who has formed a five-member group for her postgraduate entrance exam preparation ... in the UO we make our own applications. Therefore, our journey is lonelier.

The MLC students' habitus cultivated in mainland China found little echo in the field of Hong Kong HE. Instead, these students became aware of the less advantageous post-graduation employment trends in the UO as compared with those of top MLC universities. According to statistics released by the UO, only around one-fifth of its bachelor's degree graduates pursue further studies each year. Among its local Hong Kong students who continue further studies, only around 10% go abroad. In contrast, PKU and THU annually record around 80% of undergraduates continuing on to further studies, with around 26–32% going overseas (Peking University 2014; Tsinghua University 2014). To these MLC students, therefore, the UO's institutional habitus characterised by a low level of applications for postgraduate studies stood in sharp contrast to the collegial atmosphere among peers in MLC

HEIs. Their desire for what was not available at the UO arose from a disjuncture between their original habitus and the field of Hong Kong HE.

Meanwhile, these MLC students seemed to find little opportunity to tap into the institutional prestige of the UO, a prominent university with a considerable number of distinguished alumni overseas. Indeed, Liwan's account seemed to be concerned predominantly with the lack of available resources among the MLC-origin alumni of the UO. They did not benefit from the social capital conferred by local Hong Kong alumni, possibly because of their differing habitus, which was reflected in their divergent aspirations and dispositions. Rui, a second-year male business student, revealed:

> It is much more convenient and comfortable to listen to somebody sharing experience in Putonghua than in English. Also, the graduation plans and issues of concern of MLC students are largely different from local students. This means information shared by [Hong Kong] senior students is not as straightforward, useful or copyable.

All of the participants in this study explained that normally they only sought advice from MLC-origin seniors, instead of local seniors. They therefore found it harder to draw on the UO's institutional capitals in the same ways as their local Hong Kong peers could. While these students were able to benefit from the MLC-student networks in the UO, when it came to advice about employment or postgraduate application overseas, given the relatively short history, their social networks were unable to exert an equal level of influence as a strong Hong Kong social network could potentially facilitate.

Specifically, the number of MLC students recruited to Hong Kong HEIs began to increase more significantly (e.g. by 56% in 2005/06) from 2004 when Hong Kong HEIs began strategically recruiting more self-financed MLC students (Li 2010). However, as Hardy posits, due to the hysteresis effect:

> … the time lag between field change and the recognition of configurations of capital (habitus) that would support dominant field positions is always a long one, measured in decades rather than weeks. (Hardy 2008, 138)

It will take time for current MLC students and recent graduates to feed back their experience of internship and job-seeking or experience of applying for postgraduate studies to prospective MLC students. For the MLC students in this study, when they decided to choose the UO over leading MLC universities between 2007 and 2010, they did not quite anticipate the implied opportunity cost which they were currently experiencing.

Notably, while the accounts presented underline the relative disadvantages of MLC students in getting support for postgraduate application for study abroad, this does not mean that none of them succeeded in being admitted by overseas universities. In fact, according to statistics released by the UO, more than one-third of the MLC bachelor's degree graduates in 2014 enrolled in universities abroad. Of these successful cases, at least half received offers from high-ranking international universities, such as the Ivy League universities in the United States. Of the nine third-year students in this study, two obtained offers from prestigious HEIs in the United States and Europe. In contrast, the collegial atmosphere to apply for postgraduate degrees in MLC institutions would not necessarily guarantee admission to elite institutions overseas.

In fact, as these students possessed rich academic, cultural and social capitals, obtaining a job or receiving offers from overseas universities ought not to be a formidable task for them. Rather, more crucially, the hysteresis effect limited the power of these MLC students' capital in a transborder context. From a social justice perspective, these students were already in a privileged position. Their sense of double-disadvantage evoked the image of Reay's (2013) British middle-class parents who send their children to comprehensive schools. These middle-class parents, despite their advantageous social positions, still mobilise their middle-class habitus to justify their privileges and express a great deal of fear and anxiety at the prospect of not being able to retain such privileges. Similarly, these MLC students' fear of losing their advantage over students with similar credentials at top MLC universities was embedded in their sense of entitlement. Therefore, despite their privileged position, they used their elite student status to justify their disadvantaged and disconnected position in the transborder context.

Discussion and conclusion

In this article, I draw on the case of border-crossing MLC students at an elite Hong Kong university to demonstrate how the complex interrelations between the two neighbouring fields of Hong Kong and MLC HE have exerted considerable influence over transborder capital valuations. I have identified dissonances between these two neighbouring fields and expounded the MLC students' habitus. Their possession of rich capitals has engendered a strong sense of entitlement in their anticipation of experience in Hong Kong HE. In some ways, these MLC students' strategising has been successful. For example, some managed to ensure that their various forms of capital were recognised or to exchange them for other forms of prized capital in the new field. Nevertheless, due to the hysteresis effect, MLC students have experienced a mismatch between their habitus and the new field, as evidenced in, for instance, Xue's inability to appreciate the symbolic capital accorded by the Hong Kong HE field.

Specifically, in the Hong Kong labour market they perceived triple 'disadvantages', including being considered as 'educated locally', losing legitimate claim to MLC cultural capital and lacking 'local cultural capital'. In the MLC labour market, they missed opportunities to accumulate social capital and their Hong Kong education credentials were not rewarded properly.

However, I do not intend to paint a bleak picture of these MLC students' experiences. On the contrary, I emphasise that these students are highly privileged individuals who consciously or unknowingly used strategies to gain greater advantages in HE and the labour market through border-crossing. The undermining of their sense of entitlement to privileges can therefore be considered as the opportunity costs of their initial strategising. This therefore has broader implications for aspiring MLC students contemplating the prospect of studying at Hong Kong HEIs.

A Bourdieusian lens has been critical for understanding the complex capital valuations in these two neighbouring fields, especially in cases in which capital conversion becomes complicated due to changing inter-field relations. These MLC students found that they could not simultaneously embody the cultural (elite education) and social (alumni network) capitals necessary to achieve privileges enjoyed by their elite counterparts owning 'native membership' in either field (Bourdieu 1990, 66). These students thus felt trapped in their cultural distance from the Hong Kong elite students and their social and physical distance from elite students in MLC universities. Such a 'tricky' situation, I argue, is the consequence of two levels of habitus–field disjuncture.

The first level is that their habitus etched in the MLC HE field made it difficult for them to mobilise resources available in the Hong Kong HE field. They did not have adequate access to the range of academic and social capitals in the unfamiliar new field in the same way that their Hong Kong peers did.

The second level of disjuncture is that their 'Hong Kong education credential', the newly-acquired institutionalised cultural capital, had become an added layer to their original habitus. This new layer bestowed on them the identity of being 'educated locally' while also implying a critical 'absence' from mainland China. Being 'locally educated' was perceived as a deficit, devalued in the Hong Kong employment market. Meanwhile, their 'critical absence' meant that they lacked social capital accrued in mainland China, or recognition comparable with that accorded to elite MLC university graduates in the MLC job market. These two levels of habitus–field disjuncture had become intensified because of the time it takes for habitus to adapt to a new field; that is, the hysteresis effect.

Clearly, these MLC students were not 'disadvantaged' in an absolute sense. Their perception of being 'disadvantaged' was not an amalgamation of various disadvantages. Rather, it was striking that what they initially set out to pursue as an advantage, a capital – namely the Hong Kong education credential – could, in a transborder context, become a disadvantage at multiple levels. This complication added to the nuances of their identity constructions, and also demonstrated that in a transborder context, the conversion or valuation of capital forms is not a straightforward, but rather a complicated and, at times, contradictory, process.

Notes

1. *Gaokao* refers to the National College Entrance Examination.
2. This is a pseudonym, as are all the student participants' names in this article.
3. The 'locust' dispute refers to discriminatory name-calling acts between Hong Kong and MLC people; for example, some Hong Kong people refer to MLC counterparts as 'locusts' who exhaust Hong Kong's public resources, while they are called 'British dogs' in return. Maternity ward short supply is about mainland mothers flocking to Hong Kong public hospitals to deliver babies. Such behaviour is considered an exploitation of Hong Kong's welfare system, leading to inadequate space in maternity wards for Hong Kong's local mothers.
4. In 2005, China's National Bureau of Statistics categorised the annual income of a middle-class household as between RMB 60,000 and 500,000 (£6325–52,711) (Wang 2008, 58). *The Economist* suggests that Chinese urban households with an annual income between RMB 40,000 and 100,000 (£4217–10,542) are 'upper-middle class', while those with an income of between RMB 100,000 and 200,000 (£10,542–21,084) are 'mass affluent' households (Gürüz 2011, 321).
5. Before 2012, the UO had an agreement with seven top MLC universities to allow MLC students to spend a preparatory year in one MLC university before going to study in the UO.
6. The population size of Hong Kong.

Acknowledgements

The author would like to acknowledge the funding support from the Cambridge Trust for the research project on which this article is based. The author is immensely grateful for Professor Diane Reay's guidance, inspiration and invaluable feedback. The author also wants to thank Mona Jebril, David Pomeroy, Dr Selena Yanyue Yuan and two anonymous reviewers for their helpful suggestions on earlier drafts of this article. The author is deeply indebted to the students who generously shared their lived experiences.

Disclosure statement

No potential conflict of interest was reported by the author.

References

Altbach, P. 1989. "The New Internationalism: Foreign Students and Scholars." *Studies in Higher Education* 14 (2): 125–136.

Bourdieu, P. 1984. *Distinction: A Social Critique of the Judgment of Taste*. Cambridge, MA.: Harvard University Press.

Bourdieu, P. 1986. "The Forms of Capital." In *Handbook of Theory and Research for the Sociology of Education*, edited by John G. Richardson, 241–258. New York: Greenwood Press.

Bourdieu, P. 1988. *Homo Academicus*. Stanford: Stanford University Press.

Bourdieu, P. 1990. *The Logic of Practice*. Cambridge: Polity.

Bourdieu, P. 1991. *Language and Symbolic Power*. Cambridge: Polity Press in association with Basil Blackwell.

Bourdieu, P. 1993. *Sociology in Question*. London: SAGE Publications.

Bourdieu, P. 2000. *Pascalian Meditations*. Cambridge: Polity.

Bourdieu, P., and J.-C. Passeron. 1977. *Reproduction in Education, Society and Culture*. London: Sage.

Brooks, R., J. Waters, and H. Pimlott-Wilson. 2012. "International Education and the Employability of UK Students." *British Educational Research Journal* 38 (2): 281–298.

Chan, M. K., and D. J. Clark, eds. 1991. *The Hong Kong Basic Law: Blueprint for "Stability and Prosperity" under Chinese Sovereignty?*. Hong Kong: Hong Kong University Press.

Dong, X., and T. Wei. 2015. "申请学生少 '港校热'再降温 [Declining Number of Applicants: 'Craze for Hong Kong Universities' Diminishes]." 北京青年报 Beijing Youth, March 30. http://epaper.ynet.com/html/2015-03/30/content_124506.htm?div=-1

Flowerdew, J., and S. Leong. 2010. "Presumed Knowledge in the Discursive Construction of Socio-Political and Cultural Identity." *Journal of Pragmatics* 42 (8): 2240–2252.

Fong, V. 2011. *Paradise Redefined: Transnational Chinese Students and the Quest for Flexible Citizenship in the Developed World*. Stanford: Stanford University Press.

Gao, X. 2010. *Strategic Language Learning: The Roles of Agency and Context*. Bristol: Multilingual Matters.

Gao, X. 2014. "'Floating Elites': Interpreting Mainland Chinese Undergraduates' Graduation Plans in Hong Kong." *Asia Pacific Education Review* 15 (2): 223–235.

Gu, M. 2011. "'I Am Not Qualified to Be a Hongkongese because of My Accented Cantonese': Mainland Chinese Immigrant Students in Hong Kong." *Journal of Multilingual and Multicultural Development* 32 (6): 515–529.

Gu, M., and H. K. Tong. 2012. "Space, Scale and Languages: Identity Construction of Cross-Boundary Students in a Multilingual University in Hong Kong." *Language and Education* 26 (6): 505–515.

Gürüz, K. 2011. *Higher Education and International Student Mobility in the Global Knowledge Economy*. Albany: State University of New York Press.

Hansen, A. S. 2013. "Purity and Corruption: Chinese Communist Party Applicants and the Problem of Evil." *Ethnos. Journal of Anthropology* 78 (1): 47–74.

Hardy, C. 2008. "Hysteresis." In *Pierre Bourdieu: Key Concepts*, edited by M. Grenfell, 131–148. Stocksfield: Acumen.

Hui, C. Y. T., and T. W. Lo. 2014. "One Country, Two Cultures: Are Hong Kong Mock Jurors 'Mainlandised' by the Predominant Chinese Criminal Justice Concept of Confession?" *International Journal of Offender Therapy and Comparative Criminology* 59 (10): 1104–1124.

Lam, C. M.-H. 2006. "Reciprocal Adjustment by Host and Sojourning Groups: Mainland Chinese Students in Hong Kong." In *Living and Studying Abroad: Research and Practice*, edited by M. Byram and A. Feng, 91–107. Clevedon: Multilingual Matters.

Li, M. 2010. "Border Crossing and Market Integration: Mainland Consumers Meet Hong Kong Suppliers." In *Crossing Borders in East Asian Higher Education*, edited by D. Chapman, W. Cummings and G. Postiglione, 319–342. Hong Kong: Springer.

Li, Z. 2013. "A Critical Account of Employability Construction through the Eyes of Chinese Postgraduate Students in the UK." *Journal of Education and Work* 26 (5): 473–493.

Li, M., and M. Bray. 2006. "Social Class and Cross-Border Higher Education: Mainland Chinese Students in Hong Kong and Macau." *Journal of International Migration and Integration* 7 (4): 407–424.

Ma, E. K.-W. 2012. *Desiring Hong Kong, Consuming South China: Transborder Cultural Politics, 1970–2010*. Hong Kong: Hong Kong University Press.

Mathews, G. 1997. "Heunggongyahn: On the past, Present, and Future of Hong Kong Identity." *Bulletin of Concerned Asian Scholars* 29 (3): 3–13.

Montgomery, C. 2010. *Understanding the International Student Experience*. Basingstoke: Palgrave Macmillan.

Naidoo, R. 2004. "Fields and Institutional Strategy: Bourdieu on the Relationship between Higher Education, Inequality and Society." *British Journal of Sociology of Education* 25 (4): 457–471.

OECD (Organisation for Economic Co-operation and Development). 2014. *Education at a Glance 2014*. Paris: OECD.

Ong, A. 1999. *Flexible Citizenship: The Cultural Logics of Transnationality*. Durham: Duke University Press.

Peking University. 2014. *Peking University 2014 Graduate Employment Annual Report (in Chinese)*. Beijing: Peking University.

Postiglione, G. 1998. "Maintaining Global Engagement in the Face of National Integration in Hong Kong." *Comparative Education Review* 42 (1): 30–45.

Qiu, J. 2010. "Publish or Perish in China." *Nature News* 463 (7278): 142–143.

Reay, D. 2004. "'It's All Becoming a Habitus': Beyond the Habitual Use of Habitus in Educational Research." *British Journal of Sociology of Education* 25 (4): 431–444.

Reay, D. 2013. "The White Middle Classes and Urban Comprehensive Schools: Ambivalences and Anxieties of Privilege." In *Privilege, Agency and Affect*, edited by Claire Maxwell and Peter Aggleton, 167–184. Basingstoke, Hampshire: Palgrave Macmillan.

Shen, J. 2008. "Hong Kong under Chinese Sovereignty: Economic Relations with Mainland China, 1978-2007." *Eurasian Geography and Economics* 49 (3): 326–340.

Shive, G. 2010. "Exporting Higher Education Services: An Engine of Growth for Hong Kong." http://www.hkjournal.org/PDF/2010_spring/4.pdf

Tindal, S., H. Packwood, A. Findlay, S. Leahy, and D. McCollum. 2015. "In What Sense 'Distinctive'? The Search for Distinction amongst Cross-Border Student Migrants in the UK." *Geoforum* 64: 90–99.

Tsinghua University. 2014. *Tsinghua University 2014 Graduate Employment Report (in Chinese)*. Beijing: Tsinghua University.

University Grants Committee. 2015. "Non-Local Student Enrolment (Headcount) of UGC-Funded Programmes by Level of Study and Sex, 2008/09 to 2014/15." http://cdcf.ugc.edu.hk/cdcf/searchStatSiteReport.do#

Wang, X. 2008. "Divergent Identities, Convergent Interests: The Rising Middle-Income Stratum in China and Its Civic Awareness." *Journal of Contemporary China* 17 (54): 53–69.

Waters, J. 2007. "'Roundabout Routes and Sanctuary Schools': The Role of Situated Educational Practices and Habitus in the Creation of Transnational Professionals." *Global Networks* 7 (4): 477–497.

Waters, J. 2012. "Geographies of International Education: Mobilities and the Reproduction of Social (Dis)Advantage." *Geography Compass* 6 (3): 123–136.

Wu, K. 2011. "Cream of the Crop." *China Daily Asia*, August 12.

Xiang, B., and W. Shen. 2009. "International Student Migration and Social Stratification in China." *International Journal of Educational Development* 29 (5): 513–522.

Xu, C. L. 2015. "When the Hong Kong Dream Meets the Anti-mainlandisation Discourse: Mainland Chinese Students in Hong Kong." *Journal of Current Chinese Affairs* 44 (3): 15–47.

Yip, A. 2015. "Education Bureau Wants All Subsidised University Places to Go to Local Students." *South China Morning Post*, January 4.

Zhang, J. J. 2013. "Borders on the Move: Cross-Strait Tourists' Material Moments on 'the Other Side' in the midst of Rapprochement between China and Taiwan." *Geoforum* 48: 94–101.

Cultural capital as whiteness? Examining logics of ethno-racial representation and resistance

Derron Wallace

ABSTRACT
There is a significant, longstanding tradition in British sociological research that renders cultural capital synonymous with whiteness. This article suggests that one substantive factor that contributes to the enduring relationship between whiteness and cultural capital is the paucity of research on the Black and ethnic minority middle classes. Studies of social class in the United Kingdom frequently render middle-class life synonymous with whiteness and all too often fix ethno-racial identities to the working classes. The article draws on a 14-month comparative ethnography as a case study to provide an asset-based reading of cultural capital among the Black Caribbean middle classes in Britain. The findings suggest that the seemingly exclusive link between whiteness and cultural capital is problematised by Black Caribbean young people, and therefore should be further critiqued in sociological and educational research, especially when developing cultural capital analyses.

Introduction

There is a significant, longstanding tradition in British sociology of education that renders cultural capital synonymous with whiteness (Archer 2011; Reay 2007). For decades, studies of social class in Britain have frequently equated middle-class life to whiteness (Nayak 2007) and all too often confined ethno-racial identities to the working classes (Rollock et al. 2015). This development is almost entirely unintentional, but nonetheless consequential for Black and ethnic minority communities' representation in sociological research. To date, there is surprisingly little known about middle-class Black and ethnic minority young people, and even less is known about how they operationalise cultural capital in schools. The raft of research highlighting the white middle classes as bearers of cultural capital and the dearth of scholarship describing Blacks as capital-carrying subjects inadvertently results in perceptions of a fixed, long-term relationship between whiteness and cultural capital. Contemporary exegeses and current uses of cultural capital therefore necessitate critical interrogation. I ask: is cultural capital inherently and exclusively shaped by whiteness? This article intervenes in the commonplace construction of cultural capital in educational research as a configuration of whiteness and interrogates the politics of ethno-racial representation in social class research in the field of education.

I contend that the paucity of research on the Black and ethnic minority middle classes (Meghji 2016; Rollock et al. 2015) contributes to an enduring relationship between whiteness and cultural capital. This factor, among others, contributes to the proliferation of a one-sided 'class imaging' of Black and ethnic minority pupils (Archer 2010). I deploy the term 'class imaging' to signal the limited, and arguably racist, class perceptions frequently associated with Black identities – assumptions that render blackness synonymous with material and cultural poverty. To counter logics of deficiency and acknowledge the complexity of class relations among Black youth, this article draws on a 14-month ethnography as a case study to provide an asset-based reading of cultural capital among Black Caribbean middle-class young people in South London (Wallace 2016). First, I explore Bourdieu's original definition of cultural capital, after which I briefly examine recent scholarship on cultural capital sensitive to ethno-racial differences. I then outline the design of the study and discuss the findings, which illustrate how Black Caribbean middle-class young people in a large state school question the singular 'class imaging' of Blacks in British schools and society. The findings offer insights into the racialisation of cultural capital and underscore why the little-questioned affiliation between whiteness and cultural capital should be challenged in sociological and educational research.

To avoid essentialist and oversimplified renditions of whiteness, I characterise whiteness in broad, dynamic terms, acknowledging its (in)visibility and variability across time and space. Informed by critical whiteness studies, this article defines whiteness as a historical system of thought and action that affords undue structural, material and political privileges that often remains unmarked and unquestioned in contemporary British society (Nayak 2007). More specifically, whiteness is a set of unspoken norms (Gillborn 2005) and a 'category of positional superiority that exists in juxtaposition to "non-whiteness"' (Bablak, Raby, and Pomerantz 2016, 57). The unremarked normalcy of whiteness – as a political and institutional practice – is informed by decades of European colonialism and imperialism (Gillborn 2005) – forms of domination that endure through the current global political order, neoliberal economic arrangements, institutionalised racism in education and hierarchies of difference in everyday life (Ball 2015). To this end, whiteness rests at the foundation of structural inequality in British society and beyond (Rollock et al. 2015). By complicating the role of whiteness in social class research in local settings across Britain, we can better understand the racialisation of class differentiation, division and domination. The subsequent sections critique the use of cultural capital as the exclusive expression of elite and middle-class whiteness.

Cultural capital and ethno-racial dominance

Bourdieu's notion of cultural capital enjoys considerable currency in sociological and educational research. Like his other key concepts, cultural capital has become a buzzword often used without definitional specificity (Moore 2004). But the conceptual purchase of cultural capital as Bourdieu conceived of it cannot be reduced to popular parlance, nor can its theoretical complexities be diminished to common sense (Bennett et al. 2009). Bourdieu defined cultural capital as 'instruments for the appropriation of symbolic wealth socially designated as worthy of being sought and possessed' (1977, 488). Cultural capital has 'the capacity to reproduce itself, produce profits, expand and contains the tendency to persist' (Bourdieu 1986, 241). Put plainly, Bourdieu conceived of cultural capital as tastes, knowledge and skill sets (re)produced by privileged groups in homes, schools and related institutional fields that influence dispositions and the accumulation of power (Moore 2004).

Bourdieu extended the concept 'capital' beyond classic Marxist understandings of it by proposing cultural capital in three forms: an embodied state, noted as 'long-lasting dispositions of the mind and the body' that are observed through speech, stance and style choices (Bourdieu 1986, 245); an objectified state, represented in the material production of 'art works, galleries, museums, laboratories, scientific instruments, books ... [and] artefacts of various kinds' (Moore 2008, 105); and an institutionalised state, reflected in professional credentials and educational qualifications (Moore 2004, 2008). In this respect, cultural capital represents an amendment to the Marxist traditions of social class – a necessarily generative point of departure useful for considering the material and immaterial dimensions of social class (Robbins 2005).

Although Bourdieu offered insights into the composition, mobilisation and transmission of different forms of cultural capital throughout his career (Bourdieu 1977, 1990b; Bourdieu and Passeron 1977), his perspectives on the canonisation and legitimation of racialised expressions of cultural capital warrant further investigation. In the concept, 'cultural capital', whose culture indexed privilege and power? In settings where middle-class white ethnics do not constitute the dominant group, is it their cultures alone that have premium? Bennett and Silva (2011, 430) contend that while Bourdieu's conceptualisation of capital is distinctive, '... the concept of culture ... is one that Bourdieu pretty much takes for granted in assuming ... that culture is the symbolic plane of collective representations'. But the symbolic plane to which Bennett and Silva (2011) refer is not the sole preserve of any single ethno-racial group (Wacquant 2013). Based on Bourdieu's scholarship, cultural capital does not possess an inherent ethno-racial character. However, empirical engagements with Bourdieu's work suggest the opposite. Research highlighting the white middle classes as bearers of cultural capital and the paucity of scholarship describing Blacks as capital-carrying subjects fortify perceptions of whiteness as an intrinsic feature of cultural capital (Hollingworth and Williams 2009; Reay 2007; Reay et al. 2007; Savage 2015). Cultural capital is not exclusively a resource for Whites. In Bourdieusian terms, cultural capital is fundamentally a class resource that is unequally distributed across social fields through systems of inheritance, informing the habitus and the accumulation of social and economic advantages in social fields. However, as noted in the section that follows, this does not mean that ethnicity and race are not implicated in the formation and expression of cultural capital.

Cultural capital as white property?

The enduring, near-universal premium attributed to white European aesthetics as the dominant markers of cultural capital reinforces the wider historical system of ethno-racial domination. Such a provocation has been the topic of a recent wave of sociological and educational studies (Franceschelli 2014; Modood 2004; Rampersad 2014; Reay 2007), and has led to new formulations of cultural capital sensitive to ethno-racial differences. From multicultural capital (Reay et al. 2007), ethnic capital (Modood 2004) and transnational cultural capital (Ball, Reay, and David 2003) through to Islamic capital (Franceschelli 2014), racialised facilitative capital (Rampersad 2014) and linguistic capital (Yosso 2005), these new conceptualisations provide heterodox and orthodox approaches to unhinging whiteness and cultural capital. I now offer some attention to the most prominent of these theoretical amendments – specifically, multicultural capital (Reay et al. 2007), ethnic capital (Modood 2004), transnational cultural capital (Ball, Reay, and David 2003) and linguistic capital (Yosso 2005).

Reay et al. (2007) complicate understandings of the relationship between whiteness, middle-class privilege and ethnic minority communities. Based on in-depth interviews with 63 families in London, Reay et al. (2007) suggest that white middle-class families send their children to urban, inner-city state comprehensives to further enrich their middle-class identities. What appears to be 'risky' school choice decisions are in fact strategic social class investments in diversifying or accentuating whiteness through substantive associations with ethno-racial diversity in schools. White middle-class pupils gain added advantages in multiple social fields through the acquisition of 'multicultural capital' – knowledge of and familiarity with ethnic minorities relevant for signalling a mature worldliness in an increasingly diverse Britain. The surplus social profits acquired through multicultural capital allows segments of the white middle classes to distance themselves from the white working classes and differentiate themselves from the traditional white middle classes based on their heightened cross-cultural intelligence. With multicultural capital, Reay et al. contend, white middle-class pupils at inner-city comprehensives represent an emerging contingent of cultural omnivores – 'streetwise, globally knowledgeable, tolerant, inclusive' (2007, 1052). In their formulation of multicultural capital, Reay et al. (2007) gesture towards an ethnicised cultural capital that serves as a resource for the enhancement of white identities – a transactional good that can be acquired through school choice rather than sheer chance.

Ball, Reay, and David (2003) also extend the conceptual boundaries of cultural capital. In their assessment of the university selection processes and the higher education experiences of ethnic minorities, Ball, Reay, and David spotlight the often unrecognised assets among ethnic minorities from immigrant families. They address the lacuna in the literature on ethnic minorities' university choice decisions by providing more critical optics through which to understand ethnic minorities' higher education experiences. Giving credence to the pre-migration class histories of ethnic minority immigrant families, Ball, Reay, and David propose transnational cultural capital as 'forms of legitimate knowledge that have efficacy within the field of UK higher education' (2003, 345). Although Ball, Reay, and David's (2003) 'rucksack approach' to understanding migrants' cultural capital has been critiqued for its limited understandings of how 'migration-specific cultural capital re-produced intra-migrant differentiations of gender, ethnicity and class' (Erel 2010, 642), transnational cultural capital offers introductory insights into the complex formations of cultural capital among diverse constituencies whose homelands are beyond the shores of the British isles. In this regard, Ball and colleagues illustrate that the white middle classes are not the only ones with the capacity to mobilise and (re)produce cultural capital in Britain. Immigrants from sub-Saharan Africa, the Caribbean, South Asia and elsewhere come to Britain with class resources worth acknowledging and appreciating.

While multicultural capital and transnational cultural capital build upon classic Bourdieusian analyses, ethnic capital represents a departure from traditional Bourdieusian perspectives, drawing instead on Zhou's (2004) rendition of capital, which frames ethnicity as a productive resource with institutional and market implications. Modood (2004) suggests that while Bourdieu's conceptions of cultural capital is useful for explaining educational achievement disparities between advantaged and disadvantaged classes, cultural capital is often less generative in its explanatory power for elucidating why some groups of disadvantaged classes fare better than expected. Based on qualitative research among second-generation British South Asian and Chinese youth, Modood (2004) proposes ethnic capital to bridge the limits of cultural capital. Modood contends that 'the motor of the British South Asian and Chinese overcoming of disadvantage lies in migrant parents getting their children to internalize high educational ambitions and to enforce appropriate behaviour' (2004, 87). In this context, Modood complicates dominant understandings of group outcomes by spotlighting the traditions and practices deployed by groups of ethno-racial minorities that support their educational and economic advancement in a white-dominated society. This further reinforces the fact that the white middle classes are not the only ones who draw on capitals to foster social and scholastic success.

Although ethnic capital, transnational cultural capital and multicultural capital have provided different extensions of cultural capital, the most popular theoretical extension is Yosso's (2005) critical race theory exposition on community cultural wealth. In her much-celebrated paper – indeed, the most cited piece in the journal *Race, Ethnicity and Education* to date – Yosso (2005, 70) critiques the (mis)uses of Bourdieu's framework that inadvertently promote logics of ethno-racial deficiency. She argues:

> Bourdieu's theoretical insight about how a hierarchical society reproduces itself has often been interpreted as a way to explain why the academic and social outcomes of People of Colour are significantly lower than the outcomes of Whites. The assumption follows that People of Colour 'lack' the social and cultural capital required for social mobility. As a result, schools most often work from this assumption in structuring ways to help 'disadvantaged' students whose race and class background has left them lacking necessary knowledge, social skills, abilities and cultural capital. (Yosso 2005, 70)

To counter representations of cultural capital as profitable assets of which people of colour are deprived, Yosso (2005) proposes six related forms of capital that constitute cultural wealth in communities of colour. Yosso's constellation of capitals include: linguistic capital, varied language and communication skills developed across dominant and non-dominant fields; aspirational capital, the stocks of resilience to pursue goals despite obstacles; social capital, networks of peers and power useful for negotiating local and institutional fields; navigational capital, the skill sets deployed to successfully manoeuvre through institutions historically hostile to People of Colour; resistant capital, counter-cultural knowledge and skills that challenge the presence and perpetuation of inequality; and familial capital, cultural knowledge, memories and pedagogies preserved through varied formations of kinship.

Despite the popularity of Yosso's (2005) capitals scheme, the set of capitals she proposes is increasingly subject to critique, chief among which is the view that Yosso's theoretical amendments are insufficiently Bourdieusian. Crozier (2016), for example, contends that Yosso's work does not mention or engage habitus and field as part of her exposition on the inequality of cultural capital, but instead isolates capital in ways that are counterproductive to a full Bourdieusian analysis of social life. Another significant critique is that Yosso's formulation contributes to the unceasing proliferation of capitals, using the concept to signify valuable resources that are not capitals in a strict Bourdieusian sense (Bennett and Silva 2011). Not all resources, assets or funds of knowledge constitute capitals (Savage, Warde, and Devine 2005). Yet the term 'capital' is frequently used as a synonym for resources – an error that ultimately undermines the explanatory power of the concept as Bourdieu intended.

From a Bourdieusian perspective, goods and resources are not capitals if they do not produce gains in the dominant market. This is not to suggest that assets and resources which do not yield market gains are not socially legitimate or culturally credible. However, works like that by Yosso (2005) which seek to rightfully recognise cultural wealth among communities of colour long deemed culturally and materially impoverished need to showcase the market implications of such assets – in the way traditional Bourdieusian analysis requires.

Although these critiques hold significant merit, Yosso (2005) did not aim to advance a Bourdieusian analysis. She drew on the most robust, critical emancipationist programme on race and racism – Critical Race Theory (CRT) – to offer an epistemological break from ethno-racial deficiencies advanced by those using the range of Bourdieu's conceptual tools. CRT seeks to elucidate and eliminate racism as a formative feature of social life (Gillborn 2005). CRT is sensitive to the construction and consequences of whiteness in law, public policy, education and related spheres (Rollock et al. 2015). From a CRT lens, the wealth of whiteness is directly linked to constructions of poverty and pathology among communities of colour. Yosso (2005) summons CRT not simply to critique the premium placed on the white middle classes, but also to signify the intellectual and political urgency of a different theoretical framework useful for articulating the often-overlooked powers among communities of colour.

Multicultural capital, transnational cultural capital, ethnic capital and linguistic capital are all theoretical amendments to Bourdieu's theorisation of cultural capital. For Reay et al. (2007) and others, Bourdieu's own oeuvre grants some sensitising insights into ethnicity, race and migration that can prove profitable for understanding the ethno-racial elements of class relations, for challenging the forced union between whiteness and cultural capital, and for advancing rigorous analyses on the Black and ethnic minority middle classes. For Modood (2004), Bourdieu's concepts proved beneficial when combined with Zhou's rendition of capital – creating a hybrid cultural–social capital model. Still for others like Yosso (2005), critical theories of race (such as CRT) break away from a dominant white episteme, offering a theoretical source not yet substantively provided by Bourdieusians for disarming prejudicial ethno-racial logics. Despite their varying approaches, the aforementioned conceptual amendments share a common political persuasion worth noting – to challenge the political project of whiteness and the disadvantages it underwrites for communities of colour.

As stated previously, the relationship between cultural capital and whiteness endures in British sociology of education, in part, because of scant attention to the Black and ethnic minority middle classes as capital-carrying subjects. The following section examines the dearth of scholarship on Black middle classes in Britain.

Who holds cultural capital? Research on the Black and ethnic minority middle classes

To date, considerably less is known about the Black and ethnic minority middle classes than about the white middle classes in the United Kingdom. While a decades-old tradition of research on the white middle classes and elites continues with considerable gusto (Bennett et al. 2009; Savage et al. 2013; Savage 2015), the close, critical study of the Black middle classes has long been a neglected area of research. The gap in the literature on the middle classes is an invitation to shift scholarly attention beyond middle-class whiteness to examine unexplored contingents of the middle classes – including the Black middle classes. Commenting on the formation of the Black middle classes in Britain, Phillips and Sarre (1995, 91) argue that 'if social science has any claims to an emancipatory activity, it should challenge middle class Whiteness as a principle ...'. An emerging wave of critical scholarship heeds Phillips and Sarre's (1995) call to interrogate the relationship between whiteness and middle-class identity in ways that have gone unrecognised for decades.

Empirical studies on the Black and ethnic minority middle classes are small scale but significant. The works range between: discussions of the simultaneous experience of class privilege and racial subordination (Archer 2011; Ayling 2015); explorations of ethnic minority parents' engagement with teachers and school leaders (Archer 2010; Vincent et al., 2012); theorisations of a 'triangle of identity' to underscore the fluid racial and class identifications that Britain's Black middle classes negotiate daily (Meghji 2016); and examinations of Black Caribbean middle-class pupils' defence of the Black working classes (Wallace 2016). The largest of all these studies is Rollock et al.'s (2015) *The Colour of Class*.

Rollock et al. (2015) provide the first in-depth study of the heterogeneity of the Black middle classes in Britain. Rollock and her colleagues examine how Black middle-class parents train, monitor and support their children in British schools to ensure their social advancement and academic success. To this end, Rollock et al. (2015) lay bear the limits of single-axis class analyses that ignore the joint operation of race and ethnicity. Based on in-depth interviews with 62 Black Caribbean parents (49 mothers and 13 fathers) in professional and managerial occupations throughout the United Kingdom, Rollock et al. (2015) contend that while middle-class status affords participants some advantages, the challenges of racism are not thwarted by middle-class standing. They report that although Black middle-class mothers and fathers draw on cultural, economic and social capital in and outside of schools, racism constrains receptions of their middle-class identities in ways that are unusual in the experiences of the white middle classes. In response, the Black middle classes often develop strategies to counter white racism and enhance their advantages in wider racialised social fields, of which schools are a part. The wealth of middle-class whiteness, then, is not found in the exclusive ownership of cultural capital, but is located in the 'natural' alignment of one's stock of capitals with the wider racialised social field, the conduciveness of the racialised field to white tastes and styles, and the fruitful affiliation between certain expressions of (cultural) capital and the wider architecture of power relations that typically favours middle-class whiteness.

The scarcity of research illustrating how the Black and ethnic minority middle classes in Britain operationalise cultural capital arguably contributes to the affiliation between whiteness and cultural capital in the popular imaginary. With sustained study of how the white middle classes use cultural capital to enhance their social positions, and the limited representation in academic research of the Black and ethnic minority middle classes utilising dominant cultural capital for social gain, a pernicious class imaging is authorised – a racialised class determinism that equates blackness and other racial minority significations to material and cultural poverty, and whiteness to cultural visibility and social class variation (Archer 2011; Yosso 2005). The details of this study outlined in the following are motivated by a need for additional research on Black and ethnic minority young people's use of dominant cultural capital in inner-city schools. The findings showcased in this article challenge the view that whiteness and cultural capital are inevitably coterminous projects.

Methods and sample

Data presented in this article are drawn from a cross-national ethnography focused on the educational experiences of working-class and middle-class Black Caribbean young people in London and New York City. Seeing that research on the Black Caribbean population in Britain tends to prioritise the experiences of working classes among them, this article focuses on the middle-class participants in the London case to underscore the heterogeneity of Black Caribbeans in Britain. I classify Black Caribbean young people as middle class if their parents self-identified as such (N=5) or if the pupils indicated their family's middle-class standing based on degree attainment (from BA to terminal degrees), home ownership and professional occupation (e.g. The National Statistics Socio-economic Classification 1 and 2), in keeping with the UK's Standard Occupational Classification Manual. Throughout this project, the designation, 'middle class' prioritise educational attainment, as opposed to annual earnings, to underscore the linkages between education, cultural capital and upward social mobility discussed in Bourdieu's work (Bourdieu 1990a, 1990b; Bourdieu and Wacquant 1992).

Participants in the London sample were Year 10 and Year 11 pupils at Newton Secondary – one of the largest state comprehensives in South London. With a long history of serving the white working classes, Newton has witnessed a sharp increase in the number of Black Caribbean, Black African and other ethnic minority pupils enrolling in the school due to demographic changes in the school's catchment area. Between 2012 and 2013, semi-structured open-ended interviews were conducted with 30 second-generation Black Caribbean pupils whose parents consented to their participation in the study. One-on-one interviews were matched by focus group interviews and seven months of ethnographic observation in classrooms, canteens and other campus venues. Core participants included 16 females and 14 males: 17 working-class pupils (based on free school meals eligibility, parents' educational attainment and parents' employment) and 13 middle-class pupils (based on parents' university completion and professional credentials). All of these participants had at least one parent who migrated from Jamaica, Trinidad, Guyana, Barbados, Montserrat, Antigua & Barbuda, Grenada and the Bahamas. This article focuses on 13 in-depth interviews and three focus group interviews with the middle-class participants. In particular, I highlight the comments of participants who self-identified as Black middle class (N=7). The Black middle-class pupils discussed in the following sections were not only clear about their class standing, but also confident in their class position due to consistent discussions at home about Black middle-class families. Individual and focus group interviews lasted between 55 and 85 minutes, exploring topics ranging between cultural authenticity and belonging; peer group relations; urban schooling experiences; and perceptions of teacher expectations; among others. Pseudonyms are used for the site and subjects of the study to maintain the anonymity and protection of participants.

All interviews were recorded, transcribed and analysed carefully to ensure accuracy and precision. Transcripts were uploaded to and analysed through NVivo 8. To allow for inductive and deductive analyses, and transitions between the two, I conducted two rounds of coding. In the first, I labelled the data according to broad themes on racialised class distinctions such as 'cultural advantages and disadvantages' and 'Black tastes and styles'. The second stage included focused coding with categories such as 'being and acting black in school' and 'tensions between class privilege and racial identity'. I refined the coding scheme while searching for more patterns to deepen the analysis on the racialised class experiences of Black Caribbean young people.

Findings

The findings of this study suggest that Black Caribbean middle-class pupils lament the singular 'class imaging' of Blacks in British schools and society. 'Class imaging' refers to the controlling, largely unquestioned assumptions and stereotypical (mis)representations of Blacks in the popular imaginary that undermine class variation among Blacks, assuming instead a fixed relationship between Black identities and class disadvantage. Black Caribbean middle-class pupils in this study register such perceptions as examples of 'soft' racism (mobilised through recurring misrepresentations) that homogenises Black identities and discredits the gains of the Black middle classes. While it is beyond the scope of this article to present all of the findings from this study, in the following I focus on examples of how Black Caribbean pupils recognise and resist the racialised 'class imaging' they encounter in school through their use of cultural capital.

White 'straight coats' on Black identities?

Black Caribbean identities are complex, contested and contingently constituted (Mirza 2009). Indeed, all ethno-racial identities are. Yet reductionist constructions of Black Caribbean identities in British society prevail to a degree that is disproportionate to the misrepresentations of white identities. Such one-sided 'class imaging' of Blacks are not inconsequential falsehoods, but structured schemes of perception that foreclose multiple ways of being in everyday life and further legitimate mainstream media representations of Black identities throughout Britain. Challenging the prevailing class stereotypes of Blacks in Britain as either definitively poor or working class, the class-confident participants highlighted in this article deploy cultural capital in schools to signal their middle-class standing to their (often) white middle-class teachers and challenge their reductive understandings of blackness. To this end, participants' use of cultural capital in schools is at once a staged act of racial representation and resistance.

Participants in this study are acutely aware of the prevailing class imaging Black Caribbean youth are subjected to that diminishes, denigrates and even denies the full appreciation of their racial and class identities. Joseph, a Year 11 pupil at Newton, for example, takes issue with the static perceptions of blackness common in his school. He reasons:

> There's a really tight straight coat of black identity that my white teachers try to strap onto us ...They expect us to fail ... they expect us to struggle money wise ... they expect us to fight each other ... When we challenge or exceed their expectations, it's like they can't even recognise us. You move from being that Black student to that hardworking student that's different. They stop paying attention to our blackness the moment it's not a problem but the reason for your success ... but I'm like, that's not on ... I'm on to all these games ...

Joseph is not alone in his critical summation of the racialised class imaging at work in his school. Chad, a Year 10 student-leader, also comments on how such biased perceptions inform teachers' classroom engagement with Black pupils:

> ... Do you know how many times my teachers on a regular day, especially the white one dem, yeah, just assume that me and the rest of the Black students have never been to the Tate

> Modern [museum] or to Belgium or even to Oxford, which is in my own country [with tones and volume raised to a shout] ... It's not shocking for a white person to do these things here in South London, but it is surprising for a Black person? Because all Black people are the same, right? Either we are what you think we are or we are nothing...When I raise my hand in class and tell my teachers, yeah, [that] I have been here or there, they just fob me off, like, 'oh, that's cause you're a smart boy' ... but I'm like, no, my dad is a dentist and my mum's a teacher ... We can go anywhere ... you can't limit us because we are Black ... I learned that long time in Bridge [supplementary] school.

Joseph and Chad's extracts signal the (in)significance of blackness in the white imagination (Rankine 2014). Both Joseph and Chad suggest that in the expressions and behaviour of their white teachers, Black identities are constricted to narratives of struggle, conflict and underachievement. Like their peers, Joseph and Chad testify to the fact that racialised class imaging is not a historical abstraction or simply a mundane feature of the media and its related markets, but a source of daily angst in classrooms that arguably necessitates wider, public representations in predominantly white institutions of the diverse class identities of Black people. In Joseph's view, blackness is legible and legitimate to some white teachers when expressed as a polemic. For Chad, however, the stakes are not necessarily about what blackness is, but how it is perceived and projected by white powerbrokers who comprehend blackness as a construct confined to the working classes. Joseph and Chad indicate that among some white teachers at Newton, blackness is bound to an everyday hegemony – one that links Black identities with compulsory class disadvantage and ignores those that upend such racialised class perceptions.

According to participants in this study, the practice of such racialised class perceptions is illustrated by how some teachers smuggle into classroom experiences a set of negative assumptions about the social and educational experiences of Black pupils, as if pre-determined or fixed based on their racial identities (Picower 2009). In some instances, such perceptions assume little if any access to objectified cultural capital (e.g. visit to the Tate Modern museum, etc.) for Black students like Chad. In a local school context with an all-white middle-class school leadership team, a teaching staff with 92% of its faculty identified as white British and white students comprising the majority of the student population (50.5%), whiteness generally – and white middle-class identities specifically – functions as a structured position of power and privilege, and as the key lens through which blackness is perceived. Whereas the Black middle classes are subjected to unequal representation in British sociology of education relative to the white middle classes, the social and educational experiences of participants like Joseph and Chad are limited by recurring misrepresentations in schools.

Participants suggest that the misrepresentation of their middle-class identities as working class by virtue of being Black is so widespread at Newton that it forms a durable doxa throughout the school (Deer 2008). Joseph contends that:

> If the assumptions about being poor or whatnot happened with a few teachers, I could live with it ... but you hear it all over the place. Do you know how many times teachers who don't know me, yeah, see me and ask me why I'm not eating during my lunch period because they think I'm getting free school lunch? Even the admin people do it ... Sometimes, I just don't feel like eating ... These assumptions ... these expectations about being poor or disadvantaged because you are Black are straight real ... but why would you object really unless you know you're middle class and have never gotten free school lunch?

Similarly, Year 10 pupil Akilah notes the significance of her middle-class identity for critiquing racialised class essentialism. She explains:

> At a place like Newton, if you're Black, the white teachers just assume you're financially disadvantaged. I am middle class and I know how racism works in this school … the fact that these teachers assume that Black students are all poor or working class is racist to say the least … But I know how to challenge them. Don't call them racists. If you do they will become your enemy. What I do is tell them about the books I have by [Marcus] Garvey or [Nikki] Giovanni, the places I've been to, the university I want to go to, the languages I speak, the jobs my parents have … It pushes them to think differently about young Black people …

Joseph and Akilah's middle-class confidence allows them to challenge the reach and scope of misrepresentation (through class imaging) as a core doxa in their school. Bourdieu conceived of doxa as a 'set of fundamental beliefs, which does not even need to be asserted in the form of an explicit, self-conscious dogma' (2000, 15). Expounding on Bourdieu's definition of doxa, Deer argues that doxa:

> refers to the misrecognition of forms of social arbitrariness that engenders the unformulated, non-discursive, but internalized and practical recognition of that same social arbitrariness. It contributes to its reproduction in social institutions, structures and relations as well as in the minds and bodies, expectations and behaviours. (2008, 119–120)

Put plainly, doxa refers to the accepted, uncorroborated 'truths', taken-for-granted assumptions and popular cultural opinions that influence the dispositions and relations in social fields. In an inner-city state comprehensive like Newton, the misrepresentation of Black middle-class identities as working class or poor is arguably based on a doxa that consistently codes blackness as a site of inherent class disadvantage. However, it is precisely the middle-class power pupils like Joseph and Akilah are presumed not to have that enables them to recognise and resist class imaging as a protracted form of symbolic domination frequently imposed by white middle-class teachers.

To assert their racial and class identities beyond the perceptual 'straight coats' pinned to Black Caribbean youth at Newton, participants draw on dominant cultural capital in school settings in the company of middle-class white instructors. However, they resist the racist logics that undergird the racialised class imaging they encounter by deliberately racialising cultural capital as Black – in Akilah's case, referencing the institutionally validated books, languages, universities and jobs indicative of her Black middle-class position. Participants like Akilah, Joseph and others hold that the effective use of dominant cultural capital in school life does not necessitate mimicking whiteness. In an increasingly multicultural society, there is growing appreciation for alternate bodies of knowledge and diverse cultural repertoires (Desmond and Emirbayer 2009). As such, participants maintain that tastes, styles and goods which have traction in the market can be based on multiple ethno-racial traditions. During an interview with Luke, a Year 11 student, for example, he highlighted how changing dynamics in society influence his tastes, trajectory and use of cultural capital. He reasons:

> You don't have to imitate white people to get ahead … my brother and my father work in corporate, and they win over clients with what they know about other parts of the world … because it's different. It's not what all the other blokes know … At Newton, yeah, I can definitely engage in literary criticism of *Hamlet* or, John Steinbeck's *Of Mice & Men*, but most of these teachers don't know anything about Vidiadhar Naipaul [British writer and Nobel Laureate from Trinidad & Tobago] … If you mention *The Enigma of Arrival* or *The Lonely Londoners* they would look at you confused … Black Caribbean people have things that are valuable big

> time across the world ... For me, being Black is about knowing Shakespeare, yeah 'cause you have to, but also knowing Sam Selvon, Chinua Achebe, V.S. Naipaul ... I have their books ... teachers recognise these things ... they don't expect this ... but, my brother tell[s] me all the time that this is the kind of stuff that would be good in an Oxbridge interview ...

The bodies of knowledge and kinds of books Luke draws on are indicative of the stocks of cultural capital racialised as Black and acknowledged in a white mainstream society. For Luke, a critical awareness of Shakespeare's contributions to the literary canon can also be coupled with an acute appreciation of African Caribbean Letters – knowledge that is not only valuable in dominant society, but also perhaps emblematic of one's Black identity and ethno-racial consciousness. At Newton, deep knowledge of Selvon, Achebe and Naipaul (or in Akilah's case, Garvey and Giovanni) can prove profitable among teachers and peers – signalling one's intellectual acuity or deep commitment to learning (to teachers) and one's racial consciousness (to peers). Furthermore, the forms of racialised cultural capital Luke discusses yield more than mere recognition in peer and teacher networks. Racialised cultural capital – or what could be referred to in this instance as a form of Black cultural capital – produces economic returns for his father and brother in the corporate sphere and potentially for Luke too in enhancing his candidacy for admission to elite universities.

The voices of Luke, Akilah and their peers urge us towards new, generative theorisations on the racialisation of cultural capital. Black Caribbean middle-class young people in this study suggest that race generally, and blackness specifically, matters in their operationalisation of cultural capital in their local settings. Furthermore, their comments underscore the core claim of this article: that cultural capital is not tantamount to middle-class whiteness. Contemporary renditions of Black cultural capital by Rollock et al. (2015) and Wallace (2016) note the significant value of the cultural, material and symbolic assets racialised as Black for parents and pupils and legitimated in schools, university admission and in the corporate sphere. In the context of this study, forms of dominant cultural capital racialised as Black provide key means through which participants (re)present their middle-class identities and resist the prevailing class imaging mounted by white middle-class teachers in schools.

But there are significant psycho-social costs for class-confident participants that come with regularly resisting racialised class imaging in a predominantly white institution like Newton. Comments from Devon, a 16-year-old Year 11 student-athlete, underscore the psychological consequences of misrepresentation endured in school. He argues:

> I'm definitely not posh or anything, yeah, but people in my family [have] gone to uni ... I guess you could call them successful to a certain extent ... I come to school in the same uniform as everybody else and I do pretty well in school. My teachers and footie [football] mates know my background ... I know I'm going to a good uni and I'm not ashamed of that. That's the expectation in my family ... But, sometimes my mates, like, the white ones, yeah, act like I should be ashamed of my background ... like you're only really Black if you're poor. That's straight foolishness, bruv ... sometimes, I even question myself, like, should I feel bad? ... but I'm not gonna let white people tell me what is Black and what is not ...

Devon's comments point to the fact that racialised class imaging is not only a feature of teacher relations, but also an element of peer engagement at Newton that can invoke internal psychological conflicts. Racialised class imaging is at times so significant that it can induce a sense of guilt and self-doubt among civically engaged high-achieving pupils like Devon. Not unlike Devon, Year 10 student Akilah also contends regularly with misrepresentation of her class identity based on her racial identity. Her experiences disrupt the logic of Black class disadvantage, rendering her at points an uncommon and perhaps incoherent Black subject. She asserts:

> ... I get so frustrated when people assume I'm poor because I'm Black or I'm not Black because I'm not poor, working class or whatever. I get it from students, teachers and even some of my friends ... I get it from Black people, Asian people, white people ... doesn't matter ... makes me wonder if I belong here, yeah ... Thank God my mother prepared me for all this at home ...

As mentioned previously, pupils like Akilah, Joseph, Chad and Devon recognise and resist a doxa of misrepresentation – a well-received and formidable set of 'truths' that 'other' these Black middle-class pupils for differing from stereotypic expectations of Black middle-class young people's class identities. Pupils in this study did not learn to recognise skewed 'class imaging' on their own accord. As Chad and Akilah point out, they are oriented to these prejudicial expectations and representations through their middle-class parents' informal trainings at home and in supplementary schools. Such findings corroborate Rollock et al.'s (2015) claims on the centrality of Black institutions (families and supplementary schools) for the Black middle classes in a white society. With a school curriculum and context that reinforces the normativity of white middle-class identities (Gillborn 2005), pupils like Akilah learn to contend with the psycho-social challenges imposed by 'class imaging' through Black institutions. Additionally, participants forge counter-cultural representations that allow for the variance and visibility of Black middle-class identities seldom recognised in their school and the wider society. They subvert ethno-racial class determinism by persisting with expressions and achievements that confound teachers' and pupils' definitions of blackness. Class-confident participants are empowered to do so based on positive and plural representations of Black middle-class identities at home and in supplementary schools – sites where the institutional habitus aligns with their individual habitus.

In white-led institutions like Newton, ethno-racial class determinism manifests itself in everyday social life as 'acceptable' unconscious assumptions (doxa) about the class standing of Blacks in Britain. 'Class imaging' is not simply an outgrowth of a doxa of racial misrepresentation, but a form of racialised violence of which middle-class participants in this study are acutely aware. 'Class imaging' simultaneously maintains white supremacy and middle-class privilege in ways that displaces those whose identities do not rest at the intersection of whiteness and middle-class identity. What is more, even in a putatively pluralistic, post-racial context, blackness still functions as a somatic signifier of class disadvantage. Commenting on the nature of overt and covert forms of domination, Desmond and Emirbayer argue that:

> Since we are disposed to a world structured by racial domination, we develop racialised dispositions – some conscious, many more unconscious and somatic – that guide our thoughts and behaviors. We may talk slowly to an Asian woman at the farmer's market, unconsciously assuming that she speaks poor English; we may inform a Hispanic man at a corporate party that someone has spilled their punch, unconsciously assuming that he is a janitor; we may ask to change seats if an Arab American man sits next to us on an airplane. Miniature actions such as these have little to do with one's intentional thoughts; they are orchestrated by one's practical sense, one's habitual knowhow ... (2009, 345)

In Britain, ethno-racial domination may at times vary from what Desmond and Emirbayer (2009) describe, but can also extend to a set of unspoken assumptive norms that uses blackness as a code word for class disadvantage as part of everyday social awareness. Such doxic misrepresentations of the Black middle classes maintain the positional and status superiority of the white middle classes.

Conclusion

The foregoing discussion has sought to critique the function of ethno-racial class determinism in shaping the perceptions and experiences of Black Caribbean young people at a large state secondary school in South London. I privilege the perspectives of the seven self-identified Black Caribbean middle-class pupils in the London case of the larger cross-national ethnography to illustrate how some young people in multicultural contexts transform the moral and racial meanings associated with cultural capital. Participants report that teachers misrepresent their class identities by virtue of their race and thus heighten their awareness of the racialisation of cultural capital. Little analytical attention has been given to these dynamics in social class research in the United Kingdom. Concentration on these dynamics can spotlight the heterogeneous forms of ethno-racial domination and class misrepresentation at work in state schools.

Participants' commentaries suggest that there are often-ignored ethno-racial logics to the use of cultural capital and the performance of social class in local fields that can be theoretically fruitful to Bourdieusians. Firstly, their interview extracts confirm that Black middle-class pupils are not monocultural actors (Carter 2003). Indeed, they can be hybrid subjects able to recognise dominant cultural capital (e.g. deep knowledge of Shakespeare and the practice of traditional modes of talking) that they racialise as white in urban state schools like Newton, while infusing elements of Black cultural production and aesthetics credentialed as 'high brow' across the world. In this regard, cultural capital need not be culturally homogeneous or geographically constrained.

Secondly, in addition to challenging the forced union between whiteness and cultural capital, this article suggests that Black middle classes experience unequal representation in British sociological and educational research and recurring misrepresentation in state schools. Limited assumptions about their class identities are often imposed on participants based on stereotypes of blackness in British society (Rollock et al. 2015). In white-dominated institutions, the white middle classes and elites often retain the power to undermine the class gains of Black people through misrepresentations and retain the power to (in)validate cultural capital that the Black and ethnic minority middle classes deploy for market return (Wallace 2017; Stahl 2014). More needs to be done theoretically and empirically to shine light on how racism impedes the advancement of the Black and ethnic minority middle-class young people in state comprehensives in spite of their cultural capital.

Thirdly, the proliferation of capitals in sociological research should be regarded as an invitation to all Bourdieusians to re-examine Bourdieu's lesser-known selections for his critical discussions of ethnicity, race and caste – from *The Algerians* (Bourdieu 1962) to *Weight of the World* (Bourdieu 1999) and beyond. Yosso (2005), Modood (2004) and others pose heterodox renditions of capital because orthodox examinations of cultural capital hardly account for the significance of ethnicity and race. Committed Bourdieusians should interrogate and innovate – challenge mis-readings of capital and offer correctives by illustrating how cultural capital is mediated by ethnicity and race according to social fields, all the while keeping to the tradition of Bourdieu's relational analysis. Capacious, race-conscious Bourdieusian perspectives are urgently needed to explore the complexities of Black and ethnic minority young people's class identities.

Lastly, white constructions of blackness offer provocative insights into the complexities of schooling in inner-city educational institutions. In schools like Newton with an overwhelmingly white teaching force, an all-white leadership team and a national curriculum that offers far more positive renditions of whiteness than it does of racial and ethnic minorities (Picower 2009), Black identities are constrained to a set of polemics, obfuscating their richness and variability. In this regard, the accumulating wealth of whiteness is not found in exclusive ownership of cultural capital, but in the lack of injustices endured through a racialised class determinism that affiliates Blacks and ethnic minorities with cultural and economic poverty and whiteness with cultural visibility and social class diversity. British sociology of education can arguably address the unequal representation and recurring misrepresentation of the Black middle classes by moving beyond whiteness and providing more consistent analyses of the expressions and experiences of all middle-class subjects.

Disclosure statement

No potential conflict of interest was reported by the author.

Funding

This work was supported by Gates Cambridge Trust.

ORCID

Derron Wallace http://orcid.org/0000-0002-0103-6588

References

Archer, L. 2010. "'We Raised It with the Head': The Educational Practices of Minority Ethnic, Middle-Class Families." *British Journal of Sociology of Education* 31 (4): 449–469.

Archer, L. 2011. "Constructing Minority Ethnic Middle-Class Identity: An Exploratory Study with Parents, Pupils and Young Professionals." *Sociology* 45 (1): 134–151.

Ayling, P. 2015. "Embodying 'Britishness': The (Re)Making of the Contemporary Nigerian Elite Child." *Curriculum Inquiry* 45 (5): 455–471.

Bablak, L., R. Raby, and S. Pomerantz. 2016. "'I Don'T Want to Stereotype… but It's True': Maintaining Whiteness at the Centre through the 'Smart Asian' Stereotype in High School." *Whiteness and Education* 1 (1): 54–68.

Ball, S. 2015. "Subjectivity as a Site of Struggle: Refusing Neoliberalism?" *British Journal of Sociology of Education* 49 (1): 1–24.

Ball, S., D. Reay, and M. David. 2003. "'Ethnic Choosing': Minority Ethnic Students, Social Class and Higher Education Choice." *Race Ethnicity and Education* 5 (4): 333–357.

Bennett, T., and E. Silva. 2011. "Introduction: Cultural Capital-Histories, Limits, Prospects." *Poetics* 39 (6): 427–443.

Bennett, Tony, Mike Savage, Elizabeth Bortolaia, Alan Warde, Modesto Gayo-Cal, and David Wright. 2009. *Culture, Class, Distinction*. New York: Routledge.

Bourdieu, P. 1962. *The Algerians*. Boston, MA: Beacon Press.

Bourdieu, P. 1977. *Outline of a Theory of Practice*. Cambridge: Cambridge University Press.

Bourdieu, P. 1986. "The Forms of Capital." In *Handbook of Theory and Research for the Sociology of Education*, edited by J. Richardson, 241–258. London: Greenwood Press.

Bourdieu, P. 1990a. *In Other Words: Essays towards a Reflexive Sociology*. Stanford: Stanford University Press.

Bourdieu, P. 1990b. *The Logic of Practice*. Stanford: Stanford University Press.

Bourdieu, P., and J. Passeron. 1977. *Reproduction in Education, Society and Culture*. Beverly Hills, CA: Sage.
Bourdieu, P., and L. Wacquant. 1992. *An Invitation to Reflexive Sociology*. Chicago, IL: Chicago University Press.
Bourdieu, P. 1999. *The Weight of the World: Social Suffering in Contemporary Society*. UK: Alhoda.
Bourdieu, P. 2000. *Pascalian Meditations*. Stanford, CA: Stanford University Press.
Carter, P. 2003. "'Black' Cultural Capital, Status Positioning and Schooling Conflicts for Low-Income African American Youth." *Social Problems* 50 (1): 136–155.
Crozier, G. 2016. "Are Bourdieu's Ideas Useful in Analysing 'Race' ?" In Bourdieu in Educational Research: Social Class, "Race" and Ethnicity. Bourdieu Study Group Conference. Bristol, July 5, 2016, University of Bristol.
Deer, C. 2008. "Doxa." In *Pierre Bourdieu: Key Concepts*, edited by M. Grenfell, 119–130. Durham: Acumen.
Desmond, M., and M. Emirbayer. 2009. "What is Racial Domination?" *Du Bois Review* 6 (2): 335–355.
Erel, U. 2010. "Migrating Cultural Capital: Bourdieu in Migration Studies." *Sociology* 44 (4): 642–660.
Franceschelli, M. 2014. "'Islamic Capital' and Family Life: The Role of Islam in Parenting." *Sociology* 48 (1): 1190–1206.
Gillborn, D. 2005. "Education Policy as an Act of White Supremacy: Whiteness, Critical Race Theory and Education Reform." *Journal of Education Policy* 20 (4): 485–505.
Hollingworth, S., and K. Williams. 2009. "Constructions of the Working-Class 'Other' among Urban, White, Middle-Class Youth: 'Chavs', Subculture and the Valuing of Education." *Journal of Youth Studies* 12 (5): 367–382.
Meghji, A. 2016. "Positionings of the Black Middle Classes: Understanding Identity Construction beyond Strategic Assimilation." *Ethnic and Racial Studies* 40 (2): 1–24.
Mirza, H. S. 2009. *Race, Gender and Educational Desire: Why Black Women Succeed and Fail*. New York: Routledge.
Modood, T. 2004. "Capitals, Ethnic Identity and Educational Qualifications." *Cultural Trends* 13 (50): 87–105.
Moore, R. 2004. "Cultural Capital: Objective Probability and the Cultural Arbitrary." *British Journal of Sociology of Education* 25 (4): 445–456.
Moore, R. 2008. "Capital." In *Pierre Bourdieu: Key Concepts*, edited by M. Grenfell, 101–116. Acumen: Durham.
Nayak, A. 2007. "Critical Whiteness Studies." *Sociology Compass* 1 (2): 737–755.
Phillips, D., and P. Sarre. 1995. "Black Middle-class Formation in Contemporary Britain". In: *Social Change and the Middle Classes*, edited by T. Butler and M. Savage, 52–92, London: UCL Press.
Picower, B. 2009. "The Unexamined Whiteness of Teaching: How White Teachers Maintain and Enact Dominant Racial Ideologies." *Race Ethnicity and Education* 12 (2): 197–215.
Rampersad, R. 2014. "'Racialised Facilitative Capital' and the Paving of Differential Paths to Achievement of Afro-Trinidadian Boys." *British Journal of Sociology of Education* 35 (1): 73–93.
Rankine, C. 2014. *Citizen: An American Lyric*. Minneapolis, MN: Graywolf Press.
Reay, D. 2007. "Unruly Places: Inner-City Comprehensives, Middle-Class Imaginaries and Working-Class Children." *Urban Studies* 44 (7): 1191–1203.
Reay, Diane, Sumi Hollingworth, Katya Williams, Gill Crozier, Fiona Jamieson, David James, and Phoebe Beedell. 2007. "'A Darker Shade of Pale?' Whiteness, the Middle Classes and Multi-Ethnic Inner City Schooling." *Sociology* 41 (6): 1041–1060.
Robbins, D. 2005. "The Origins, Early Development and Status of Bourdieu's Concept of 'Cultural Capital'." *The British Journal of Sociology* 56 (1): 13–30.
Rollock, Nicola, David Gillborn, Carol Vincent, and Stephen J. Ball. 2015. *The Colour of Class: The Educational Strategies of the Black Middle Classes*. New York and London: Routledge.
Savage, M., A. Warde, and F. Devine. 2005. "Capitals, Assets, and Resources: Some Critical Issues." *British Journal of Sociology* 56 (1): 31–47.
Savage, Mike, Fiona Devine, Niall Cunningham, Mark Taylor, Yaojun Li, Johs Hjellbrekke, Brigitte Le Roux, Sam Friedman, and Andrew Miles. 2013. "A New Model of Social Class: Findings from the BBC's Great British Class Survey Experiment." *Sociology* 47 (2): 219–250.

Savage, M. 2015. *Social Class in the 21st Century*. London: Penguin Press.

Stahl, G. 2014. "White Working-Class Male Narratives of 'Loyalty to Self' in Discourses of Aspiration." *British Journal of Sociology of Education* 37 (5): 663–683.

Vincent, C., N. Rollock, D. Gillborn, and S. Ball. 2012. "Being Strategic, Being Watchful, Being Determined: Black Middle Class Parents and Schooling." *British Journal of Sociology of Education* 33 (3): 337–354.

Wacquant, L. 2013. "Symbolic Power and Group-Making: On Pierre Bourdieu's Reframing of Class." *Journal of Classical Sociology* 13 (2): 274–291.

Wallace, D. 2016. "Reading 'Race' in Bourdieu? Examining black cultural capital among black Caribbean Youth in South London." *Sociology* 52 (3): 1–17.

Wallace, D. 2017. "Distinctiveness, Deference and Dominance in Black Caribban Fathers' engagement with public schools in London and New York City." *Gender and Education* 29 (5): 594–613.

Yosso, T. 2005. "Whose Culture Has Capital? A Critical Race Theory Discussion of Community Cultural Wealth." *Race Ethnicity and Education* 8 (1): 69–91.

Student retention in higher education: the role of institutional habitus

Liz Thomas

This paper examines some of the issues surrounding student retention in higher education. It is based on the case study of a modern university in England that has good performance indicators of both widening participation (i.e. increasing the diversity of the student intake) and student retention. The two-fold nature of this success is significant, as it has been asserted that greater diversity will necessarily lead to an increase in student withdrawal. Furthermore, changes to student funding in the UK put greater financial pressures and stress on students, especially those from low-income groups. Nevertheless, many students cope with poverty, high levels of debt and significant burdens of paid work to successfully complete their courses of study. Drawing on the work of Reay *et al.* (2001), this paper adopts and explores the term 'institutional habitus', and attempts to provide a conceptual and empirical understanding of the ways in which the values and practices of a higher education institution impact on student retention.

Introduction

There is currently much interest in not just access to higher education, but student success too (NAO 2002). Using a case study of a modern university in England that has both increased the diversity of the student intake and supported their academic success, this paper examines some of the issues surrounding student retention in higher education (HE). The research, which is still in progress, utilized focus groups with students, which were supplemented by the collection of data via a questionnaire. Many students are experiencing financial pressures, including poverty and concern about debt, a comparative lack of money (in relation to previous income levels and/or peers not in HE) and significant burdens of paid employment, but despite these issues many students persevere in HE. This raises the important question: what prevents these students from leaving before the completion of their course of study? This is explored here considering the concept of 'institutional habitus', drawing particularly on the work of Reay *et al.* (2001). The aim is to provide a conceptual and empirical understanding of the ways in which the values and practices of a HE institution impact on student retention.

The following section provides an overview of access and retention in HE in England, and provides further details of the research undertaken. Next, there is a brief review of the literature, which identifies seven topics that are perceived to influence student success. Drawing from the empirical research the paper then examines the significance of financial issues to 'non-traditional' students, but as this is an insufficient explanation of student withdrawal the concept of institutional habitus is considered. The paper reflects on how the notion of institutional habitus relates to the experiences of these students, in particular the academic and social experiences are explored. The paper concludes by considering the utility of 'institutional habitus', and makes recommendations for improving institutional policy and practice to enhance the success of students from under-represented groups in HE.

Research context

In most developed countries, there have been major increases in the number of students participating in HE (see, for example, Green *et al.* 1999). In the UK in 1985/86, there were 599 000 full-time students in HE; in 12 years the number more than doubled to 1 230 400 in 1997/8 (DfEE 1998). Now approximately one third of the age group (API) participate in HE in England, and in Scotland the API is 45% (Ward and Steele 1999: 198), and the government aim is that by 2010, 50% of young people will have participated in HE by the time they are 30.

There is a temptation, especially for 'cultural restorationists' (see Ball 1990, Sand 1998) to link greater participation in HE with declining input standards (Wright 1996). In other words, to blame students for being poorly prepared for HE, and/or for lacking academic ability. For example, in the recently published House of Commons Select Committee Report on student retention one commentator suggests that a 'gentle rise' in non-completion rates is the consequence of taking 'risks' in the admissions process ($1:15).

Although participation in HE has expanded significantly in recent years, the proportional figure for non-completion has remained relatively stable, and even fell slightly in 1997/8 (the last year for which figures are available). In 1982/3, the rate of non-completion was 13% (in Great Britain) and in 1997/8, the rate was 17% (in the UK). Predictably, there have been variations in these rates in the intervening years with a peak of 18–19% in 1995/6. Significantly, this increase in non-completion took place before the mass expansion of HE following the transformations of the Further and Higher Education Act of 1992. (All figures quoted above are from the Select on Education and Employment, Sixth Report, 2001, para. 1.11.)

It seems to me that it is too easy and somewhat irresponsible to 'blame' new student constituencies for the small increase in early withdrawal from HE; such a response lets the HEIs and the HE sector in general off the hook. Tight (1998) describes this process as 'victim blaming', and comments that: 'stigmatizing non-participants from the start hardly seems the most sensible approach' (quoted in Parry and Fry 1999: 109). Furthermore, in the Select Committee Report the Secretary of State for Education appears to stress the importance of institutional responsibility:

> 'The evidence shows that there are unacceptable variations in the rate of 'drop-out' which appear to be linked more to the culture and workings of the institution than to the background or nature of the students recruited' David Blunket, then Secretary of State for Education ($18).

It is, therefore, pertinent to examine how these students can be supported to succeed in HE given that their access is more of a struggle and less of a 'right' than for other students. The research discussed in this paper does not focus on the question posed by the Select Committee 'why do students fail to complete?' as this reinforces the notion that students are culpable for withdrawal and have *failed*. Instead, it seeks to address the question: 'In what ways can institutions support non-traditional students to succeed?'

The research is based on a case study of a modern university with a commitment to widening participation and student retention (these are key commitments in its corporate plan). This dual commitment is reflected in the institution's ratings in the HEFCE performance indicators, which are above the national average by between 5 and 11 percentage points for participation of students from state schools (national average is 85%), from social classes III, IV and V (national average is 25%) and from the poorest postcode areas (national average is 12%). The case study institution is also above its own benchmark performance indicators, which are 92%, 31% and 15% respectively, by at least two percentage points.[1] Furthermore, the retention rate is high. The non-completion rate is below the national average of 16%, but more significantly, it is lower than other institutions with similar widening participation profiles.

This research project aims to investigate the reasons why students both consider withdrawing from their course, and, more crucially, what influences them to progress to completion. It is not concerned primarily with statistical analysis, in the way that the recent Irish Higher Education Authority report is (Morgan *et al.* 2001). Nor is the research examining withdrawal in relation to specific disciplines or subjects, although students from a wide range of courses and schools are involved in the research. Instead, it adopts a qualitative approach to promote greater understanding of student retention and withdrawal at the level of the institution.

The research is employing a range of research methods, including a literature review, focus groups, questionnaires, interviews, policy review and statistical analysis. The research discussed in this paper is concerned with the student perspective; it draws from the initial literature review and discussions with senior members of staff, but primarily it is based on focus groups with students, and a follow-up questionnaire completed by the participants. Six focus groups were undertaken with between five and six participants in each, with a total of 32 students were involved. The students were drawn from across the university, and represent a mix of gender, subject, year of study, qualification sought and age; none had responsibility for dependents and all students were registered for full-time study. The research took place within my own institution, but this was not viewed as particularly problematic. Firstly, I and the other researchers do not have direct contact with these students, secondly the team included researchers of different ages and from different backgrounds, and perhaps most importantly we took care to construct an identity that was acceptable and re-assuring to students; we dressed casually, used more informal language and aligned ourselves with the students' perspectives rather than defending the institution or colleagues when they were criticized.

Factors influencing student retention in higher education

There is a large body of international research and theory exploring the individual, social, and organizational factors which impact on student retention in HE (Tinto 1975, 1993, Benn 1982, Astin 1984, Johnes 1990, Pascarella and Terenzini 1991,

Moortgat 1997, Berger and Braxton 1998, Ozga *et al.* 1998). Much of this literature suggests that there is a wide range of interacting personal and social attributes, as well as institutional practices, which impact on both retention rates and performance. Drawing on our initial literature review and preliminary discussions within the case study institution, seven topic areas to investigate through the empirical research were identified. These were academic preparedness; the academic experience (including assessment); institutional expectations and commitment; academic and social match; finance and employment; family support and commitments; and university support services.

Academic preparedness

Mass HE has been associated with increases in student withdrawal, although as was noted earlier, there is not a clear correlation between *wider* participation and early withdrawal in the UK in recent years. There is however a tendency to attribute lower levels of completion to greater student diversity and a lack of 'academic preparedness' of these new student groups. In this study 'academic preparedness' is interpreted as the extent to which students feel they are ready to study at HE level, and the ways in which the institution provides academic support if it is needed.

Academic experience

In addition to the academic preparedness of students (i.e. input quality of students) a second, related issue is the 'academic experience'. This embraces curricula, teaching and learning issues, accessibility of and relationships with staff, flexibility (e.g. timetable and deadlines) and both modes of assessment and opportunities for re-taking courses.

Institutional expectations and commitment

The third category is related to institutional expectations and subsequent commitment to the institution. Research on elite universities in the USA suggests that most students entering such colleges have high levels of institutional commitment. This commitment arises from, and is reinforced by, the very strong traditions or 'social charters' of these universities enabling their graduates to enter prestigious areas of employment (Berger and Braxton 1998). The research therefore sought to examine the expectations that students had about HE, and the extent to which they thought the institution they were attending would realize their goals. Students were asked about whether they were attending their first choice institution, whether they entered via the 'clearing system', and if they felt they had made an informed choice to enter the university, which was based on sufficient information. The researchers also enquired about their main reason for entering HE, and the extent to which they felt this university would help them achieve their objectives.

Academic and social match

The fourth area investigated was 'academic and social match' – in other words the degree of academic and social integration into their institution. This area of interest stems from the work of Tinto (1975, 1993, 1997). Tinto's 'interactionalist theory' views retention as a function of the match between the student's academic capabilities and motivation and the institution's academic and social characteristics. That is to say, all other things being equal, the fit between the individual's and the institution's characteristics strongly influence the student's goal commitment (of obtaining a degree, diploma etc.) and her/his institutional commitment (to the College) (Berger and Braxton 1998). What Tinto's work and allied research has suggested therefore is that the more students interact with other students and staff, the more likely they are to persist (Astin 1984, Tinto 1997).

The research considered the extent to which students felt they fitted in at their institution, and this included both academic and social and cultural inclusiveness. Students were asked about how they perceived their relative academic position; in other words, did they feel academically less able than peers, equal to peers or more able than peers? The research tried to gauge the extent to which students did or did not feel that they came from similar social and cultural backgrounds, and consequently whether or not they felt accepted by the institutional environment. A further area of interest was living arrangements, and the importance of participation in social groups, activities and other 'networks'.

Finance and employment

The relationship between financial issues and withdrawal is currently receiving considerable attention in the UK since the abolition of student grants, total reliance on student loans and the introduction of tuition fees. HEFCE-funded research in 1997 (carried out before these changes were implemented) found that financial hardship exercised some impact on early withdrawal. In particular, students from the two lowest socio-economic groups were more likely to withdraw because of financial difficulties than students from the top two social groups (Ozga and Sukhnandan 1997). The HEFCE report acknowledged that finance was likely to be of greater significance in the future. The House of Commons Select Committee Report on student retention found finance and part-time employment to be contributory factors to early withdrawal ($107 and $109). In the field of further education in the UK, statistical research commissioned by the Kennedy Committee revealed that 'student withdrawal rates in further education colleges were higher for those qualifying for income-related fee remission than for others' (1997: 72). This does suggest that financial hardship has significant impacts on student retention and withdrawal.

The Select Committee Report on retention was concerned about the need for students to engage in part-time employment in order to generate a supplementary income. Research in Scotland by Sinclair and Dale (2000) found that 68% of students were working part-time in 1999–2000, compared with 43% three years earlier in 1996/7 (2000: 10). Furthermore, their research showed that almost a quarter of first year students in 1999/2000 were working more than 16 hours per week. The Select Committee recognized the potential impact of part-time employment on both studying and retention, and thus recommended that institutions should provide guidance to students that they should not work more than 12 hours per week

This research therefore sought to explore the ways in which financial issues influence students' decisions to stay or leave university. This was related to whether or not students paid fees, whether they had student loans and how much and/or other debts, such as overdrafts and outstanding credit card balances. Students were also questioned about part-time employment, in terms of type of work, number of hours and impact on studying. In the survey, students were asked to identify the extent to which, (if at all), they worried about finance. In addition, the degree to which students were aware of the levels of debt they would incur *before* they made their decisions to enter HE, and whether or not this did, or would have influenced their decisions was considered.

Family support and commitments

A sixth area of interest was family and community support and commitment. Much of the previous research on retention, in both the USA and the UK, stresses the importance of the external environment, especially the family. For example, families or communities with little or no experience of HE may be less supportive of members' participation. Moortgat's (1997: 11–12) review of case studies of non-completion in a European context suggests that socio-economic factors are important in understanding non-completion. In addition, family responsibilities, particularly childcare, have been shown to have a negative effect on retention, especially for women (Moortgat 1997). Ozga and Sukhnandan (1997) found that family commitments were more crucial determinants of non-completion amongst mature students.

This research, therefore, tried to take account of the external family and community environment of students, including whether other family members had attended university or college, support or hindrance from family and friends in relation to HE, the impact of care responsibilities and any assistance provided by the university. The main focus of this part of the research however was students who did not have full-time care responsibilities.

University support services

The final, and overarching, area of interest in this research project is the ways in which the institution provides support to overcome factors that might contribute to early withdrawal. In general, the ways in which the university assists students to stay in HE, and how it could be more supportive. This theme is addressed in relation to each of the preceding six topics.

Having identified and discussed the seven topics that were investigated in this research, I want to turn to the research findings and interpretations.

The significance of financial issues

Bearing in mind the composition of the student cohort it is not surprising to discover that financial issues featured strongly in this student-focused research. In each of the focus groups the first question asked was: 'Have you ever thought about dropping out of university?' In response to this, finance was the predominant concern. This consisted of three inter-related issues. The first was a general lack of money and concern about debt: 'When you go to the bank and see how much you are in debt. You sit down and work out how much money you'll have spent. I'll have been here for four years by the time I finish, and I'll have spent £41 000'.

In the supplementary questionnaires 14 (43.5%) students said that they frequently have financial concerns that effect their studying, and only 4 (12.5%) said they never have financial concerns that effect their studying. Thus, the majority of students (87.5%), therefore, feel that at some time they worry about finance.

Most students seemed to be aware that they would be in debt before they started university. But, some students felt that the concept of debt was meaningless until 'some thing brings it home to you':

> I knew I was going to be a lot in debt, but I think that when I came up here it wasn't a reality. It was something you thought was going to happen, until the point you've got the debt collectors knocking on your door, or you get your Switch card taken off you.

The second financial issue was a comparative lack of money, either with respect to one's previous income levels or friends in full time employment. For example, one student commented that she did not feel like going back to university to start her second year because over the summer she had been earning money. In other groups, students compared themselves to friends who had not entered HE, but who were in paid employment, and thus had money to spend on going out, clothes and so forth. One student commented: 'It's difficult if you've got mates at home who are working and they've got jobs and you've got nothing'.

The final issue was the need to work to supplement income, and the resultant pressure on students. Many undertake paid work, either during term time and/or during the vacations. Employment includes bar work, call centre staff and secretarial and administrative tasks. Some students hold senior positions (e.g. assistant manager in bars), but they tend to be paid the minimum wage. They work a wide range of hours during term time, with at least one student in each focus group working up to 30 or 40 hours per week when the work is available. Similarly, some students report working between 50 and 60 hours during the holidays to earn enough money for term time. One student explained how the pressure of working long hours to support himself made him think about leaving university:

> 'I actually thought about giving up as well because of money, lack of money . . . ' (interrupted)
> 'Yes.'
> 'Definitely.'
> '. . . that was my reason why I was considering it. I have to work 30 hours a week to keep myself here, the cost of being here, tuition fees, etc, etc. It just gets on top of you'.

Many students, especially those from non-traditional groups are struggling with all of these aspects of financial pressures, as this account demonstrates. A mature student, who has been working, explains how this has made it much more difficult for him to be a student than he had anticipated, and so at the end of his first year he seriously considered withdrawing from his course:

> I worked full time, I'm 27 now, for eight years, and I've got the debts that come from when you work full time. I have to pay out about £200 per month, before I start paying anything else out. And because I live with my parents still, I was only getting the basic loan, and it wasn't enough, and so I ended up working every hour that god sends when I wasn't actually in lectures, and it just got too much towards the end of the first year. You try to find time to fit in all your work, but you're also thinking 'if I don't go to work

> tomorrow, or whenever, then the week after you're going to be really short or have no money. I ended up getting the hardship loan from the university, the one that you don't have to pay back, and that helps with my loan, but even then it works out that I've got something like £20 a week to myself if I don't go to work. I've had to stop work the last three weeks because I'm coming to the end of my second year, and I want to get my work done without having to rush it or do last minute again. So even though we got the loan last week . . . after two weeks I'll have no money left at all, and that's having the hardship fund as well. It's all my own fault, the debts, but I didn't realise how hard it would be, I virtually have to work three or four full days a week, to pay my loan at the end of the month and to live.

Despite the poverty, high levels of debt and term-time and vacation employment, the students still valued both coming to university, and more interestingly, the cost of having a social life. Of the 69% who did know the levels of debt they would be in at university, only 36% said that this made them think more carefully about entering HE. Similarly, of the 31% who did not anticipate being in debt to such an extent, the majority (80%) said that if they had known this would not have influenced their decision.

The financial strain is significant, but a large majority of students are resigned to poverty, debt and working long hours in poorly paid employment in order to support themselves through university. This raises an important question: what prevents these students from leaving before the completion of their course of study?

Institutional habitus

In order to make sense of the empirical research, and in particular to answer the question of why some students persist in HE despite the difficulties encountered, I have found it useful to employ the concept of 'institutional habitus'. The term 'habitus' was coined by Bourdieu, and the notion of institutional habitus draws strongly on this work, and develops the idea in relation to organizations.

'Habitus' is used by Bourdieu to refer to the norms and practices of particular social classes or groups (Bourdieu and Passeron 1977). The habitus refers to a set of dispositions created and shaped by the interaction between objective structures and personal histories, including experiences and understanding of 'reality'. Thus, a person's habitus is acquired, at least in a significant part, through the family, and this, for example, structures their educational experiences. These experiences in turn impact and modify the habitus, which again goes on to structure further experiences (such as additional learning or employment). Robbins describes habitus as 'the disposition to act which individuals acquire in the earliest stages of socialisation and which they consolidate by their subsequent choices in life' (Robbins 1993: 159). Habitus refers to more than norms and values, because it is embedded within everyday actions, much of which is sub-conscious, hence the use of the term disposition. Although there is an on-going process of re-structuring of the habitus, change is slow. Indeed, Reay *et al.* (2001) note that 'habitus produces action, but because it confines possibilities to those feasible for the social groups the individual belongs to, much of the time those actions tend to be reproductive rather than transformative' (para. 1.2). Central to Bourdieu's notion of habitus are two ideas. Firstly, is the need of classes and groups to reproduce themselves. Secondly, in society certain classes and groups are dominant and so control access to educational and career opportunities. Bourdieu attributes this to the dominance of 'cultural capital', which legitimizes the maintenance of the status and power of the controlling classes. The dominant classes have symbols such as language, culture and artefacts that enable them to subjugate other social classes.

Drawing from the work of McDonough (1996), Reay (1998) and Reay *et al.* (2001), institutional habitus can be understood as 'the impact of a cultural group or social class on an individual's behaviour as it is mediated through an organisation' (Reay *et al.* 2001, para. 1.3). The significance of organizations is apparent in Bourdieu's work: he viewed the education system as the primary institution through which class order is maintained. He analysed students in French higher education institutions, and concluded that working class students were less successful not because they were of inferior intelligence or not gifted, but because the curriculum was 'biased in favour of those things with which middle-class students were already ex-curricularly familiar' (Robbins 1993: 153). In other words, educational institutions favour knowledge and experiences of dominant social groups (e.g. white, middle-class men) to the detriment of other groups. Hence, the education system is socially and culturally biased, and this is played out in the relations between staff and students, and amongst students.

Reay *et al.* (2001) argue that, in relation to HE choice, 'a school effect' or 'institutional habitus' is a significant variable that interacts with class, gender and race to impact on secondary school pupils' and further education college students' lives and HE choices. Institutional habitus should be understood as more than the culture of the educational institution; it refers to relational issues and priorities, which are deeply embedded, and sub-consciously informing practice.

This is possible as educational institutions are able to determine what values, language and knowledge are regarded as legitimate, and therefore ascribe success and award qualifications on this basis. Consequently, pedagogy is not an instrument of teaching, so much as of socialization and reinforcing status. This process ensures that the values of the dominant class are perpetuated and individuals who are inculcated in the dominant culture are the most likely to succeed, while other students are penalized. This is summarized by Robbins:

> Bourdieu's conclusion seemed to suggest that the working-class students were at an unfair disadvantage and that there was a conspiratorial collusion between middle-class staff and middle-class students which meant that these students received a structurally preferential treatment which was a kind of cheating (Robbins 1993: 153).

In relation to student retention in HE the notions of habitus and institutional habitus appear to be useful tools. If a student feels that they do not fit in, that their social and cultural practices are inappropriate and that their tacit knowledge is undervalued, they may be more inclined to withdraw early. This can be contrasted to a student from the dominant social class who, in Bourdieu's words 'encounters a social world of which it is a product, it is like a "fish in water": it does not feel the weight of the water and it takes the world about itself for granted' (Bourdieu and Wacquant 1992: 127). Conversely, a student from a non-traditional background may therefore feel like 'a fish out of water', and thus return to their familiar habitus. I want to argue that if an institutional habitus is inclusive and accepting of difference, and does not prioritize or valorize one set of characteristics, but rather celebrates and prizes diversity and difference. Students from diverse backgrounds will find greater acceptance of and respect for their own practices and knowledge, and this in turn will promote higher levels of persistence in HE.

In order to apply the concept of institutional habitus to issues relating to retention in HEIs it is necessary to develop, explore and understand different institutional practices that can impact on the extent to which students feel that they are accepted. The following discussion therefore is not intended to provide a definitive list of institutional factors, but to explore issues and relationships that students identified as being important to their decisions not to withdraw early and to persist in HE.

The academic experience: attitudes of staff, teaching and learning and assessment

Relationships between students and teaching staff seem to be fundamental to attitudes towards learning and coping with academic difficulties. Within a particular 'field' individuals, groups and institutions exist in structural relations to each other, which are mediated by habitus, thus the relations between staff and students are key to understanding the institutional habitus. This point is supported by James (1998: 109), who argues that contrary to the way student experience is usually conceptualized in HE in the UK, the student experience has to be understood in relation to practices of teaching and research, as part of a larger picture. In other words, the way in which the HE field is structured is significant, and he points to the tension between research and teaching, and the lack of parity of academic status and economic capital. Research with HEIs that have a good track record in both recruiting and retaining under-represented groups suggested that the former polytechnics accorded higher status to teaching, which had benefits for these student groups in particular, but that this priority was being challenged by the need for more academics to be research active, and for all institutions to perform well in the research assessment exercise (Thomas *et al.* 2001).

If learning and teaching is accorded a reasonably high status, and furthermore, if the learning and teaching of students from under-represented groups is prioritized this will enhance the position of these students in their relationships with staff. The significance of these relationships for student success were explicit in the focus group discussions. If students feel that staff believe in them, and care about the outcomes of their studying, they seem to gain both self-confidence and motivation, and their work improves, as these comments suggest:

> Those tutors that really care about you, and care about your learning, I care about making an effort into those assignments to give to them, because, although it's not, I feel like I'm letting them down a bit, because of the amount of effort you can tell they've invested in me, I sort of feel that I should make an effort.
>
> It makes a hell of a difference if you like your tutor. Your work just comes on leaps and bounds I find. If they don't give a stuff, you just think . . . although it's my mark, I'm still not as motivated . . . If someone cares about my work, I'll go out and do that extra bit of research or look in to this.

Students seem to be more likely to feel that they are accepted and valued by staff if lecturers and tutors know their names and exhibit other signs of friendship, are interested in their work and treat students as equals. Thus, their position in relation to teaching staff, and in comparison to peers, is significant. For example, one student commented: 'The fact that you can call staff by their first name is a major thing'. Furthermore, acts of kindness demonstrate greater equality and confirm students as accepted:

> We can get hold of lecturers at any time . . . They do help, especially when I had my accident. I said I wasn't going to lectures for three weeks because I was in hospital. They said 'OK, we'll get the work to you'. So that helped. I thought 'yeah'. They're really kind and helpful, I liked it.

Students who feel respected by staff are more able to take problems to staff, and thus sort them out. Academic difficulties that are not resolved may well lead to failure, and ultimately involuntary withdrawal. One student was able to contrast the response between staff in two departments in order to illustrate the importance of staff attitudes to both the ways students view work, and the extent to which they are likely to seek support with academic difficulties:

> Doing a joint honours, I've got two sets of people in charge of my course. On the one side I've got [department A], who are very, very accommodating to any problems you may have, they're very approachable, you can talk to them about anything, they'll encourage you to do your work, and they're there if you need them. If you can't find a book or a theorist or something they will probably have it, and if they haven't they know where you can get it. Whereas on the [department B] side, I never see them, I can never find them, they're of no help whatsoever. If you don't see them for one week and you go to see them, they're very condescending, they're boring, they do talk down to you a lot, and you're sought of standing there thinking . . . surely you should be giving me the information that I need, and they're not doing . . . You don't feel that if you do have a problem with an essay or a deadline or something like that, you don't feel that you can say anything to them, because they're very scathing.

This again demonstrates the significance of relationships, related to the position of students and the status of teaching within two different departments within the same institution. Furthermore, because students are treated in a certain way by staff in department B, this in turn impacts upon the way in which the students behave – for example, not asking for academic support. Conversely, another student commented that having a 'personal' relationship with staff enabled her to approach them with problems:

> If they know you personally it's easier to go to them with problems because they remember what you've done in the past and it's easier. They can say 'you didn't have problems with this, so why?', and so on. But if you go to a lecture and you answer one of their questions, and they say 'what's your name?' it just doesn't feel like they value your presence. If they can't be bothered to learn my name . . .

It is not surprising that staff-student relations are so important, as it is through these that relative positions are reached. The habitus of the institution does much to shape these interactions, as do those of the individuals involved; but these exchanges in turn contribute to shaping the habitus of both the individuals involved, and the institution itself, and influencing future relations between staff and students, and students and HE. Closely allied to the attitudes of staff, and the relationships that students have with them, are the issues of teaching, learning and assessment.

Methods of teaching, learning and assessment provide sites for interactions between staff, students and their peers, and with institutional structures, and thus have a central role in both changing and reproducing social and cultural inequalities. A traditional institutional habitus assumes that the habitus of the dominant group (i.e. white, male, middle class, able bodied etc) is not only the correct habitus, but treats all students as if they possessed it, and this is reflected in teaching, learning and assessment strategies. Thus, in a number of different ways 'non-traditional' students are positioned at a lower status than 'traditional' peers, and are effectively discriminated against, indeed in Bourdieu's work five levels of practice through with inequalities are perpetuated are identified (Harker 1990: 88–89). For example, a traditional institutional habitus tends to reinforce initial inequalities, and these expectations are internalized by students so they *expect* to do less well than their middle-class peers, but equally the language of instruction, the assumed knowledge and the prioritizing of style over contents favour students from a dominant background, rather than those for whom HE is not the norm. Thus, according to Bourdieu's work in France, the habitus of the dominant social group acts as a multiplier of educational capital (i.e. family has a stronger influence on success than the education system), but this is not necessarily applicable to *all* societies and *all* educational systems (Harker 1990: 97). This suggests that it is possible to create an institutional habitus that does not reinforce the habitus of the dominant groups in society and education, but which is inclusive of difference. The discussions with students in the case study institution demonstrated ways in which teaching, learning and assessment were either inclusive, or contributed to alienating those not from the dominant habitus.

The survey data from the focus groups indicates that the majority of students felt academically either 'quite well' or 'very well' prepared to study in HE. Even students who are not well prepared for HE in a traditional sense (i.e. with high A level scores) seemed to feel supported by inclusive teaching and learning approaches, which is responsive to the varying levels of academic preparedness. One student commented: 'They do try and get everyone to the same level 'cause people have come from different backgrounds'.

Similarly, a mature student, with an Access Course qualification, who had withdrawn from a more traditional university explained how previously he had not coped with the transition from college to university: 'When I did drop out it was mainly the teaching methods that were off putting coming from college to university. They were so suddenly academic that it was a real shocker!' This comment suggests that in the 'other' institution the teaching assumed the dominant habitus to be the norm, and was therefore not accommodating of the different habitus and experiences of this 'non-traditional' student. Conversely, in the case study institution both pedagogy and attitudes reflect the acceptance of difference. A student (who had also withdrawn from another institution) contrasts the attitudes of teaching staff; this suggests that in the former institution students, especially those who struggling are not regarded as equals:

> I do think the tutors here are more forgiving. In tutorials they will be more forgiving and more easy going in comparison to the tutors [name of previously attended institution]. They will actually discuss it with you, not ridicule you if it's bad or something like that.

A central aspect of the academic experience of students relates to assessment. In one focus group for example, the students thought it was difficult to fail as long as you put the work in. This can be attributed to the fact that the staff are supportive and work through academic difficulties with students: 'I don't know many people who have failed. It isn't hard as long as you put the work in'. This statement suggests that success is seen to be within the grasp of all students (as long as they put the work in), and that cultural capital (such as language, style and other symbols) does not dominate the assessment process. While not all students had experienced assessment success and some felt it was easy to fail, the opportunity to re-take assessments, or even the whole year helps to reassure students that the system is not biased against them. But in some departments there were said to be practical problems that made completing assessed work more difficult for particular students. Students complained that deadlines for assignments are all at the same time, and asked 'Surely they could spread it out?!' This is especially problematic for students who have part-time work commitments. Some students also pointed out that all assignments need to be word-processed, but there is 'always a queue for computers. Not everyone can afford to buy one'. This lack of resources is clearly likely to have greater impact on low-income students than those from more affluent backgrounds. An awareness of the differing economic circumstances of students (and the need to work part-time, and to access university IT facilities) would therefore assist students to complete their assignments on time and to the best of their ability.

There therefore seem to be important lessons for institutions regarding the attitudes of staff and the relationships that they have with students; and teaching, learning and assessment issues. This suggests the need for an institutional habitus that challenges the assumption that the habitus of traditional HE students is the 'proper' habitus, and students without this should not be assisted, or even penalized. In general, staff need to be aware of the different social, cultural and academic backgrounds of students, to accept and respect students and develop an inclusive model of teaching, learning and assessment. Perhaps the case study institution has gone some way to achieving this type of institutional habitus; a third-year student describes her perceptions, and indicates that the teaching and learning takes account of difference:

> There doesn't seem to be that much difference across our field. I do know that there are people who always get firsts, and there are people who just about scrape 2:2s. It doesn't seem to make that much of a difference, because we all work together, we all get mixed together doing different presentations, different group work, that it doesn't matter.

A student in a different focus group makes a similar observation: 'Our course is really diverse and nobody really cares, nobody really cares where you're from, we all work together'. These comments suggest that although different entry qualifications and previous experiences can be divisive, sensitive and supportive teaching and learning can contribute to overcoming such differences, rather than reinforcing the social and academic distance between students, and to the HE 'norm'.

The social experience: friendship, mutual support and social networks

HE can be defined as a 'field', in which there is a struggle for position, thus not only do students need a learning environment that is inclusive and accepting of difference, but they need similar social relations. The empirical research demonstrated that an aspect of the university experience that seems to be fundamental to the decision of students whether or not to stay at university was the extent to which they had good friendships and social networks that provided support to overcome difficulties. For example, one student who had thought about leaving was asked 'What made you decide not to leave then?' On reflection, he seems to conclude that friendship is a key to HE persistence:

> I've got a lot of really good friends here. I think that's one of the major things for most people that'll keep them here. Most people I know have made the best friends they've ever had at university. That keeps people. That will keep people here. That was a major factor for me. And I didn't want to walk away from, what is in effect, for its good and bad points, some of the best times of my life, and I'm ever likely to have. That's what kept me here.

The importance of friends and social networks whilst participating in HE can perhaps be understood by recourse to the concept of 'social capital', which is said to be important in communities for overcoming social exclusion. It is used to signify the extent to which people have access to networks, their levels of political and civic engagement and membership of associations (Thomas and Jones 2000: 16). Social capital – or mutual support – seems to be occurring within the case study university, and enabling students to overcome the internal and external problems that they face. Social relations are shaped largely by the habitus: 'One's habitus form the basis of friendship, love and other personal relations' (Mahar *et al.* 1990: 10), and therefore it is instructive to observe the extent to which the institutional habitus and associated practices can challenge the familial habitus (which Bourdieu shows to be more influential in France).

It is revealing to note how students talk about their living arrangements by recourse to the word 'family'. This represents the importance of the interaction between the institutional habitus and the familial habitus of the student, and indicates how friendship helps to bridge gaps and overcome difference. For example, the students identify their friends as their new 'family', and explain that living with people necessarily puts a strain on friendships, but liken it to families:

> The people I live with now are really great. They're my new family – but every now and then they wind me up so much.
>
> It's like when you're at home with your family, you fall out all the time.

One element of the importance of friendship is revealed by the discussion below. This demonstrates how students, particularly those from non-traditional backgrounds, tend to lose their friends at home as their interests and tastes change.

> I went home a few weeks ago and I saw a couple of friends, people that I used to hang about with. And we went out and I had to dress differently to the way I dress. I had to put on shoes and trousers . . .

This sounds familiar, this story does. (General agreement by other members of the focus group).

> I just don't do that anymore. We didn't go into one single bar, club, etc., that played any music I liked, we didn't go anywhere were the people weren't all really pretentious, and at not one point did any of them show any interest in what I was doing. They've made their own little clique, and I'm not part of it anymore because I've dared to be different and move away. So I don't really fit in anymore.

This vignette illustrates the need to develop social networks at university to replace or complement the networks that students have at home. Again, this portrays the differences between the institutional habitus and the habitus of students from communities where participating in HE is not the norm, and the importance of institutions actively seeking to develop an institutional habitus that is accepting of diversity, and that promotes social networks.

Our research identified three ways in which the institution can play a role in promoting social networks: firstly through student living arrangements, secondly by the provision of appropriate social facilities and thirdly via collaborative teaching and learning practices.

Living arrangements help students to identify common ground with peers (i.e. those with a similar habitus), and this in turn appears to strengthen their perception of their relative position within the HE context. For example, living with other students, people who are 'in the same position' means that issues of poverty, debt and working shifts are the norm, and are thus accepted, as this student notes: 'It's good living with people in the same position, because, you know, you're not the only person who's got no money and staying in every night'.

Communal living can also enable students to live with people who they view as different; this provides insight that there is not a single dominant habitus that they are outside of, but again it appears to strengthen their relative perception of themselves within the field. The following comment was made by a student who had experienced racism in his first year:

> I live with another fine art student. Everyone in the house is completely different, which is good . . . I've got to know so many more people, and this helps you fit in and overcome racism.

Those students who do not live in 'student' accommodation (i.e. either halls of residence or a shared house in the private sector) are more likely to feel marginalized from their peers, and thus that they occupy a lower position. In our research, local students who live at home said that they would have liked to have had the chance to go away to university, and so live with other students: 'In a way I feel that I miss out, living at home'.

Students appear to need choices to enable them to meet their living arrangement needs, and flexibility and support to allow them to find the solution that best suits their needs. For example, some students felt that halls of residence were very important, as they provided a way of being with other people and preserving independence:

> The best thing about coming to university was halls. Living with that many different people, 30 people, all in one place.
>
> I actually lived at home for my first year, and the main reason I did that was because I would have come here if I could come into halls, but I didn't want to have to move into a house with people I didn't know.

Other students however did not like the idea of living in halls, and thus appreciated the option of alternative living arrangements.

This discussion indicates that institutions need to examine the accommodation arrangements. Firstly, students need to have choices and flexibility with regard to their living arrangements. Secondly, it should be acknowledged that local students may find themselves in an inferior position as they are excluded from the socialization of living in student accommodation, and thus institutions many need to develop ways to enable local students to develop friendships and social networks, then they too will be able to access mutual support.

Another way in which institutions can promote the development of social networks is via the Students Union. Talking about the Student Union bar, one student commented:

> There's a real community because you can sit there and in your group of friends there'll be somebody who knows that group of friends and somebody who knows that group of friends ... Basically everybody in here knows everyone, it's like a family. You rely on your friends more than any thing at university to get you through the hard times, to help you out and to be there to have fun with.

Another student added: 'There's a sense of belonging ... even down to the clothes you wear and the attitudes you have'. Part of this sense of belonging seems to comes from the security of knowing people: 'I know that at any point in the day, any day, I could walk in and know one or two people'.

The students in this focus group attributed their likelihood of knowing people to the size of the Union bar that they frequented:

> Over here it's much more of a community that it is at [other venue] ... It's much smaller, it's a lot more intimate. You have the possibility of seeing faces that you recognize as opposed to people you'll never see again.

This perhaps starts to point to the value of smaller social venues, where students can more readily feel comfortable, and be more certain that they will meet people they know. It also highlights the potential problems that students who do not drink (e.g. students from certain religious groups), or those who feel uneasy in bars (e.g. women on their own) may experience. This suggests the need for alternative venues for socialization, that are not in direct opposition with the familiar habitus, to be available to assist students to make friends for support and pleasure.

A third way in which institutional practices can promote friendship and social networks is via the induction and teaching processes when students commence at the university. A student, who describes himself as having two learning difficulties, including a nervous problem, explains the importance of team building activities and group work within his programme of study:

> I do loads of team activities . . . If it's a big assignment it gets broken up between a certain amount of people. And obviously, if you're doing an assignment you can't just say, 'you do that, you do that, you do that and we'll all meet up when it's done', cos, it's just impossible, you've got to look at everyone's work, and make your own analysis from that, so there's loads of team activities happen on our course . . . We sat around for a couple of hours discussing it. It's also a really good way of making friends as well, or socializing with people, cos it leads on to other things. Like when I said before, when I first came here I didn't really know that many people, so I sort of found that really helpful, having to work as a team, as it really got the whole course to gel together, so it was good, yeah it is a good idea.
>
> Kim (focus group facilitator): 'Do you feel that you belong to the group . . . ?'
>
> Yeah, definitely. You'd have to be really quiet not to. I don't know about other courses, but the people on my course are fairly easy going. I suppose it's not just my course, it's going to be the university in general, because it's such a different mix of people, because you've got rich people who live in rich areas, and you've got other people, and other people, and they're all chucked together, and everyone's got different views, and you don't just talk about the assignments, you just talk about everything, and cos' everyone's from everywhere all round the country there's always something to talk about, someone's always got something interesting to say. It's good.

This final example of a way in which institutions can facilitate the development of social networks, illustrates the close interrelationship between the academic and social experience of students. The institutional habitus should not restrict itself to influencing only the academic, but it should link together the academic and the social spheres within the field of HE. If this can successfully be achieved the education institutional habitus can be seen to be more influential than the family habitus. These ideas are developed in the conclusion.

Conclusion

Retention in HE, like access to HE, is complex, and it is widely acknowledged that there is an interaction between institutional and external factors. In particular, this research has found that external pressures created by the student funding mechanisms for HE in England, and the resultant pressure on students are high. These financial issues tend to be exacerbated for students from non-traditional backgrounds. But, despite these problems, significant numbers of students in the institution under study have persevered with their HE. It is argued here that the notion of an institutional habitus that is accepting of difference, and which facilitates greater match with the familial habituses of students from different social and cultural backgrounds goes some way to explain higher rates of student retention in some widening participation institutions compared to others. I will conclude this paper by reviewing the utility of the concept of institutional habitus in relation to student retention, identifying the characteristics of an institutional habitus that promotes participation and success by students from 'non-traditional' backgrounds, and using this to make tentative recommendations for institutional policy and practice.

Reay *et al.* (2001) have noted that different educational establishments have different institutional habitus, and their research suggests that the habitus of some institutions is less likely to be in tension with the familial habitus of 'non-traditional' students (e.g. mature students, para. 4.5) than others. When students were talking in the focus groups they seemed to feel that they fitted in at their university. For example, the students brought up and discussed class bias at Oxbridge, and one student commented: 'I don't want to go somewhere that treats people like that. I'd rather go somewhere where I'm allowed to be who I am, and do what I want to do'. This clearly suggests that some more elite institutions are perceived to have a habitus that is alien to students from 'non-traditional' backgrounds, and in which these students will be made to feel that their habitus is not 'correct' as it is not the dominant habitus. Furthermore, it indicates that students are more likely to persist within an educational institution that does not require them to radically deviate from their habitus (which after all is at best difficult, and at worst impossible to achieve).

The institutional habitus helps to determine the way in which difference is dealt with, and thus the way students encountering difference for the first time react. For some students attending this university it was the first time they were exposed to such diversity: 'Coming here was the biggest shock of my life. It was a great learning experience. It was like an awakening'.

Within this institution, difference is not problematized, and the institutional habitus appears to be strong, and thus it is not overshadowed or even captured by the habitus of the elite. For example, the following statement illustrates the way in which one student feels that the institutional habitus, which has a strong community focus, influences the practices of students: 'Nobody flashes any wealth about. Everybody classes themselves as a "student", you all start to mould into one person, and pick up a local accent and stuff like that'.

I think that 'institutional habitus' is a useful notion when exploring student persistence and success, but to operationalize the term it is useful to identify the characteristics of an institutional habitus that promotes access and retention of students from lower socio-economic groups. A recurring theme in the discussion above relates to the willingness of institutions to embrace and value diversity, and thus to respond positively to the differing needs of student groups who are traditionally under-represented in HE. The institutional habitus of HEIs determines the practices of the university, for example, flexibility, willingness to change and the extent to which it embraces or suppresses diversity. The specific characteristics that have been identified from this on-going empirical research and from a student's perspective are:

- staff attitudes, and relationships with students, which minimize the social and academic distance between them, and enable students to feel valued and sufficiently confident to seek guidance when they require it;
- inclusive teaching and learning strategies which do not assume that the habitus of 'traditional' HE students should be the habitus of new cohorts. This includes an awareness of different previous educational experiences, the language of instruction and implied requirements, alternative learning styles and needs and other assumed norms.
- collaborative or socially-orientated teaching and learning which promotes social relations between students through academic activities.
- a range of assessment practices that give all students, irrespective of their preferred method of assessment, the opportunities to succeed, and which do not assume the same access to time and other resources. This includes utilizing a range of assessment tools, providing opportunities and support for re-assessment and consulting students about other (academic and non-academic) commitments when planning assessments.
- choice, flexibility and support with regard to accommodation, which allows students to find the living arrangements that best suit them and to move if necessary;
- a diversity of social spaces: the Students Union bar is an important social facility for some students, but alternative spaces need to be provided for students

with different needs. Particular attention is needed with regard to local students who are not able to socialize through their living arrangements;
- students are allowed to be themselves, and not expected to change to fit in with institutional expectations which are very different to there own habitus.

The habitus involves a set of complex and diverse predispositions, and although it is a dynamic concept, in which the past and the present, and the individual and the collective interact, change is slow. It is, therefore, not possible for HEIs to 'adopt' an institutional habitus that accepts and values diversity. But, it seems clear to me that one implication for HEIs is the need to develop a strategic or holistic approach to widening participation, that moves widening participation away from marginal projects, to being integrated throughout the institution's activities. Particular recommendations include:

- widening participation is an institution-wide activity and not limited to specific (short-term projects), or the responsibility of a few who 'care';
- leading by example: senior staff need to demonstrate their commitment to widening participation, and structure their own relationships with both other staff and students in a way which demonstrates respect of difference;
- staff development to promote inclusive attitudes and teaching, learning and assessment procedures;
- validation and quality assurance measures that emphasize a collaborative pedagogy and an inclusive curriculum;
- a review of assessment procedures and timing to ensure students are given a range of opportunities to succeed (i.e. different types of assessment and the opportunity for re-assessment);
- a review of both the accommodation options available, and the extent to which students are able to move. This might involve staff development to create greater awareness of importance of letting students transfer to alternative living arrangements;
- a review of the social facilities available, and a consultation to ensure the needs of all learners are being met;
- other actions that demonstrate diversity through the curriculum, timetabling, availability of staff and services, teaching and learning approaches, role models in terms of staff and other students, and so forth.

This research indicates that efforts to improve the retention and success of students from 'non-traditional' backgrounds require substantial and thorough commitment on the part of institutions. It is not merely the need to provide some additional student support services, nor is it an external student finance problem that can be ignored. The empirical research suggests that relationships and positions are at the heart of student success; institutions must be willing to examine their internal structures of power and representation, including the spheres of governance, curricula and pedagogy. The responsibility for change is, therefore, laid squarely at the feet of the HE sector and institutions in particular; it is not acceptable to continue to blame new student cohorts, because unless the institutional habitus is changed they will continue to be discriminated against. Such fundamental changes are necessary if the government's target of 50% of the under 30s having participated in HE by 2010 is to be reached, but Ward and Steele (1999: 197) are sceptical about the commitment of senior staff and academics to the widening participation objective. The HEFCE's requirement for HEIs to prepare a widening participation strategy that makes links with learning and teaching strategies, human resource strategies, estates and facilities, disability statements, marketing strategies, communication and information technology and child-care arrangements must therefore be welcomed (HEFCE 01/36).

In this paper, I have used the concept of institutional habitus to examine ways in which institutions can seek to improve retention of students by seeking to change their practices. An institutional habitus that embraces diversity will be less discordant with the habituses of students coming from 'non-traditional' backgrounds, and enables them to feel less like 'a fish out of water'. This, in turn is likely to improve retention directly, and furthermore will provide them with resources to cope with the pressures that students, especially those from non-traditional backgrounds, will necessarily face. It is significant because, firstly, it starts to indicate ways in which HEIs, and the HE sector as a whole, can take responsibility for student completion and early withdrawal, and seek systemic change to promote the former and reduce the latter. Secondly, this approach does not blame students for failure, but addresses the more pertinent issue of how institutions fail students.

Acknowledgements

Sarah Williams and Kim Slack, both of the Institute for Access Studies, Staffordshire University, have contributed to the empirical research and the literature review that this paper is based on.

Note

1. Benchmarks are calculated by HEFCE to address institutional variation within the HE sector, and to facilitate meaningful comparison. A benchmark is constructed for each institution with respect to each performance indicator; they take into account an institution's entry qualifications, subject mix and proportions of young and mature entrants.

References

ASTIN A. W. (1984) *Preventing Students from Dropping Out* (San Francisco, CA: Wiley, Jossey-Bass).

BALL, S. J. (1990) *Politics and Policy-Making in Education: Explorations in Policy Sociology* (London and New York: Routledge).

BENN, R. (1982) Higher education: non standard students and withdrawals, *Journal of Further and Higher Education*, 19 (3), 3–12.

BERGER, J. B. and BRAXTON, J. M. (1998) Revising Tinto's interactionalist theory of student departure through theory elaboration: examining the role of organisational attributes in the persistence process, *Research in Higher Education*, 39 (2), 103–119.

BOURDIEU, P. and PASSERON, J. C. (1977) *Reproduction in Education, Society and Culture* (London and Beverly Hills, Sage Publications).

BOURDIEU, P. and WACQUANT, L. (1992) *An Invitation to Reflexive Sociology* (Chicago: Chicago University Press).

DFEE (1998) *Participation in Education and Training by 16–18 year olds in England:* 1987 to 1997. Statistical Bulletin 335/98 (London: DfEE).

GREEN, A., WOLF, A. and LENEY, T. (1999) *Convergence and Divergence in European Education and Training Systems* (London: University of London Institute of Education).

HARKER, R. (1990) 'Bourdieu: education and reproduction, in R. Harker, C. Mahar and C. Wilkes (eds), *An Introduction to the Work of Pierre Bourdieu. The Practice of Theory* (Basingstoke and London: The MacMillan Press Ltd), pp. 86–109.

HEFCE 01/36. Strategies for widening participation in higher education. A guide to good practice.

HOUSE OF COMMONS SELECT COMMITTEE ON EDUCATION AND EMPLOYMENT (2001) Sixth report. Higher Education: Student Retention. Available online: www.publications.parliament.uk

JAMES, D. (1998) Higher education field-work: the interdependence of teaching, research and student experience, in M. Grenfell and D. James (eds), *Bourdieu and Education: Acts of Practical Theory* (London: Falmer Press), pp. 104–121.

JOHNES, J. (1990) Determinants of student wastage in higher education, *Studies in Higher Education*, 15 (1), 87–100.

KENNEDY, H. (1997) *Learning Works – widening participation in further education* (Coventry: FEFC).

MAHAR, C., HARKER, R. and WILKES, C. (1990) The basic theoretical position, in R. Harker, C. Mahar and C. Wilkes (eds), *An Introduction to the Work of Pierre Bourdieu. The Practice of Theory* (Basingstoke and London: The MacMillan Press Ltd), pp. 1–26.

McDONOUGH, P. (1996) *Choosing Colleges: How social class and schools structure opportunity* (New York: State University of New York Press).

MOORTGAT, M. (1997) *Retention Rates Research Project.*

MORGAN, M., FLANAGAN, R. and KELLAGHAN, T. (2001) *A Study of Non-Completion in Undergraduate University Courses* (Dublin: HEA).

NATIONAL AUDIT OFFICE (NAO) (2002) *Improving student achievement in English higher education.* Report by the Comptroller and Auditor General (London: The Stationary Office).

OZGA, J. and SUKHNANDAN, L. (1997) *Undergraduate Non-Completion in Higher Education in England.* Report 2 (Bristol: Higher Education Funding Council for England).

OZGA, J. and SUKHNANDAN, L. (1998) Undergraduate non-completion: developing an explanatory model, *Higher Education Quarterly*, 52 (3), 316–333.

PARRY, G. and FRY, H. (1999) Widening participation in pursuit of the learning society: Kennedy, Dearing and 'The Learning Age', in A. Hayton (ed.), *Tackling Disaffection and Social Exclusion: Education perspectives and policies* (London: Kogan Page Ltd).

PASCARELLA, E. T. and TERENZINI, P. T. (1991) *How College Affects Students: FIndings and Insights from Twenty Years* (Oxford: Jossey-Bass Publishers).

REAY, D. (1998) 'Always Knowing' and 'Never Being Sure': institutional and familial habituses and higher education choice, *Journal of Education Policy*, 13 (4), 519–529.

REAY, D., DAVID, M. and BALL, S. (2001) Making a Difference? Institutional habituses and higher education choice, *Sociological Research Online*, 5 (4). Available online: htttp://www.socresonline.org.uk/5/4/reay.html

ROBBINS, D. (1993) The practical importance of Bourdieu's analyses of higher education, *Studies in Higher Education*, 18(2), 151–163.

SAND, B. (1998) Lifelong learning: vision, policy and practice, *Journal of Access and Credit Studies*, 1 (1), 17–40.

SELECT COMMITTEE ON EDUCATION AND EMPLOYMENT (2001) *Higher Education: Student Retention.* Sixth Report (London: House of Commons).

SINCLAIR, H. and DALE, L. (2000) The effect of student tuition fees on the diversity of intake within a Scottish new university. Paper presented at British Educational Research Association Annual Conference, 7–9 September 2000, Cardiff University

THOMAS, E. and JONES, R. (2000) Social exclusion and higher education, in E. Thomas and M. Cooper (eds), *Changing the Culture of the Campus: Towards an Inclusive Higher Education* (Stoke on Trent: Staffordshire University Press), pp. 8–22.

THOMAS, E., YORKE, M. and WOODROW, M. (2001) *HEFCE Pilot Study: Access and Retention. Final Report* (Bristol: HEFCE).

TIGHT, M. (1998) Education, Education, Education! The vision of lifelong learning in the Kennedy, Dearing and Fryer reports, *Oxford Review of Education*, 24 (4), 473–485.

TINTO, V. (1975) Dropout from higher education: a theoretical synthesis of recent research, *Review of Education Research*, 45, 89–125.

TINTO, V. (1993) *Leaving College: Rethinking the Causes and Cures of Student Attrition*, 2nd edn (Chicago: University of Chicago Press).

TINTO, V. (1997) Classrooms as communities: exploring the educational character of student persistence, *Journal of Higher Education*, 68 (6), 599–623.

WARD, K. and STEELE, T. (1999) From marginality to expansion: an overview of recent trends and developments in widening participation in England and Scotland, *Journal of Access and Credit Studies*, 1 (2), 192–204.

WRIGHT, P. (1996) Mass higher education and the search for standards, *Higher Education Quarterly*, 50 (1), 71–85.

Index

Note: Page numbers followed by 'n' indicate notes section.

Printed in Great Britain
by Amazon

37113178R00130